The
Future Compatible
Campus

The Future Compatible Campus

Planning, Designing, and Implementing
Information Technology in the Academy

DIANA G. OBLINGER
SEAN C. RUSH
Editors
Global Education Industry
IBM

ANKER PUBLISHING COMPANY, INC.
Bolton, MA

The Future Compatible Campus

Planning, Designing, and Implementing
Information Technology in the Academy

ISBN 1-882982-19-3

Composition by Deerfoot Studios
Cover design by Deerfoot Studios

Anker Publishing Company, Inc.
176 Ballville Road
P.O. Box 249
Bolton, MA 01740-0249

ABOUT THE AUTHORS

Martha A. Beede. Martha Beede has 12 years experience assisting institutions in planning, systems implementations, and improving service and efficiency through the use of enabling technologies and processes. Specializing in helping institutions transform their student service operations, Ms. Beede joined IBM after managing a large student system project at the University of Vermont. Prior to joining the University of Vermont, she worked as a manager at Coopers and Lybrand, where she was responsible for marketing, planning, management, and delivery of information technology and audit services to higher education institutions. Ms. Beede holds an M.S. in information systems from Northeastern University and a B.S. in business administration from the University of Vermont.

David L. Bellamy. David Bellamy is with the Higher Education consulting organization of IBM. He has 18 years experience implementing systems and managing complex projects. He specializes in the integration of people, process, and technology for new systems. At IBM, David has held technical, sales, and management positions and is currently managing a practice for universities implementing integrated student information systems. Mr. Bellamy received a B.A. in organizational management from Eastern College.

D. Lawrence Bivins. Lawrence Bivins is the IBM Project Coordinator for the IBM Global Campus Affiliates program. Previously, he was the IBM Project Coordinator for the Institute for Academic Technology (IAT), a partnership between IBM and the University of North Carolina at Chapel Hill. Mr. Bivins' background includes work in state government, public policy, and association management, including four years as the executive director of a nonprofit lobbying organization based in Washington, DC. Mr. Bivins received a B.A. in political science and economics from Louisiana State University, Baton Rouge, and holds graduate degrees from The American University, Washington, DC, and the London School of Economics.

David G. Brown. Dave Brown is the Provost at Wake Forest University. He has held previous positions as President of Transylvania University (Kentucky), Chancellor of the University of North Carolina at Asheville, and Provost at Drake University and Miami University (Ohio). He has chaired the American Association for Higher Education, the Provosts of the Land Grant Universities, and the Chief Academic Officers of the American Council on Education. In Winston-Salem, Dr. Brown currently chairs the Futures Council, Project 2020, and the Education Division of the Chamber of Commerce. He has authored three books. Dr. Brown received his B.A. and Ph.D. in economics from Denison and Princeton Universities.

Darlene J. Burnett. Darlene Burnett is the solution manager for student services with Higher Education, IBM North America, specializing in helping colleges move to student and faculty-centered environments with an emphasis on productivity, effectiveness, accountability, and improved access and quality. Before joining IBM, Ms. Burnett was responsible for the computer instruction program at Johnson County Community College and has held a variety of management positions with IBM. Ms. Burnett holds an M.B.A. in organizational behavior and marketing from the University of Missouri at Kansas City and a B.S. in computing from Kansas State University in Pittsburg.

Kathryn L. Conway. Kathryn Conway is a senior analyst and consultant at the Institute for Academic Technology with the University of North Carolina at Chapel Hill (UNC-CH) where she currently focuses on the design and use of learning environments. She combines ten years experience in distance education and classroom design with a diverse background including instructional technology and mass communications. In addition, Ms. Conway has held several positions involving the development and support of technological initiatives at UNC-CH over the past 20 years. Previously she was the Director of Research in Learning Technologies, the Director of Instructional Technologies, and the Associate Director of the Media and Instructional Support Center. Ms. Conway holds a B.F.A. in directing for theater and an M.A. in communications from the University of North Carolina at Chapel Hill.

James W. Cortada. James Cortada is a member of the IBM Consulting Group where he consults in the area of business transformation. He is the author of over two dozen books dealing with a wide range of management issues, including measurements and information processing. He is the coeditor of McGraw-Hill's *Quality Yearbook* and serves on the board of editors of several business journals. He is the Chairman of the Board of Trustees of the Charles Babbage Institute at the University of Minnesota and serves on other industry boards. Dr. Cortada has a B.A. in history from Randolph-Macon College, and an M.A. and Ph.D. from Florida State University, both in history.

William H. Geoghegan. William Geoghegan is the solutions manager for teaching and learning for Higher Education, IBM North America. Since joining IBM in 1984, he has held a variety of management and staff positions. Prior to joining IBM, Dr. Geoghegan served for 17 years in faculty, research, and administrative positions at the University of California at Berkeley, including nine years as Associate Dean of the Graduate Division and ten years as founder and Director of the Quantitative Anthropology Laboratory, a first-of-its-kind academic computing facility supporting teaching and research in the social sciences and humanities. Dr. Geoghegan holds a B.S. in humanities and science from the Massachusetts Institute of Technology, and M.A. and Ph.D. degrees in anthropology from Stanford University.

William H. Graves. William Graves is the interim Chief Information Officer at the University of North Carolina at Chapel Hill where he also is a professor of mathematics and information and library science. He founded and is responsible for the Institute for Academic Technology, a national technology partnership with IBM. Dr. Graves chairs the planning committee for EDUCOM's National Learning Infrastructure Initiative, and serves on the CAUSE Board of Directors and the steering committees for the Networking and Telecommunications Task Force, the Coalition for Networked Information, and the Internet Project. Dr. Graves has given over 300 invited presentations on the role of information technology in higher education and has written extensively on the subject. Dr. Graves earned his Ph.D. in mathematics from Indiana University.

Kristine A. Hafner. Kristine Hafner is Director for Business Initiatives with the Office of the President of the University of California where her role is to introduce and implement new management practices with the nine University of California institutions. Previously, Dr. Hafner was a senior consultant and engagement manager with IBM Consulting where she specialized in strategic planning and business systems redesign in higher education institutions. Dr. Hafner has 14 years of experience working with large, complex organizations in the private, public, and nonprofit sectors to design and implement change. Dr. Hafner holds a B.A. in modern languages, and an M.A. and Ph.D. in French language and literature from the University of Wisconsin-Madison where she taught in the Department of French and Italian, and in the Women's Studies Program. She also studied business administration at the University of Pennsylvania Wharton Graduate School of Business and at IBM Advanced Business Institute/Harvard Business School seminars.

Richard P. Hulser. Richard Hulser is a digital library consultant with IBM Higher Education and has over 17 years of experience working in information management. His specialties focus on working with university, college, library, and museum clients in strategic technology planning and implementation. Before joining IBM, Mr. Hulser was a library director at a community college. Mr. Hulser is active in the Special Libraries Association and the Coalition for Networked Information. Mr. Hulser received his M.A. in librarianship and information management from the University of Denver, his M.Ed. in instructional media from Utah State University, and a B.A. in earth and space sciences from the State University of New York at Stony Brook.

Danuta C. McCall. Danuta McCall is with the Higher Education consulting organization of IBM where her focus is on the management of change in post-secondary educational institutions. She consults with universities implementing institution-wide information systems. At IBM Ms. McCall has held numerous marketing and management positions and is currently developing a consulting and services partnership with a leading supplier of institution-wide administrative application software. Ms. McCall received an M.B.A. from the University of California, Los Angeles, and a B.A. in marine biology from the University of California, Berkeley.

James R. Mingle. Jim Mingle has served as the Executive Director of the State Higher Education Executive Officers (SHEEO) since 1984. Dr. Mingle's work has involved him in numerous public policy issues. He has served as an advisor and consultant to states and institutional boards as well as national and professional associations. He is the author of numerous books and articles. His most recent work has focused on how states and institutions should respond to emerging technological developments, especially in computing and distance learning. Dr. Mingle has a Ph.D. from the Center for the Study of Higher Education at the University of Michigan, and B.A. and M.A. degrees in history from the University of Akron in Ohio.

Charles R. Moran. Charlie Moran manages the Higher Education consulting practice for Blackwell Consulting Services. Previously he was with the IBM Consulting group's higher education management consulting practice. Mr. Moran has worked with clients in a wide range of industries, including higher education, manufacturing, and telecommunications. His areas of expertise include strategic planning, information systems planning, networking architectures, data center management, and application development, as well as management issues surrounding the integration of information systems within changing organizations. Mr. Moran has more than 19 years experience in the information systems industry. He graduated from the University of Notre Dame with a B.S. in electrical engineering. He also holds an M.B.A. with a concentration in finance from the University of Chicago.

Richard Nichols. Dick Nichols is a Senior Network Consultant with IBM Education Consulting. He specializes in data, voice, and video networking activities helping clients to analyze existing networks, evaluate user requirements, provide logical and physical designs, prepare implementation plans for campus-wide networks, create information technology plans, and integrate these various networks where common technologies permit. Mr. Nichols has over 40 years experience working with commercial and government telecommunications organizations. Mr. Nichols studied at Wisconsin State College, Wilson Junior College, and Memphis State University.

James S. Noblitt. James Noblitt is a Senior Fellow at the Institute for Academic Technology. Previously, he has been a research linguist at the Center for Applied Linguistics in Washington, DC and a professor of linguistics at Cornell University where he headed the French language program and taught courses in medieval French and applied linguistics. Dr. Noblitt is the coauthor of a program for writing assistance in French, "Systeme-D," winner of the EDUCOM Best Foreign Language Software Award for 1988. His multimedia CD-ROM program for listening comprehension in French, "Nouvelles Dimensions," was the Grand Prize Winner in the 1995 Video Breakthrough Awards, sponsored by Asymetrix, Creative Labs, and *Multimedia World* magazine. He was awarded the 1996 EDUCOM/Modern Language Association achievement medal for his work with information technology in language learning. Dr. Noblitt holds B.A. and M.A. degrees in French literature from the University of Virginia, was a Fulbright scholar, and received his Ph.D. in French linguistics from Harvard University.

Diana G. Oblinger. Diana Oblinger is Manager, Academic Programs and Strategy, Higher Education, IBM Global Education Industry. She is known for her leadership in teaching and learning, including advancing the concept of student mobile computing and distributed instruction. Dr. Oblinger also serves as the program manager for the Institute for Academic Technology, is an adjunct professor at North Carolina State University, and serves on the steering committee for EDUCOM's National Learning Infrastructure Initiative. Prior to joining IBM, Oblinger was responsible for managing the academic programs of 17 departments with 250 faculty and over 2,000 students at the University of Missouri-Columbia. She also spent several years on the faculty at the University of Missouri and at Michigan State University in teaching, advising, and research. Dr. Oblinger is the author of numerous papers on multimedia and enhancing instruction with technology. She has received three outstanding teaching awards, an outstanding research award, and was recently named Young Alumnus of the Year by Iowa State University. She has received several awards since joining IBM.

Edwin J. Pinheiro. Ed Pinheiro is a worldwide teaching and learning solution manager for IBM. He specializes in helping colleges plan and implement enhanced curricula using multimedia and instructional tools and has in-depth knowledge of multimedia, personal computer software, development, and authoring systems as well as the application of these tools and technologies to higher education. He holds six U.S. patents and is the author of a book on multimedia. Mr. Pinheiro received a B.S. in electrical engineering from Case Western Reserve University.

Mark Resmer. Mark Resmer is Associate Vice President for Information Technology at Sonoma State University, a campus in the California State University System, where his responsibilities include management of all institutional information resources, including instructional technology, information management, telecommunications, and institutional research. In addition, he is extensively involved in system-wide network and information technology policy issues. He currently heads a project that has implemented universal access to information technology for all incoming freshmen at Sonoma State. He led an EDUCOM NLII working group on universal student access, and is currently project manager for the NLII Instructional Management System. Previously he was the Director of Academic Computing at Vassar College. Dr. Resmer earned his B.A from Vassar College and LTCL from Trinity College, London.

Sean C. Rush. Sean Rush is the General Manager, IBM Global Education Industry, which includes the sales, consulting, and industry solutions teams dedicated to education issues. Mr. Rush has 25 years of professional experience working with service sector organizations. Prior to joining IBM in 1994, he spent 14 years as a consultant for Coopers and Lybrand, LLP in Boston where he served as chairman of the firm's National Higher Education and Not-for-Profit practice which is responsible for more than 2,000 clients throughout the United States. He concurrently served as partner-in-charge of Coopers and Lybrand's Higher Education Consulting practice, providing financial, operational, and planning services to colleges, universities, and other nonprofit organizations. Throughout his career, Mr. Rush has worked with more than 75 public and private institutions in the areas of total quality management, business process reengineering, and operations management. Mr. Rush has published numerous books and articles in the area of higher education and is a member of several higher education organizations.

Thomas C. Wunderle. Tom Wunderle is a consultant with IBM Higher Education, specializing in helping colleges and universities develop strategic plans for information technology. His experience in technology grant writing and strategic planning provides unique insights into the leveraging of external resources and partnerships that can help support technology initiatives. His experience at IBM includes administration management, communications/advertising, satellite broadcast production, and financial management. Mr. Wunderle has a B.A. from Eastern Kentucky University, an M.A. from Kent State University, and has served as an adjunct professor at a community college.

CONTENTS

About the Authors   *v*

Preface and Chapter Summary   *xv*

Acknowledgments   *xxii*

PART 1: THE RATIONALE
FOR THE FUTURE COMPATIBLE CAMPUS

1. Transforming the Academy   2
   Kristine A. Hafner and Diana G. Oblinger

PART 2: PLANNING FOR THE FUTURE

2. A Strategy for I/T Investments   26
   William H. Graves

3. Strategic Information Technology Planning   36
   in Higher Education
   Charles R. Moran

4. Staging for the Launch: An Implementation   53
   Planning Framework
   Thomas C. Wunderle

5. Student Services for the 21st Century:
   Creating the Student-Centered Environment   68
   Martha A. Beede and Darlene J. Burnett

PART 3: MOVING TOWARD THE FUTURE
IN TEACHING AND LEARNING

6. Student Mobile Computing   88
   Diana G. Oblinger, Mark Resmer, and James R. Mingle

7. Wake Forest University's Strategic Plan for Technology   109
   David G. Brown

xiii

8. Collaborative Learning   118
   Edwin J. Pinheiro

9. Instructional Technology and the Mainstream:
   The Risks of Success   131
   William H. Geoghegan

10. Making Ends Meet: A Faculty Perspective
    on Computing and Scholarship   151
    James S. Noblitt

PART 4: DEVELOPING THE INFRASTRUCTURE

11. The Importance of the Campus Network Infrastructure   166
    Richard Nichols

12. Planning for Success: Are You Ready for Client/Server?   178
    David L. Bellamy and Danuta C. McCall

13. Designing Classrooms for the 21st Century   198
    Kathryn L. Conway

14. Prepare Today for the Digital Library of Tomorrow   218
    Richard P. Hulser

15. Managing Innovation: Project Implementation
    in Higher Education   230
    D. Lawrence Bivins

PART 5: MEASURING SUCCESS

16. Knowing How It Is All Working:
    The Role of Performance Measurements   248
    James W. Cortada

Index   273

PREFACE
AND CHAPTER SUMMARY

The purpose of this book is to help our clients and colleagues in higher education design the "future compatible campus." There are many problems with our existing campuses, ranging from deferred maintenance to inadequate computer technology. Because our expertise is in technology and education, we are often approached by those who have decided to "do technology." These conversations frequently begin with the expressed desire to create a more competitive college or university now and in the future. Technology is often the centerpiece of this competitive posture. When we ask what the vision or the plan is, the reply is often, "We hoped you could tell us what to do."

It is not a simple answer. Just as no two institutions are alike, the plan for creating a future compatible campus is unique to each institution and its culture. However, our work with colleges and universities has led us to conclude that there are some critical elements. All involve planning. All involve transformation. All involve the appropriate use of technology to make education more productive and personal.

As a colleague often says, "If you don't know where you're going, any road will get you there." Where do we think higher education is going? In part, our vision of higher education's future was described in our previous book, *The Learning Revolution* (Oblinger & Rush, 1997). As Greg Farrington wrote,

> How will the new information tools change the structure of the university and the process of education and learning? Several changes seem inevitable. One is that learning and education will become more informal, accessible, and learner-centered. Another is that the demand for education, particularly lifelong education, will grow significantly, as will competition in the education market. The new tools will open new markets for traditional educational institutions and also expose them to vigorous competition. Those universities and colleges that can change, innovate, and lead are likely to thrive; those that cannot will be at risk. Surely some will disappear (Farrington, 1997).

The phraseology varies, but the "future compatible campus" is synonymous with the "connected campus." The connected campus will allow higher education to develop a technology-enabled environment that consists of three components: connected learning, connected service to the community, and connected management. Enabled by the network infrastructure, higher education will be able to use technology to redesign the academic and administrative aspects of colleges and universities to further enhance the quality of the learning experience. This new approach will be based on networks, communications, and computer technology using learning-on-demand, learner-centered instruction, student-centered services, and digital libraries.

Residential colleges and universities will still be in demand for many learners. However, technology expands the reach and range of these traditional settings, allowing for more personalization and communication. Hybrid organizations may be formed where students can synthesize on-campus with on-line experiences. Other students, particularly working adults, may opt for on-line educational experiences that provide them with the education and flexibility they need. Preparing for any of these futures will require transformative approaches—to the curriculum, to the use of faculty time, to how we support and nurture students—plus a technology infrastructure.

How do you create the future compatible campus? The starting point is to know where you are today. The current higher education environment is increasingly complex. Shifts in the workplace are driving changes in higher education. Technology trends are affecting individuals, institutions, and societies. In general, information technology places pressure on the "middleman." Computer networks offer the possibility of "disintermediating" both learning and student services. Demographics are shifting; students are behaving more like consumers. Public confidence in higher education is at an all-time low.

But the picture is not always grim. Demand for higher education has never been greater. Plus, there is a renewed emphasis on instruction in most colleges and universities. Information technology is being used to expand the learning options for both students and faculty. Internationalizing the curriculum has taken on increasing relevance in light of the permeability of international boundaries by the Internet.

In this decade we will move to global connectivity which will be embodied in a worldwide, highly distributed computing infostructure. Connectivity enabled by the infostructure will profoundly change access to content, services, and communications. There are likely to be three social impacts that result from the infostructure:

▶ Everyone will become a technology user because costs will be low enough and compatibility will be high. New software will allow the broader population of users to easily deal with ever more complex systems.

▶ Inter-enterprise integration will become pervasive. We already see this in the form of electronic links among suppliers, distributors, and customers. The "virtual university" and sharing of courses will be another form of inter-enterprise integration.

▶ We will process and transport bits instead of people and things; information will displace the physical. Working this way will be faster and less costly, as well as less harmful to the environment.

CHAPTER SUMMARY

Each of our authors touches themes ranging from strategy to measurement. It will take wise planning, thorough execution, and many midcourse corrections to become a future compatible campus. To help you begin the process, many questions are posed throughout this book.

Hafner and Oblinger, in their chapter on transforming the academy, establish the rationale for transformation in higher education. In order to become and remain compatible with the demands of the future, many institutions will need to fundamentally rethink what they do and why. Streamlining administrative processes, increasing operational productivity and efficiency, and focusing on customer satisfaction are often first steps. Along the way, they provide examples from instruction, student services, and the library of where starting with a clean slate, asking probing questions, and enabling new processes with technology lead to greater efficiency, effectiveness, and better service. Their examples illustrate how reengineering instruction can break the cost constraints of our existing instructional model. In another example—purchase orders—processing time is reduced from three weeks to three days.

We assume that technology will be part of the future compatible campus. However, if you were designing the information technology (I/T) strategy for your institution, what guidelines would you follow? Bill Graves begins from the premise that most higher education executives are investing in I/T to add quality to business as usual, thereby adding costs. Unfortunately, most uses of I/T in higher education have failed to be transformative in their impact. If I/T is to become more than an added cost and a personal productivity tool for higher education, then its transformative power must be institutionally focused on increasing the productivity of higher education's primary business—instruction. Graves outlines how an institution might approach its I/T strategy.

Capitalizing on his experience helping numerous organizations create strategic plans, Charlie Moran relates the common planning errors and describes some common pitfalls of strategic plans. He goes on to describe a new planning methodology for higher education: the strategic alignment framework. This framework focuses on an alignment between both the strategic and tactical needs of an institution as well as the vision and actions of its information technology (I/T) investments and personnel. This framework focuses every I/T planning recommendation on supporting specific institutional strategies and/or goals.

Having a strategic plan is one step. The next step is to make it work. How can the institution ensure that the plan will be implemented? Tom Wunderle describes an implementation planning framework that was designed and developed for large, complex projects. Implementation planning requires greater detail and more thorough analysis when people, money, time, and other resources must be committed to the project. For most of us, translating strategy into action can be a significant challenge. Wunderle introduces an alternative approach to implementation planning: the planning template. The template is a planning approach or framework that includes a methodology as well as supporting tools and techniques designed to facilitate the development of a business case plan.

Remembering that the focus of higher education should be on students, Martha Beede and Darlene Burnett describe the transformation of student services. With only a few exceptions, today's student services are neither student-centered nor future compatible. If the future compatible institution is to serve both residential and distant students whose educational experiences will span a lifetime, reengineering student services will be essential. Burnett and Beede describe the activities that can affect student satisfaction, retention, and success. Beginning with a conceptual framework, they detail the characteristics that will need to be embedded in future compatible student services. Exemplars from several institutions illustrate how the principles can be put into practice.

The next section of the book focuses on the learning environment. We begin with a chapter on student mobile computing because it has been recognized as one of the most powerful strategies for transforming the learning environment. The transformation caused by student mobile computing is about much more than just computers. The strategy—providing computers and network access 24 hours a day to all students and faculty—extends a technology-enhanced learning opportunity to all students. As observed by

Oblinger, Resmer, and Mingle, ubiquitous availability of technology acts as a catalyst that changes not only what is taught but how; it changes the infrastructure, and it changes student and faculty behavior. This chapter documents the rationale behind student mobile computing, how it is implemented, and the outcomes of the process.

Dave Brown provides a synthesis of planning rationale and implementation strategies for student mobile computing at Wake Forest University (WFU). WFU began with clearly defined goals and a strong sense of institutional mission. It chose to use technology to enrich learning opportunities for faculty and students. Consistent with its mission, technology was introduced as a tool of the liberal arts to foster more and timelier communication among faculty and students. The Plan for the Class of 2000 has been implemented based on principles such as personal and individual education, putting students first, communication, and community.

Collaborative learning may not be a new instructional technique, but when implemented using communication and computer technology, it has the potential to extend and enhance the classroom environment as well as reach new groups of learners. The trend is for higher education to change the mode of instruction. As Edwin Pinheiro describes, collaborative learning will play an important role in enhancing the quality of the teaching and learning experience for both faculty and students by lowering the barriers to communication and allowing collaboration to occur independent of time and place. Those interested in adopting a collaborative style will find guidance in the questions to ask as well as the examples provided in this chapter.

Bill Geoghegan's chapter helps us understand the instructional technology revolution. Predicted over the last few decades, it is a revolution that went into apparent hibernation toward the end of the decade but now seems to be reawakening. Through the application of diffusion theory, Geoghegan explains who adopts technology and why. Certainly, faculty adoption of technology and faculty support will be critical in creating the future compatible campus. Geoghegan also discusses the implications of the rapid expansion in the demand for instructional technology and how the risks of renewed growth can be managed.

In another perspective on faculty adoption of technology, James Noblitt describes both the top-down and the bottom-up approach to technology. He offers suggestions from the faculty perspective for how to gain support for innovation, such as providing examples within the faculty member's discipline, demonstrating feasibility, accommodating the faculty value system, and ensuring quality. He makes the case that bottom-up innovators are most successful when they start with a real problem; that is, they do not simply transfer current curricular materials to electronic form. Rather, they leave alone what is working well, and innovate where it will do the most good.

Implied in all scenarios of the campus of the future is an underlying infrastructure. Dick Nichols describes the importance of the campus network infrastructure. As he explains, planning pays. He details the common user expectations of the network, the benefits to campus-wide networking, and the components to consider in a technology plan. Technology planners are beginning to realize the benefits of building one network infrastructure which will support all modes of communications, especially as digital video becomes more cost-effective. With computer communications inherently digital, most modern telephone systems digital, and the emergence of digital video, digital information will allow the true integration of all modes of communication. Other key features of the network to incorporate in the I/T plan, such as scalability (the key to longevity), are discussed.

In the future, more and more of higher education will exist in a distributed environment. As Dave Bellamy and Danuta McCall explain, for a distributed environment, changes in business processes will demand client/server technology. In their chapter, they explain a management model that can be used to plan successful client/server projects. Also highlighted are the benefits and pitfalls. Using six indicators to determine the degree of the project's success, they show that those most likely to succeed align technical complexity with organizational readiness. The pitfalls lie in areas such as institutional culture, focus on customer service, and a mismatch of expectations. Many of their observations extend beyond just client/server implementations and may be valuable, whether or not a project is based on client/server.

Another component of the infrastructure on campuses is the classroom. In contrast with today's classrooms, the classrooms of the future will be more complex learning environments because they are part of an integrated human and technological system that enables students to learn in a more dynamic and participatory way. One of the points Kathryn Conway makes is that the foundation of any learning experience is what happens in the learner, not what happens with the technology. To avoid high-tech classrooms filled with low-tech teaching, she outlines principles that can be followed and provides an overview of several types of technology-enhanced learning environments.

None of our institutions would be complete without the library. Throughout their history, libraries have played many important roles in archiving, information retrieval, and knowledge dissemination. There are many reasons for wanting to use technology in libraries, which Richard Hulser describes. With the library's critical information role, the first step is to be sure the library is integrated into any strategic plan. In addition, faculty, students, and administrators will need new capabilities to manage information as institutions migrate toward a digital environment. The emergence of vast, distributed repositories of educational materials will necessitate new capabilities for storing, searching, retrieving, and managing digital information.

Effective project management is a critical component of any strategic technology initiative. Lawrence Bivins' chapter explores various approaches to managing complex projects. Project management, defined as a set of methods, principles, tools, and techniques for the effective management of objective-oriented work, is an often forgotten component of technology initiatives. Among the sound project management principles he describes are careful planning, effective implementation strategies, coordination and communication, and strong top-level leadership. The bottom line: A project management approach is strongly recommended as a way of ensuring that the resources invested into technology initiatives are maximized.

What we have observed in many industries, including higher education, is that change can be harnessed in very positive ways. Those best at it recognize that the one basic tool that helps obtain the best insight on what to do next and why is a robust set of measurements. In the final chapter on measurements, Jim Cortada describes how to know whether your initiative is working. Intuition is not good enough. The more we change, the more we need to understand the consequences of change. Cortada describes measurement techniques that can help higher education understand how they are progressing with their transformations while gaining insight that will make it possible to continue the process of change safely, cost-effectively, and to the satisfaction of all the constituencies that depend on them.

Creating the future compatible campus is a challenge for all of us. We hope this volume will help you design a vibrant future for your institution.

REFERENCES

Oblinger, D. G. & Rush, S. C. (Eds.). (1997). *The learning revolution: The challenge of information technology in the academy.* Bolton, MA: Anker.

Farrington, G. C. (1997). Higher education in the information age. In D. G. Oblinger & S. C. Rush (Eds.), *The learning revolution: The challenge of information technology in the academy.* Bolton, MA: Anker.

Acknowledgments

We would like to thank our colleagues—in IBM and higher education—who helped us begin to understand how to create the future compatible campus. These chapters do not describe all that we need to know to create the future, to be sure, but they represent a beginning.

Diana G. Oblinger and Sean C. Rush

I would like to thank my own ".com" generation—Brian and Adam—for keeping me focused on the future. Their thirst for knowledge and ease with technology provide me with a source of motivation and energy. I would like to particularly thank my husband, Jim, for encouraging me, supporting me—and helping me remember the things that really matter.

Diana G. Oblinger

I would like to thank my good colleague and coeditor Diana Oblinger, whose hard work made this a reality, much more so than mine. In addition, my thanks to the many colleagues at IBM who have taught and tutored me enormously during my first years with the company. My hat is off to them for the fabulous job they all do. Finally, I would like to thank my children, Alison and Christopher, for supplying me with their abundant energy; it uplifts me every day.

Sean C. Rush

PART 1

THE RATIONALE FOR THE FUTURE COMPATIBLE CAMPUS

TRANSFORMING THE ACADEMY

Kristine A. Hafner and Diana G. Oblinger

Society is being transformed by global competition and the power of technology. Futurists have coined a variety of phrases to describe our emerging world: knowledge economy, information age, or digital economy are only a few. No matter what the term, change is the focus with technology increasing the pace of transformation. Higher education is under increasing scrutiny even though it has held a steady course on its traditional missions of not only grooming society's future thought leaders through instruction and research, but also contributing to society through public service.

The Wingspread Group on Higher Education (1993) stated that there is a dangerous mismatch between what American society needs from higher education and what it is receiving. This disparity has led American organizations, in both the public and private sectors, to rely less and less on higher education, and to invest heavily in alternate sources of employee training and development to ensure their ability to compete in a global economy. This parallel "higher" education delivery system is a growing, billion dollar business, and it has driven an even deeper wedge between the "ivory tower" and the more pragmatic needs of American society (Davis & Botkin, 1995).

Part of this reduced ability to compete may be due to what Gregorian calls "the greatest challenge facing modern society." This theory holds that the challenge for modern civilization is "how to cope with information and transform it into knowledge. Universities, colleges, libraries, and learned societies more than ever before have a fundamental historical and social task to give us not merely training but education; not only education but culture; and not just information but its distillation—knowledge" (Gregorian, Hawkins, & Taylor, 1992).

It is a great irony that American higher education institutions have historically been unable to become effective learning organizations—where self-assessment and continuous improvement are deeply integrated into the fabric of governance and decision-making. Colleges and universities have remained largely insulated from the quality principles that have guided industry, and more recently government, toward greater efficiency and a more service-oriented culture. Only recently has the stable, safe, traditional, insular world of academe been challenged to the core by forces which threaten its identity, and, in some cases, its very existence.

SERIOUS CHALLENGES TO HIGHER EDUCATION

Among the many issues accelerating the pressure for change in higher education are:

▶ *Public disinvestment* in higher education is increasing. In many states, public funding for building prisons far outweighs investments in higher education.

▶ *Declining federal and state government funding* have forced unprecedented faculty, staff, and program reductions.

▶ *Tuition increases* have spiraled out of control. While the cost of living in the United States increased 80% since 1980, tuition costs increased 300%. Students and parents have reached the limits of their ability to pay.

▶ *Changing demographics* predict a greater percentage of nontraditional students in the future, many of whom will need special services and remedial education in order to pursue standard programs of study.

▶ *Greater needs for flexibility* in education delivery systems will force institutions to ensure student access to instruction and information anywhere, any time, through a variety of media. The teaching paradigm of the past may be inadequate to move higher education into the 21st century.

▶ *Student recruitment challenges* magnify as students shop for competitive financial aid packages, tuition waivers, and customized courses of study.

▶ *Loss of human potential* is significant in all but the most selective institutions. Freshman retention rates and graduation statistics reinforce the perception that higher education is on a course to weed out those less likely to succeed.

▶ *Demands for accountability* are forcing institutions to measure their performance and communicate it effectively to stakeholders. As the push for accreditation reform gains momentum, many agree that college and university accreditation has focused too much on input measures and that more needs to be done to measure outcomes and the value-added by the educational process.

▶ *Demands for increased productivity* arise from the common perception that faculty do not teach enough, that students do not learn the right things, and that administrators are reactive "firefighters" instead of effective managers.

▶ *High fixed costs of doing business* (e.g., aging, decaying infrastructures, and massive deferred maintenance) give institutions a hefty bill to pay regardless of the number of students they attract and retain. Higher education institutions have no easy outlet for excess capacity.

In this environment, higher education leaders are called upon to transform an "industry" that is notorious for its resistance to change. Embedded in this challenge is the need to rally support for the good of the whole in an environment which optimizes the autonomy, independence, and self-reliance of the parts.

How can education change quickly and dramatically? The answer is by focusing on transformation. Three forces are causing institutions to consider transformation: 1) Customers are taking charge; 2) Competition is intensifying; and 3) Change is becoming a constant (Hammer & Champy, 1993). Institutions of higher education, which were designed in an environment of stability and growth, are not well-positioned to succeed in a world where customers, competition, and keeping pace with change demand flexibility, quick response, and different assumptions about how work should be done.

In many colleges and universities, work is performed in "functional silos," vertical organizational structures that are built to preserve internal order, but not necessarily to serve the learner. These vertical silos (e.g., admissions, registration, bursar, financial aid) are hierarchical in nature, and have managers and supervisors to review and approve the work of others. When staff in a given department (e.g., admissions) complete a work task (e.g., admit a student), they hand off to another work group where the next set of specialized tasks are performed (e.g., register the student, process financial aid applications, etc.). This model of student services delivery, more the norm than the exception today, produces frustrated students who wait in lines and who cannot request and receive the information they need from a single source in a timely manner. How has higher education managed to avoid integrating the notion of customer service into their operations for so long?

As customers of higher education institutions, students are interested in a smooth, integrated process which will produce the results they need. They expect to go seamlessly from admissions to registration, file their financial aid application and receive their awards, pay their fees, attend classes, receive advising and grades, and graduate, with the least possible disruption to their learning experience. They expect to initiate these tasks themselves via technology from their homes and dorm rooms. Like customers of any successful service delivery operation, they expect the institution to make their interactions with it easy, fast, and painless. To transform an institution, the focus must be on what its customers want and need. Many tasks that employees perform have nothing to do with meeting customer needs; they are done simply to satisfy the internal demands of the organization, hence the world of multiple reviews, four-part forms, and complex certification stamps and approval signatures. Often things are done simply because they have always been done that way. There is growing recognition that the academic enterprise must operate more effectively, more efficiently, and with greater accountability.

Any institution may benefit from considering the challenges driving change. Important questions to ask include:

▶ What internal and external factors are driving the need for change in your institution?

▶ What are the strategic issues confronting your college or university which, if they are not addressed, will threaten your future?

▶ What strengths will well-position you to change? What weaknesses will be obstacles?

Opportunities for Change
Along with the challenges which are accelerating the pace of change, opportunities have surfaced which make transforming academic institutions more achievable.

▶ At a large institution, the share of the budget devoted to technology and information can reach ten percent. There is increasing awareness that substantive gains in efficiency and productivity cannot be achieved without the application of information technology.

▶ Increased focus on the Internet and the World Wide Web as a transaction-processing platform has spawned a variety of applications predicated on electronic access to and sharing of information anywhere in the world, any time, by anyone wanting to participate. The cyberworld is changing how colleges and universities do business.

▶ Students not only accept, but demand, that essential services be provided to them electronically (course selection, registration, library catalog, and information retrieval services, etc.). Students are eager users of new technologies.

▶ There is a recognized need for lifelong learning and ongoing education in our society. Colleges and universities have the opportunity to define new ways of creating and disseminating information that take into account the changing educational demands of new learners.

▶ There is increasing familiarity with and acceptance of business models focused on increasing effectiveness, quality, efficiency, and accountability in higher education.

▶ The competitive environment in higher education is forcing an interest in comparative benchmarking of both academic and administrative operations and in the identification of best practices. Strategic performance indicators for higher education are being redefined to focus more on outcomes.

▶ There is increasing recognition of the need for flexibility and readiness for change as a survival issue.

The Importance of Vision

Institutional transformation implies an evolution from a present state to a future state. To ensure that the collective actions of an institution are focused and directed toward a common goal, there must be a clear understanding of the institutional vision, mission, and goals. According to Dill (1994), "Planning requires a sense of community; community implies we have values in common." In many respects, the sense of community in higher education is low. "At work over these more than four decades is an academic ratchet that has loosened the faculty members' connection to their institution. Each turn of the ratchet has drawn the norm of faculty activity away from institutionally defined goals and toward the more specialized concerns of faculty research, publication, professional service, and personal pursuits" (Massy & Zemsky, 1990).

Developing a vision of future success and a set of clear, achievable, measurable goals to achieve this success is the first step in institutional transformation. In an environment where strategic planning is traditionally seen as synonymous with the budgeting process (predicting the future by looking backward), this forward looking approach will greatly benefit institutions, whether they are healthy or caught in a financial and bureaucratic stranglehold. A compelling vision of the future will

▶ Provide focus at both the strategic and operational levels

▶ Give specific, reasonable, and supportive guidance to members of the organization about what is expected of them and why

▶ Guide decision-making as well as help to avoid and resolve conflict

▶ Affirm the future in the present, thereby creating a meaningful contrast between the world as it is and the world as the institution would like it to be

▶ Inspire and motivate constructive behavior among administration, faculty, and staff

Transformation involves first determining what should be done and then determining how to do it. It ignores what *is* and concentrates on what *should be* (Hammer & Champy, 1993).

In developing a strategic context for transformation, questions to ask include:

▶ Do you have a vision of your future success? ("What do you want your institution to look like in the future?")

▶ Is your mission clearly stated? ("Why do you do what you do?")

▶ What strategic goals will allow you to fulfill your vision of success? ("What should you do? Where should you focus your resources?")

▶ What are you doing well today that should continue in the future? What policies, practices, programs, or processes need to be changed or discontinued?

Once the common goals of the institution are defined, most institutions find that they need to take a hard look at their academic and administrative functions in order to identify opportunities for cost savings, reduction of bureaucracy, measurable improvement in educational outcomes, and in the institution's competitive posture.

Even though many are calling for the transformation of higher education, an equal number see no reason to change. These "traditionalists" often cite how stable higher education has been for hundreds of years. Since the

Gutenberg Bible was printed in 1456 using movable type, the technology of information storage, retrieval, and transmission—the university's basic technology—has remained essentially constant until the current era. Indeed, the use of written records to supplement oral teaching goes back to the fifth century B.C. Since their inception, universities and colleges have relied upon lectures, discussions, and the written word because these were the only technologies available.

Information technology has opened new, fundamentally different options for teaching and learning. History demonstrates that fundamental technological change ultimately begets significant structural change, regardless of whether the affected participants choose to join or resist the movement. The changes that universities have weathered over the centuries did not upend their basic technology. Information technology does.

Education process reengineering means challenging tried and true pedagogical methods, many of which have been in place for decades or even centuries. Examples include the lecture and laboratory, the course as the basic unit of instruction, the academic calendar, and in some cases the role of campus-based instruction itself. Higher education is ripe for reengineering because extant processes have been frozen for a long time, because student needs are changing, and because technology has opened important new possibilities (Massy, 1997).

THE ELEMENTS OF SUCCESSFUL TRANSFORMATION

A variety of approaches have been advocated to address cost and quality pressures in higher education, including across-the-board cuts or budget freezes. Standard across-the-board cost-cutting methods have not worked. This approach simply reduces the number of people available to do the work; it does not eliminate the work. Those left behind bear the stress of doing more with fewer resources. Campus-wide budget freezes can lower overall quality. Critical, value-added programs are affected to the same degree as less essential programs. Services are often reduced to the lowest common denominator. Reduction without transformation is unlikely to yield positive results.

Introducing technology without rethinking processes or human resources is not likely to be successful either. Early information technology investments may not necessarily have reduced costs or made processes easier to manage. Humorously referred to as "paving the cow paths," introducing new systems to automate cumbersome and ineffective work processes can create gridlock. As a result, multiple, independent "shadow" systems spring up, filling the gap left by unresponsive centralized systems.

In this case, processes have not been simplified; they have merely been automated. No wonder staff have not always embraced new systems and have continued to do the work of a paper system, plus the work of the information system. Their work has actually become more difficult and more frustrating.

A successful institutional transformation effort must design a system where effective cross-departmental or cross-functional processes deliver products or services to customers.

▶ It must help people develop the beliefs and behaviors to meet the requirements of the new system.

▶ It must identify and implement the appropriate technology to support the new system.

▶ It must establish measurable performance objectives and continually assess progress in achieving strategic goals.

Such transformations involve people, process, and technology (Figure 1.1).

FIGURE 1.1

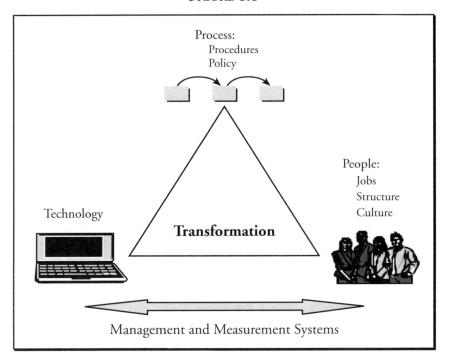

Processes

Processes are a series of definable, repeatable, and measurable tasks leading to a valuable result for internal or external customers. Processes enable an institution to deliver the products and services required to meet its mission. Taking a process view of work (versus an organizational hierarchy view) allows an institution to identify and prioritize core processes, to analyze the performance of these processes, and to redesign them for greater efficiency and effectiveness.

People

People are a critical success factor in designing radical change. Institutional transformation must address how people should be organized to work effectively together, how the culture and work environment need to change in order to support the "to be" world, and how to integrate these changes in a positive way into the thinking and behavior of each and every member of the college/university community.

Information Technology

Information technology plays a critical role as the enabler of transformation. Technology can dramatically improve the efficiency of work processes, as well as ensure accuracy, timeliness, and increased access to information.

Consider the role information technology has played in the transformation of libraries. For example, the U.S. Copyright Office at the Library of Congress receives over 600,000 registrations each year. To process this flow of materials, the Copyright Office is developing a Copyright Office Registration, Recordation, and Deposit System (CORDS). CORDS will enable the processing of electronic copyright registration, deposit, and recording of materials transmitted in digital form over communications networks.

In another effort to improve customer service and efficiency, the Library of Congress implemented in 1995 a new on-line legislative system named THOMAS (after Thomas Jefferson, the so-called father of the Library of Congress). Prior to THOMAS, the *Congressional Record,* containing all of the discussion and record of the legislative process, was most easily available through printed form delivered every morning following a congressional session to its subscribers. Today, this on-line index of legislative activity is updated daily and is available for anyone in the world to search freely. This presents a major change in the quality and timeliness of legislative information available to U.S. citizenry. Currently anyone with electronic access can search the 103rd or 104th editions on-line and have associated materials, such as the full text of legislation under consideration, displayed by the system immediately (Thorin & Sorkin, 1997).

Management and Measurement Systems

Management and measurement systems provide the assessment and decision-making framework to ensure the continuous feedback and learning required to adequately balance these essential drivers of change. This book's final chapter discusses the critical role of performance and diagnostic measurement both as a management decision-making tool and a communication vehicle. Any effort to transform from the status quo to a different, brighter future requires a means to assess progress and to take corrective action along the way. Good measures are road signs on the journey to future success.

When transformation efforts take this broad view of the critical drivers of change, the return on the investment of time and resources is greatest. In addition, it is important to look at the institution as a whole and to identify the processes which have

1) The greatest impact on the college or university's ability to achieve its strategic goals

2) The greatest impact on the satisfaction of its internal and external customers

3) The most significant potential for tangible and intangible benefits to the institution.

Administrative processes (registering students, administering financial aid, managing facilities, etc.) as well as academic processes (teaching, conducting research, creating course schedules) must be examined. Regardless how familiar, the traditional patterns and styles of education are not absolute. Courses do not have to be taught by the lecture method nor subjects in semester-long units. Students do not have to gather in a classroom to interact and learn. The goal of educators, having been presented with the most interesting set of educational tools in decades, should be to choose those most appropriate to each task and not to cling to old methods and notes, assuming that they are best simply because they are familiar. The new tools should be used for what they do best so that humans can be liberated to do what they do best (Farrington, 1997).

Incremental improvement models (total quality management, continuous quality improvement) which gained the attention of the higher education community in the late 1980s and early 1990s shifted the focus to business processes, presented benchmarking as a model for measuring performance, introduced the voice of the customer, required decisions based on facts, and offered tools and techniques for improving process efficiency.

The terms business process reengineering or redesign were coined in the private sector to describe radical change initiatives at the business systems level. According to Hammer and Champy (1993), reengineering is the fundamental rethinking and radical redesign of business systems to achieve dramatic improvements in measures of performance such as cost, quality, service, and responsiveness. Business process reengineering expanded the framework of continuous improvement to address the need for radical change through innovation, organization of work around results, and a more significant role for automation of work processes. In the simplest of terms, business process reengineering means starting with a clean slate.

Not surprisingly, most transformation efforts (e.g., process redesign or reengineering) in the academic community have taken place on the administrative side or in professional schools. Very little transformation has been attempted (successfully) in academic programs. Even so, many believe that teaching and learning can and should be redesigned. Massy (1997) presents a scenario based on the teaching of microeconomics that is illustrative.

The traditional method of teaching microeconomics usually involves a combination of lecture and discussion sessions on a fixed schedule, supplemented with reading and homework assignments. The reengineered method might employ a combination of lectures, interactive studio sessions using simulations and multimedia packages, as well as small group discussions with faculty about meaning and relevance—discussions rich in personal interaction and mentoring as well as knowledge transmission—all on a flexible schedule geared to student needs.

Massy describes how a hypothetical reengineered course might appear to students as they learn microeconomics theory and its practical applications, and to faculty as they carry out their teaching duties. The following scenario illustrates the kinds of qualitative benefits—for students and for faculty—that can be achieved through reengineering.

A Reengineered Course

"What is microeconomics and what is it good for?" These natural questions are addressed in a series of three or four lectures at the beginning of the learning process. The department recruits its most charismatic lecturer for this assignment, and the professor gives her all in preparing and delivering the material. Being chosen for this assignment becomes an important element of recognition by one's colleagues. Convening in a large group provides a sense of excitement, which the professor reinforces by using state-of-the-art multimedia to illustrate and punctuate important points—the students will remember these sessions many years later when much of the detail that comes later will have faded.

Next the student embarks on a series of interactive studio and individual exercises using simulation and multimedia applications (supplemented with the familiar textbook) to develop competence in the course's first content module. The courseware's interactive character produces real-time diagnostics about student progress and difficulties as a byproduct of the learning process itself—diagnostics that can be used to design mitigations or control entry to the next learning stage. From the department's standpoint, the fact that much of the intellectual content is built into the materials enables more independent student work and more flexibility in staffing. For example, much of the work needed to bring students to proficiency with the courseware is handled by graduate students or support staff without any loss of effectiveness.

Once students have mastered the codified knowledge specified for a course module, they move into small group discussions with faculty about the noncodified dimensions. "What does the theory say at its deepest level? What objections have been raised, and are there competing world-views? How can these concepts help in one's career and life generally?" Because students move into the small group sessions only after they have demonstrated a requisite degree of understanding, the time with the professor is not dominated by elemental questions. These sessions take better advantage the faculty's unique skills than restating codified wisdom in class after class.

Students advance to the subsequent course module when they have completed the cycle for a given module. This may be gated on an individual basis, as when a student begins the next phase of technology-based independent work, or control may be through completion of the discussion sessions described in the previous paragraph. Either way, student progress will not be bound to a fixed syllabus determined by the average student's ability and motivation. Students needing more time will get it—and still pass the course providing they attain the requisite learning threshold in a reasonable period of time. Better students can move ahead quickly, thus enabling them to gain more education or, at their discretion, reduce the time and cost of attaining the degree.

The scenario also illustrates another benefit from reengineering: It relaxes traditional constraints on the economics of the educational process. For example, faculty labor is applied at the times and in the circumstances needed rather than in fixed quanta defined inflexibly as courses per semester (teaching loads). Technology substitutes for some of what has traditionally been viewed as faculty work, but faculty labor is redeployed to tasks that professors can do best. Support staff and graduate student time may be used to a greater extent than in some kinds of institutions currently, but it is concentrated in areas where faculty do not have a comparative advantage—not in places, like small group discussion sections, where a professor's wisdom can confer important benefits. The basic economic message is that reengineering breaks the widely perceived linkage between expenditure per student (or the student-faculty ratio) and educational quality (Massy, 1997).

Challenge Assumptions

Transforming higher education begins with setting aside current assumptions about how the college/university operates and for whom. When institutions succeed in challenging their current assumptions and in redefining them in the context of a broader transformation effort, the picture that emerges is surprisingly different.

FIGURE 1.2

AREA OF TRANSFORMATION	CURRENT ASSUMPTIONS	NEW FOCUS
Instructional mission	Task to teach	Task to enable learning
Human resources	Select talent	Develop talent/skills
Strategic focus	Budget-driven	Goal-driven
Market focus	Students	Customers
Value to student	Degree by courses	Student learning outcomes
Organization	Working hierarchy	Networked groups
Worker focus	Manager hierarchy	Teams
Rewards	Loyalty/seniority	Performance
Resources	Physical assets	People value
Competitive indicator	Institutional budget/reputation	Student achievement
Governance	Faculty autonomy	Collective responsibility
Size	Growth	Right-sized
Scale of delivery	Large	Flexible
Competition	Regional	National/global

When did you last ask yourself what assumptions your institution needs to challenge or what assumptions your department or work unit needs to reassess? For example, if we focus on learning, there are many traditions that we might question. Where is the proof that 120 credit hours makes an educated person? What does the baccalaureate degree certify? How did we come to believe that education parceled out in 50-minute increments, three times a week, was optimum for all of our students? What caused educators to decide that the length of the semester should be constant while student learning is allowed to vary? Why did we decide that mastery of the subject was less important than the time spent in the classroom? (Hooker, 1997).

This paradigm paralysis may exist because of the administrative structures we have inherited. If the accumulation of student credit hours is an insufficient measure of learning, why are we wedded to funding formulas that award dollars based on seat-time? If courses could effectively be shared among campuses—even within the same university system— why are there barriers to sharing the student credit hours? If students can learn any place at any time, what is the justification for residency requirements that mandate students enroll at a campus for their last two years of college? If education can be made available worldwide, thanks to technology, is there sufficient rationale to prohibit interstate sharing of courses? (Hooker, 1997).

TAKING A PROCESS VIEW OF HIGHER EDUCATION

Seeing your college or university's mission as a set of discrete but interrelated systems and processes will provide new insight into what you do, how to do it, and why. The first step is to translate the organization chart into the processes performed at the institutional level. Processes play different roles with respect to an organization's mission.

Some processes are directly associated with the institution's identity of teaching, research, and public service: These are *identity processes*. Other priority processes must be performed in order for these identity processes to be successful; for example, hire faculty, enroll students, obtain grants. Other categories of processes provide the infrastructure support for the institution, such as managing financial operations, purchasing goods, managing facilities, paying faculty/staff, and managing information. Finally, some processes are mandated for regulation and compliance (Figure 1.3).

FIGURE 1.3

PROCESSES	EXAMPLES
Priority processes	Hire faculty
	Admit students
	Enroll students
Operational processes	Manage financial operations
	Manage facilities
	Purchase goods
	Pay faculty and staff
Regulation and compliance processes	Hazardous waste disposal
	Health and safety regulations
	Fair Employment Act regulations

The next step is to identify those processes which have the greatest impact on institutional performance and represent the most significant opportunities for productivity and efficiency increases, customer satisfaction improvements, or cost reductions. Many business processes found in campus administration cross multiple organizational boundaries and, as a result, are both complex and cumbersome due to the number of hand-offs within the process. Each hand-off is an opportunity for errors, delays, and lost accountability. To process a purchase order in a typical state university, for example, involvement is required from academic departments, academic administration, and both the government and university procurement office. Much of what occurs within the process is outside the direct span of control of the director of procurement (Figure 1.4).

In order to take a process view of work, it is important to identify several factors:

▶ The requirement that initiates or triggers the process

▶ The customers of the process as well as their wants and needs

▶ The primary activities or steps within the process and the process participants who perform them

▶ The information that is required by each step within the process

▶ The process "owner" who is responsible for the overall performance of the process

FIGURE 1.4

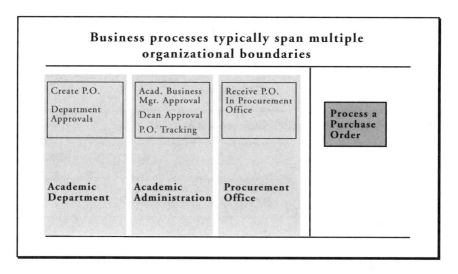

> The process performance measurements that provide information for management decision-making

Among the questions to ask as you analyze a process are

> Who are the customers of the process?

> What key outputs do they receive?

> What are the important characteristics of these outputs?

> How important is each characteristic, and how well are we currently performing?

> What performance measures should we use?

> What level of performance would customers like to see on each measure?

> What needs to improve?

> How does our process performance compare to that of our peer institutions?

> How do we track our performance over time? against our goals?

> Can we identify best practices to help us redesign our processes?

The following example illustrates a typical travel expense reimbursement process with an average cycle time of three weeks (Figure 1.5). Initial root cause analysis has identified the following as problems within the process: mathematical calculation errors, currency conversion problems, missing signatures, travel expense coding errors, and incorrect routing.

FIGURE 1.5

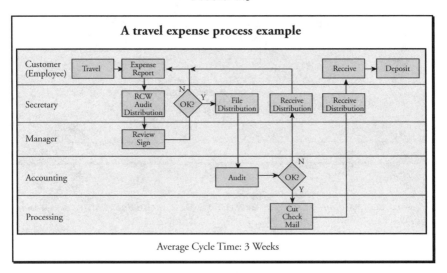

To design a process that avoids these pitfalls and ensures accurate, timely reimbursement of expenses, the following questions need to be asked at each step in the process:

▶ What problems originate in this step of the process and contribute to the poor performance of the process as a whole?

▶ Could we eliminate this activity if some prior activity were done differently?

▶ Does technology exist that would eliminate this activity?

▶ Could this activity be eliminated without affecting the final product or service from the customer perspective?

▶ Is this activity required by the customer and will the customer pay for it?

If the answer to any of the last four questions is "yes," then it is a step that provides no clear value to the customer.

In analyzing and simplifying processes, it is not unusual to find that bureaucracy results in some of the following:

❱ Unnecessary checks and balances

❱ Inspection or approval of someone else's work

❱ More than one sign-off required

❱ Unnecessary copies required, made, and stored

❱ Participants involved who add no value in the process

❱ Unnecessary written correspondence

❱ Procedures which interfere with, rather than facilitate, the process

❱ Duplication of effort

❱ No clear linkage between the output of one step and the input of the next step

Analysis of the travel expense reimbursement process revealed a high degree of "non-value-added" activity—steps in the process which have no value in the eyes of the customer (Figure 1.6).

FIGURE 1.6

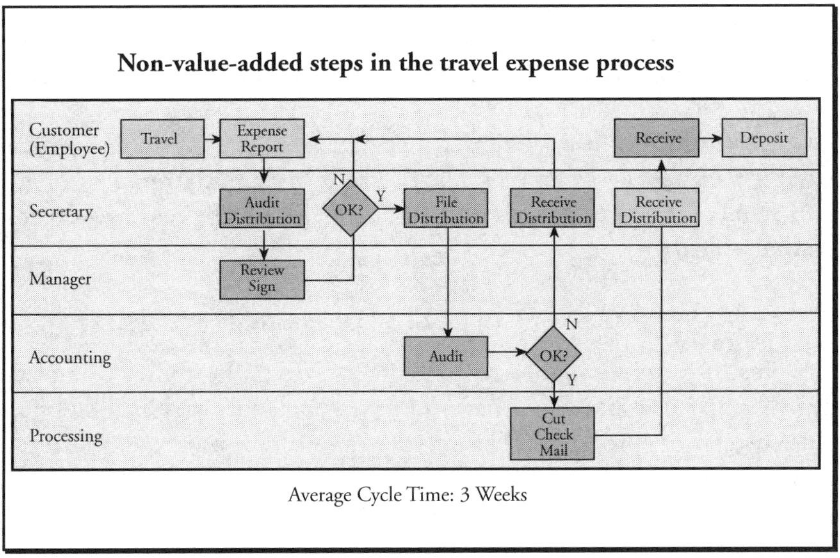

Non-value-added steps in the travel expense process

Average Cycle Time: 3 Weeks

Following the analysis of the existing process to understand problems and inefficiencies, the process was redesigned by eliminating the steps that contributed no value and by introducing new technology and work policies to expedite the process (Figure 1.7). The redesigned travel expense reimbursement process has reduced cycle time from three weeks to three days, reduced errors, eliminated unnecessary reviews and approvals, and placed the money directly in the employee account. Some organizations would take this redesign a step further by eliminating the audit step by the accounting department during processing and instituting an ad hoc post audit review process.

FIGURE 1.7

A redesigned travel expense process

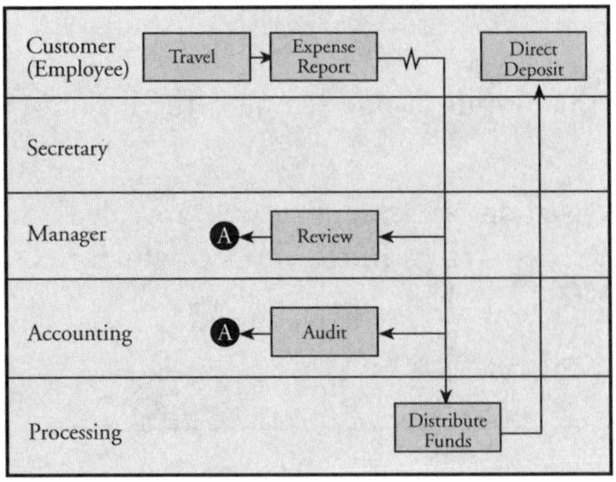

New Process
- Outcome oriented
- Captures information at the source
- Control built into the process
- Eliminates non-value-added activities
- Exception steps are removed from the main process flow

Results
- Reduced administrative processing time
- Reduced cycle time — 3 days
- No requirement for manual deposit

By focusing on the customer, challenging assumptions, and using information technology as an enabler, the results demonstrated dramatic improvement in the time and cost associated with processing travel expense reimbursements.

MANAGING THE PEOPLE SIDE OF TRANSFORMATION

The most critical component of transformation is the ability to manage change in the attitudes and behaviors of the people involved in and responsible for critical processes. The travel expense reimbursement example implies different roles for staff responsible for the redesigned process. They need to be trained in a new computer application and become proficient in its use. They are being asked to assume greater accountability for their work, as management reviews have been eliminated. They must be willing to let go of work procedures that they have been performing comfortably for years. The secretary's role has been eliminated entirely. In most process redesign efforts, people are asked to move from individual tasks to teamwork as well as to broaden their skills and responsibilities.

These kinds of changes in people's work life are not always welcomed; in fact, resistance to change is one of the greatest obstacles for transformation efforts to overcome. Any successful transformation effort focuses attention on the management of change, assesses the readiness for change in the affected organization, and develops and deploys a concrete plan to implement the desired change. The following are typical changes that must occur in order for institutional transformation efforts to be successful.

CHANGE AREA	FROM	TO
Work units	Functional departments	Process teams
Jobs	Simple tasks	Multidimensional work
People	Controlled	Empowered
Job preparation	Task-specific training	Decision-making skills
Focus on performance	Individual activity	Team/process results
Major focus	Please the boss	Please the customer
Values	Protective	Productive
Managers	Supervisors	Coaches
Senior management	Scorekeepers	Leaders

KEYS TO SUCCESS IN TRANSFORMING BUSINESS PROCESSES

While the subject of business process reengineering is relatively new to higher education, much has been learned from experience in the private sector. Given the complexity of college and university costing and funding structures, the high degree of fragmentation in job roles and responsibilities, the lack of accountability ingrained in the academic governance and decision-making model, and the extreme autonomy and independence fostered by the culture, transforming the way academic institutions conduct their "business" presents unique challenges. Following are critical success factors identified by organizations who have redesigned their business systems and processes:

▶ Recognize and articulate the compelling need for change

▶ Start with and maintain a high level of executive support and involvement

▶ Understand the organization's readiness for change

▶ Communicate constantly throughout the transformation initiative to cultivate support and buy-in from all levels of the institution

▶ Create transformation teams populated by your best people

▶ Use a structured approach that creates a common language and framework

▶ Use consultants effectively

▶ Link transformation goals directly to the institution's strategy (vision, mission, goals)

▶ Listen to the voice of the customer

▶ Select the right processes for redesign

▶ Maintain momentum and contain the focus to a reasonable number of processes

▶ Maintain the teams as the vehicle for change after the redesign activity is completed

▶ Quickly come to an understanding of the "as is" in order to devote more energy to the creation of the "to be"

▶ Choose the right performance indicators and metrics, and integrate them into your management practices

▶ Understand the risks associated with transformation and develop contingency plans to address them

▶ Develop a process for continuous improvement after the redesigned process has been implemented

CONCLUSION

In order to become and remain compatible with the demands of the future, many institutions will need to fundamentally rethink what they do and why. Streamlining administrative processes, increasing operational productivity and efficiency, and focusing on customer satisfaction are often first steps to ensuring that the college or university is allocating the maximum share of its resources to its core missions of teaching, research, and public service. In order for schools to reinvent themselves as more competitive institutions prepared to survive and thrive in the global education marketplace, they must be flexible, highly efficient, and adaptable to change. The principles discussed in this chapter provide institutions with a roadmap for better self-management.

REFERENCES/SUGGESTED READINGS

Davis, S., & Botkin, J. (1995). *The monster under the bed.* New York, NY: Simon & Schuster.

Dill, D. (1994). Rethinking the planning process. *Planning for Higher Education, 22,* 8-13.

Farrington, G. (1997). *Higher education in the information age.* In D. G. Oblinger & S. C. Rush (Eds.), *The learning revolution: The challenge of information technology in the academy.* Bolton, MA: Anker.

Gregorian, V., Hawkins, B. L., & Taylor, M. (1992, Winter). Integrating information technologies: A research university perspective. *CAUSE/Effect, 15* (4), 5-12.

Hammer, M., & Champy, J. (1993). *Reengineering the corporation.* New York, NY: Harper Business Publishers.

Hooker, M. (1997). The transformation of higher education. In D. G. Oblinger & S. C. Rush (Eds.), *The learning revolution: The challenge of information technology in the academy.* Bolton, MA: Anker.

Massy, W. F. (1997). Life on the wired campus: How information technology will shape institutional futures. In D. G. Oblinger & S. Rush (Eds.), *The learning revolution: The challenge of information technology in the academy.* Bolton, MA: Anker.

Massy, W., & Zemsky, R. (1990). The lattice and the ratchet. *Policy Perspectives, 2* (4), 5. Philadelphia, PA: The University of Pennsylvania.

Thorin, S. E., & Sorkin, V. D. (1997). The library of the future. In D. G. Oblinger & S. Rush (Eds.), *The learning revolution: The challenge of information technology in the academy.* Bolton, MA: Anker.

Wingspread Group on Higher Education. (1993). *An American imperative: Higher expectations for higher education.* Racine, WI: The Johnson Foundation, Inc.

PART 2

PLANNING FOR THE FUTURE

2

A STRATEGY
FOR I/T INVESTMENTS

William H. Graves

Twenty years ago, transaction processing, administrative database applications, and support for research in the quantitative disciplines justified a limited investment in information technology (I/T) infrastructure, accessible only to some researchers and the back-office staffs in colleges and universities. Today, however, I/T costs are increasing rapidly in higher education in response to broad demands from the faculty, staff, and student body. Information technology is now an essential tool used not just to administer records and transactions or to automate computation in research, but to create, locate, store, deliver, and analyze information and knowledge. I/T is adding value, as well as costs, to an industrial age infrastructure of buildings and rigidly scheduled classrooms designed long ago to support the textbook-aided and library-aided lecture. I/T is enhancing individual productivity—at additional cost to the institution and the individual. Paradoxically, it is not significantly increasing the productivity of the institution.

Overall, higher education executives are investing in I/T to add quality to business as usual, thereby adding costs. So far, most uses of I/T in higher education have failed to be transformative in their impact. If I/T is to become more than an added cost and a personal productivity tool for higher education, then its transformative power must be institutionally focused on increasing the productivity of higher education's primary "business"—

instruction. Perhaps this quote from the Pew Higher Education Roundtable says it best:

> The changes most important to higher education are those that are external to it. What is new is the use of societal demand—in the American context, market forces—to reshape the academy. The danger is that colleges and universities have become less relevant to society precisely because they have yet to understand the new demands being placed on them.... [Americans need] real assurances that shifting economic and political fortunes will not place a higher education beyond their grasp.... It is precisely that promise that is being imbedded in the new electronic superhighway—which may turn out to be the most powerful external challenge facing higher education, and the one the academy is least prepared to understand (Zemsky, 1994).

To take advantage of the transformative promise of I/T, colleges and universities will have to embrace and work within a basic tenet: The network is the keystone of the I/T revolution. Any I/T-enabled educational revolution will be based on easy and affordable access to the network from any place at any time.

"The network is the computer" may be an overused phrase, but it underscores a fundamental shift in the way information technologies are being used. Sharing resources over the network mitigates many of the constraints of time and place and enables the manipulation of information in an almost infinite variety of ways. It is the network which will allow the creation of innovative instructional models designed not just to increase access to instruction and to add quality to the learning experience, but also to contain the overall cost of instruction.

Linked to the Internet and based on open Internet standards, an institutional intranet of ubiquitously and easily accessible communication, computation, and information resources can provide:

▶ A globally-connected, robust digital communications environment to enhance the reach, timeliness, and effectiveness of human communication in every aspect of instruction, research, public service, and institutional management

▶ A learning infrastructure with attendant services to increase the quality of student and faculty academic work and to increase access to academic resources and instruction beyond the boundaries of the traditional classroom, lab, and library

▶ An information and transaction infrastructure with related services which enable an institution to streamline its management and outreach functions by redesigning their underlying processes

It will be ironic if higher education, which pioneered the Internet, fails to adapt its academic programs and administrative structures to take advantage of networked opportunities for institutional and collective productivity. The heft of higher education's costs lies in instruction, mostly in instructional personnel. To help contain operating costs per student, whether paid from private or public coffers, I/T must be deployed to ensure that prevailing investments in instructional personnel and programs produce higher levels of instructional productivity. That is seldom the case today.

BEWARE THE BOLT-ON

Today's tendency is to bolt I/T onto prevailing instructional practices. Even those executives who have encouraged technology-enabled innovation in their institutions' core business—instruction—have too often followed a path of least resistance by funding individual instructors who step forward to lead the charge but whose collective work results in little more than episodic innovation. These efforts often improve the quality of students' learning, but do little to alter the basic economics of instruction since they are typically overlaid on an existing classroom-based course.

Some colleges and universities have funded special projects to demonstrate the high-tech nature of the campus of the future. By failing to take a systemic, institutional approach, these institutions fail to address the fundamental issue: the future of the campus. Building high-tech classrooms of the future today, for example, parrots the early days of motion pictures when stage plays were filmed.

A case in point is distance education. The typical practice of distance education, which relies on real-time interactive video to remove the geographic constraints of the classroom lecture, is a bolt-on application of technology. While this form of distance education can increase access to instruction and even avoid the bricks-and-mortar costs of new campuses, it does not alter the fundamental time-bound classroom communication model or the basic economic measure of the labor intensive classroom—the student-teacher ratio. The contact-hour lecture delivered from any distance is labor intensive.

The contact hour constrains the current instructional model. Few would argue that the contact-hour lecture is the best mechanism for human contact between mentor (instructor) and student. Instead, the lecture too often represents a trade-off, a way to deliver information while ensuring some contact between an instructor and students to produce a return on an institutional investment in a classroom teaching infrastructure and a semester-based or quarter-based currency of certification. Many academic executives, having managed mandated efficiencies by trading off a more Socratic faculty-student interaction against a contact-hour instructional infrastructure, now face the proverbial rock and hard place. Any further attempts to optimize the productivity of instructional investments within today's labor intensive contact-hour paradigm by increasing class sizes or course loads are likely to compromise quality beyond a point acceptable to either the public or the professoriate. Tinkering at the margins of this instructional model which is already buckling under increasing demands for productivity and accountability is a high risk. More flexible and productive instructional models are needed.

DISTRIBUTE INSTRUCTION

The phrase "distributed instruction" implies a shift from today's institution-centered model of education to a society-centered model. It also implies new possibilities which are not connoted today by the phrase "distance education." Distributed instruction offers new possibilities through a form of distance instruction which is more flexible and affordable than that associated solely with real-time interactive video. Several key factors differentiate distributed instruction from purely distance instruction and with the result that distributed instruction is more scalable than distance education.

Economies at the Margin

An important differentiator is the contrast between the economics of computer networks and those of real-time interactive video networks. The incremental cost of adding one more node to an interactive video network is approximately the same as the cost of an original node—a fairly high cost. In contrast, the institutional intranet required to participate meaningfully in the Internet community requires a large initial capital investment, but the incremental cost of adding one more node to it is relatively low—the cost of a personal computer and its support.

Disintermediation

Another critical difference between the two forms of distance education is that a real-time video network, as typically deployed for distance education, is not only time-dependent, but also highly mediated. The space, equipment, personnel, and other resources needed for a teleclass or teleconference are scarce and must be negotiated and scheduled. Also, the required time-dependent interconnections must be managed by a technician. In contrast, a student at a computer connected to the Internet can have access any time to any available Internet resource; this access is mediated by computers without additional human intervention.

Time Independence

Another obvious difference is that computer networks, unlike real-time interactive video networks, remove the constraints of time while still supporting some forms of real-time communication. Computer networks, moreover, provide for the capture, storage, and retrieval of video in digital form.

Resource Sharing

Although video networks allow a professor to be shared, computer networks can be deployed more ubiquitously for asynchronous and real-time communication and for the delivery of shared instructional resources. Indeed, a campus intranet developed around Internet standards can readily be connected to the Internet and, thereby, to other institutions' intranets. This amplifies an institution's investment many times over. It is at the heart of the collaborative possibilities inherent in the Internet.

Interoperability

The characteristics of interactive video networks argue for using them when real-time interaction is necessary or when a societal need justifies their expense. However, it is not always possible to connect one institution's interactive video network to another's. There are neither standards nor a nationwide fabric of interconnection points to ensure sharing—as there are for the Internet.

Flexibility and Social Relevance

The ultimate goal of creating distributed instructional opportunities is to meet the rising societal expectation for affordability, relevance, and flexibility in higher education—the point of the earlier quote from the Pew Roundtable. Society expects higher education to link its curricula, its research agendas, and its public service offerings more closely to social and economic needs. Society also expects higher education to become more flexible in its course and degree offerings in order to meet new educational needs. Rapid changes in discipline areas, along with rapid growth in the volume of the overall knowledge base, are fueling an emphasis on lifelong learning and learning to learn. Moreover, not all students are interested in a residential experience. Many consumers of instruction prefer tightly focused, self-selected learning objectives. This is especially the case with nontraditional learners and lifelong learners who may have legitimate educational needs neither relevant to nor easily accommodated by the time-and-place constraints of traditional campus-based study or the time constraints of multiple-year degree offerings.

Overall Return on Investment

All of this means that an institutional intranet can be the key to restructuring instruction. The opportunity is for higher education to experiment strategically with alternative models of distributed instruction which draw on the Internet's communication technologies, information resources, and capacity to deliver interactive learning applications. The promise of distributed instruction is to increase access to instruction, to enhance the quality of students' learning, and to reap a better overall return on investments in instruction.

STRATEGIZE WISELY

As noted earlier, focusing on those instructors who are willing to try I/T-based innovation is a strategy that has often resulted in episodic, individual successes but seldom in institutional transformation. Wiser strategies are needed.

Some colleges and universities are focusing instructional I/T investments on institutional continuing education service units. These groups understand the value of alternative instructional models. However, many are isolated from the institutional mainstream, so there is the danger that an investment in continuing education might not pay off for the entire institution. An alternative is to focus on those schools or departments within the institution which are ready to take leadership positions in distributed instruction. Many professional schools and departments, such as business and the health-related academic units, understand the need to deploy I/T in their continuing or executive education programs.

Perhaps the most appealing strategy is to focus on major and/or costly educational problems within the institution or within a consortium of institutions—basic math skills, for example. There is little risk in trying new approaches to major problems which have resisted resolution. Successes in such highly visible areas of the curriculum, which typically are also high enrollment areas, can seed innovation elsewhere. This is an institutional strategy which focuses on a few select high-enrollment courses to optimize the instructional return on investment in I/T.

Access to the global information infrastructure (the Internet) allows higher education to look at its services in a new context, which need not be from a strictly competitive perspective. The roles of academic institutions as both consumers of services as well as providers of services can be redefined. The individual institution need not be the sole owner of knowledge and talent in an environment in which resources can be shared (for a fee or for free). Institutions can work together to provide distributed instruction while retaining the valuable competitive institutional distinctions that guide and certify an individual's higher education. This is a strategy of "collabotition"—precompetitive collaboration to create an enhanced foundation for competitive differentiation. Indeed, the high costs of creating a ubiquitously accessible institutional intranet and the difficulty of widespread cultural change in the academy argue for an approach in which the costs and risks associated with major change are shared among institutions.

Any strategy for using I/T as a tool for transforming instruction relies on ubiquitous access to the institutional intranet and the Internet, therefore on an overall strategy or plan for creating and using such infrastructure. I/T planning should have three primary components:

▶ A long-term strategic framework for prioritizing and funding those uses of technology which are most strategic to the institution's mission—in instruction, for example

▶ A continually evolving, standards-based I/T architecture and a more specific, central implementation of shared infrastructure and technologies to guide the purchase of information technologies and the provision of attendant technology services at all levels of the institution

▶ A collaborative process for ensuring that I/T architecture and investments support the institution's strategy

Technology planning is not solely about developing a plan for managing and using centrally-purchased technologies. Much of the responsibility for technology planning lies outside the central technology organization(s). The strategic framework, for example, must be developed, funded, and monitored in collaboration with the leadership of mission-critical academic and administrative units. Even the I/T architecture and the shared, centrally managed technologies must have the confidence of, therefore input from, the independent technology support organizations which span a range of mission-critical units, such as the libraries, the schools and colleges in a large institution, and various administrative offices.

An institutional technology officer can facilitate an attempt to link technology as a tool to issues and initiatives strategic to the institution's future, such as new instructional models, new student services models, and new business process models. But only the chief executive and academic officers can ensure the involvement of academic and administrative leaders in identifying institutionally strategic needs and the funding to meet them. There are many mechanisms for connecting I/T spending and implementation to mission, but the key is to create a mechanism to provide a sounding board for I/T priorities and to advise the institutional technology officer on how to structure a collaborative process that will take into account mission-critical issues and needs while identifying the financial resources required to meet those needs.

The institutional technology officer also must give I/T leaders from across the campus a voice in designing the I/T architecture and implementing the central technology blueprint. In addition to convening this group of technologists and creating a strategic mechanism for connecting the technologists' planning to mission-critical needs and directions, organizing customer focus sessions can be useful when they are constituted and convened as needed to address a range of specific service and application areas.

It is important to understand that the central technology blueprint will have to be constantly adjusted both in its scale, to keep pace with unprecedented and often unpredictable demand, and in its implementation to keep pace with changes in technology. The institution's technology environment will be in constant evolution for the foreseeable future, exacerbating the need to ensure the participation of decision-makers from mission-critical academic and administrative units in formulating the strategic framework for deploying technology.

I/T planning as described above is almost tantamount to institutional planning. Consider, for example, just a few of the issues raised by the use of technology as a tool in the instructional program:

▸ How should the center of campus be configured to serve the future goals of the institution?

▸ Which students need to be on campus, to what extent, and when?

▸ Can any time/any where Internet communications increase the frequency and quality of faculty/student contact and decrease dependence on the rigid, labor intensive contact hour model and thus on the classroom?

Consider the emergence of new educational service providers and their impact on the institution's mission-critical competencies.

▸ Will commercially delivered courses and on-demand learning enabled by digital technologies allow some institutions of higher learning to concentrate on the synthesizing aspects of general education?

▶ Will some academic institutions move away from instruction in basic skills by insisting on externally certified competence in these skills as a condition of admission?

I/T planning raises all of these issues if such planning is connected to the institution's mission, as it should be.

ACT SOON

Higher education executives cannot awaken too soon to the need to view information technology as a strategic investment rather than a cost. Most academic executives are aware that the problems facing their institutions do not beg short-term solutions, but few have seriously challenged the culture of traditional instruction. The development and adoption of new instructional models will not be painless and will not happen overnight. If academic leaders hesitate to act as partners to create a national educational fabric, viable alternatives to the present model of institution-based education will present themselves, and higher education as an institution may be hard-pressed to compete.

REFERENCES/SUGGESTED READINGS

Graves, W. H. (1994, March/April). Toward a national learning infrastructure. *EDUCOM Review, 29* (2), 32-37. http://www.educom.edu/educom.review/review.94/mar.apr/graves_article.

Graves, W. H. (1993, September/October). Educational ecosystem of information and computation: Medium and message. *EDUCOM Review, 28* (5), 9-12. http://ike.engr.washington.edu/iat/director/graves.html.

Heterick, R. C., Jr. (1993). *Reengineering teaching and learning in higher education: Sheltered groves, Camelot, windmills, and malls.* CAUSE Professional Paper Series, No. 10. Boulder, CO: CAUSE. http://cause-www.colorado.edu/information-resources/ir-library/abstracts/pub3010.html.

Oblinger, D. G., & Maruyama, M. K. (1996). *Distributed learning.* CAUSE Professional Paper Series, No. 14. Boulder, CO: CAUSE.

Twigg, C. A. (1994, July/August). The changing definition of learning. *EDUCOM Review, 29* (4), 22-25. http://www.educom.edu/educom.review/review.94/jul.aug/Twigg_Article.

Twigg, C. A. (1994, November/December). Navigating the transition. *EDUCOM Review, 29* (6), 20-24. http://www.educom.edu/educom.review/review.94/nov.dec/twigg.

Twigg, C. A. (1994, September/October). The need for a national learning infrastructure. *EDUCOM Review, 29* (5), 16-20. http://www.educom.edu/educom.review/review.94/sept.oct/Twigg_Article.

Zemsky, R. (Ed.). (1994, April). *To dance with change.* Policy Perspectives: The Pew Higher Education Roundtable, Vol. 5. Philadelphia, PA: The University of Pennsylvania.

Strategic Information Technology Planning in Higher Education: A New Roadmap to the 21st Century Academy

Charles R. Moran

Mythical State University's (MSU) mission statement and institutional philosophy declare that the university's primary goals are to graduate students who are highly competitive in today's job market. MSU prides itself on being closely attuned to the needs of today's employers and on providing curricula that prepare students to effectively respond to those needs. A few years ago, MSU's executives recognized the importance of staying current with technology to maintain a competitive edge and to provide their students with high value technology skills. A committee was formed to develop a strategic plan for technology. The committee, representing administrative services, academic affairs, and the information technology staff quickly developed a list of high priority initiatives that the membership felt were strategically important. The list was approved, budgeted, and implementation was begun. The key projects included:

▶ Expansion of the campus backbone (network) to handle greater bandwidth demands

▶ Creation of a state-of-the-art multimedia courseware development studio

▶ Upgrading the mainframe to better handle administrative tasks

▶ Enhancing the computer science and engineering labs to accommodate the latest personal computers

Two years later, the executive committee began hearing that potential students were not attending MSU because they perceived it to be a "low-tech" school. What went wrong? Technology was going to be one of the keys to the future for MSU. Hadn't MSU developed three highly regarded multimedia courses that had been demonstrated at a number of higher education conferences? Didn't the mainframe have more than enough capacity to handle the new human resources package that personnel had been requesting for several years? Weren't the faculty happy with the Internet capabilities available through the new network?

Enrollment services commissioned a survey of the student body, area high schools, and prospective students who had gone elsewhere in order to understand student perceptions. They discovered that, from the students' perspective, little had changed since the technology plan was approved. They found:

▶ There is more bandwidth on the network, but the public labs have not been expanded to provide access to the network. and most classrooms have no network access.

▶ Most of the labs are department owned and not generally accessible.

▶ Computers owned by the students and faculty often cannot access the campus network and labs.

▶ The multimedia studio provides high visibility for a handful of MSU faculty, but does little to build practical technology skills among the student body or to improve the overall instructional technology abilities of the faculty.

▶ The mainframe has great capacity, but little or none of it is being directed toward student or faculty needs.

▶ When something breaks, the help desk doesn't help.

After two years of planning and implementation, along with the major associated expense, the executive committee realized that its technology plan was out of synch with the primary goals and needs of the institution. Rather than a focus on developing competitive students, the plan was focused on high visibility technology. If the planning committee had consistently tested the emerging plan against MSU's mission/goals, it would have noticed the disconnect that was developing. If the committee had taken the time to carefully assess what was working and not working in the current environment, it might have developed a more pragmatic set of projects. Perhaps most importantly, if the committee had actively included representatives from the key stakeholder groups—students and faculty—in the planning process, these issues would probably have been addressed early in the process.

IT'S NOT WORKING ANYMORE...

Many higher education institutions have for years engaged in strategic technology planning similar to that at MSU. Having a technology plan is a requirement at many institutions and is often included in national accreditation review processes. Despite this long history of planning, many campus executives are beginning to realize that information technology has not had the dramatic impact that many thought it would or should have on the lives of faculty and students nor on the critical needs of our institutions. Most students still struggle through poorly automated services, nonintegrated information systems, and an inadequate focus on the real impediments to institutions using technology in support of learning. Most faculty have minimal access to technology and even less access to the support they need to integrate technology with pedagogy. Most institutions have not begun the critical discussions to decide how, if at all, teaching and the student/faculty relationship will change to take advantage of technology. Most institutions do not have the necessary infrastructure (network, support, equipment, etc.) to meet their needs, nor do they have a clear-cut plan for reducing the gap. A more effective strategic planning approach would have included focused recommendations for these issues as key components of the technology plan.

The way most institutions do strategic planning today is not working. We keep planning the same old way for this rapidly changing environment, then find ourselves unprepared to keep up with the changing needs of our institutions and our stakeholders. It is not rational to keep doing the same thing over and over again yet expect a different result. We need to stop repeating the traditional approach to technology planning. It is not working, and it never will. We need a new way to plan.

Our view is that higher education must reflect and reevaluate every facet of its traditional planning approach. We propose that higher education adopt a new model for strategic planning: the strategic alignment framework. This framework focuses on driving alignment between both the strategic and tactical needs of an institution as well as the vision and actions of the school's information technology (I/T) investments and personnel. This framework focuses every I/T planning recommendation on supporting specific institutional strategies and/or goals.

CURRENT STATE OF INFORMATION TECHNOLOGY PLANNING

Think of a strategic plan as a roadmap to the future. If you were asked, "Can you give me directions to your campus?" your first question would be "Where are you coming from?" To describe how to move to a future destination, we must clearly define both the current location and the future destination. Armed with these two items we can begin to build a pragmatic roadmap to the new location. This concept, while seemingly simple, describes some of the fundamental problems with most campus I/T plans today. After reviewing dozens of campus plans, we have observed that they usually fall into one of two categories: a vision without substance or a budget without vision.

A Vision Without Substance

Many schools spend long months, even years, defining a vision for the future state of technology at their institution. These vision statements are often four or five lines of text describing the role of technology in the future of the institution. Sometimes it includes several paragraphs to further define this future state. There are problems with many of these vision statements.

Problem #1: Vagueness. First, they are often too vague and general. Here is the test. If we replace the school's name with the name of almost any other school in the world, is the vision still appropriate? While it's not necessarily wrong to have a vision that many others share, it speaks to the need for a more detailed, campus specific definition of the future vision.

Along with the vision, it is important to define the strategies for achieving the vision. These strategies should include definable goals for success. If we do X or raise/lower a measurement to Y, then we have achieved this strategy and part of the vision. We rarely see these types of quantifiable statements and goals in campus strategic technology plans.

Problem #2: Lack of institutional vision. The second problem relates to why it takes months and even years to describe the I/T vision: There is no defined institutional vision. Forget technology for a moment. As an institution, where is the college or university trying to go in the future? How will it get there? What are the inhibitors to the institution reaching its desired future? These questions are rarely asked. It is even more rare that they are clearly answered, if at all. If the institution cannot define what it is evolving toward—as an institution—how can we safely define how technology should help the school evolve? Is the institution moving aggressively in distance learning, with a goal of 20% of student full-time equivalents (FTEs) attending a distance learning course by the year 2000? Or is the institution talking about distance learning only because it is politically correct to do so? Will the campus aggressively pursue nontraditional groups as a new source of students in its science and engineering school? Does the institution see the role of the faculty and the faculty's relationship to students remaining fairly constant for the next 10 years or changing greatly? Must the campus rapidly reduce the cost of its administrative overhead by X% over the next three years to balance its budget? Is the curriculum planning process evolving to make programs more attractive to prospective students and faculty? Is there a process or a plan to change the curriculum to take advantage of technology in instruction or to modify faculty merit criteria? In defining the unique strategies and goals for any institution it is important to move the vision from global generalizations to actionable institutional goals.

The benefit of developing these types of institutional strategies is that they can help achieve a major goal of "best practices" strategic planning: They describe a focused set of actions to be taken. Perhaps more importantly, they define what will not be done. Institutional leaders need to make these decisions, focusing often less than adequate resources on doing the right things right whether for technology or nontechnology planning. This is not to say that the things we stop doing are bad or wrong; we just can't afford to do everything right. We need to stop doing some things in order to do higher priority things in a more effective manner. It is axiomatic that if everything is a priority, nothing is a priority.

Problem #3: Where are you today? The third major problem with most technology plans is that they do not accurately define where we are today. In the analogy mentioned before, it is like giving directions to your campus without asking from where you are starting. A major obstacle to defining where you are is that it requires an objective assessment of what is working today and what is not. Nobody is entirely comfortable with having their work evaluated (we carefully said "evaluated" not "judged"), but if we do not assess ourselves, how can we ever improve?

Assessment requires finding out what is important to students, faculty, and the institution and evaluating performance at meeting these needs. This is difficult to do without a strong sense of trust in the organization as well as the process. These assessments should not be perceived as "witch hunts."

Consider them more like a midterm report card on results. We need to see this as a constructive exercise to document successes and address weaknesses. The quality of assessment efforts will directly influence the quality of the final plan.

Problem #4: Time. Another problem with these type of plans is that they take too long to create. Often, we find that a technology planning committee has spent 14 months defining the vision and does not have the energy to effectively build a high quality implementation plan. How do you effectively plan for rapidly changing technology if your planning process takes years? Who has the energy to be part of a planning process that lasts that long? Because the process is so lengthy we often find campus I/T plans that are three, four, and five years old, and therefore are completely out of date. These plans usually sit on the shelf and gather dust. Many plans are physically (and intellectually) covered with dust—something that doesn't occur with a plan that is being continually reviewed, implemented, and updated.

Building a strategic plan must be considered an ongoing process, not an event. The economics and capabilities of information technology are changing so rapidly that plans must be regularly reviewed and updated (probably annually) just to keep pace. If this is true, we need a process that can be done quickly (three-year reviews might require three to five months; annual update booster shot reviews might last one month). We must not allow the critical need to obtain a buy-in to be an excuse for a planning process that takes forever. When you spend two years building a technology plan, three things occur:

▶ Nobody wants to be involved with implementing the plan.

▶ The plan is out of date before you get it bound and distributed.

▶ Nobody wants to be on the next planning team.

Planning processes that take longer than a year are ineffective and waste everyone's good efforts. Single campus plans should be completed in less than six months.

A Budget Without Vision
Because of the problems with the first type of plan, many institutions have moved to a budget-without-a-vision type of plan. This plan has a quick vision statement (taken and customized from somewhere else) attached to the annual I/T budget plan. It goes straight from a quick vision to "We need three of these @ $5,000 each, ten of these @ $1,600 each...." These plans

look both strategic and practical. However, they are often a collection of transactions without any strategic, integrated rationale.

Problem #1: What problem is solved? The key problem with a budget-without-a-vision plan is that you can rarely get good answers to the questions: "After you buy and install all of this stuff, how will the school's goals and the needs of its stakeholders be improved?" "Will the problems that keep the president up late at night be fixed?" We often receive blank stares in response to these questions. In other cases, the responses still miss the heart of the matter; for example, "Isn't it obvious that moving to a 100 mb fast Ethernet is the best thing for the school?" "Isn't it obvious that we have to wire every classroom, office, and lab?" "Isn't it obvious that the model 500 machine is out of date and needs to be upgraded to the 700 model for $750K?"

The simple answer to these questions should be: "No, it is not obvious." If you cannot define outcomes for each recommendation in the plan which clearly provide identified value to the institution, a faculty, student, or staff member, then maybe you should not implement that recommendation. Use this test for all ongoing I/T projects. You may be surprised to discover how many projects don't pass the test.

A characteristic of these plans is the presence of I/T strategy components which seem to have been chosen in a vacuum. Does anyone, outside of the I/T group, understand why we need to embrace the "ZZZ" architecture? We owe it to our stakeholders to help them understand, on a nontechnical level, the pros and cons of any technology decision which will consume significant funding. We owe it to them to involve them in selecting their future technologies. The approach of "I know what you need, so just trust me, and fund this . . ." is no longer acceptable to many campus executives. It should not be.

Problem #2: Prioritization. In the budget-without-a-vision plan, there is often little or no prioritization of recommendations: Everything in these plans must be done. What happens when we find that we cannot afford to implement the whole I/T plan? Which task(s) should we take off the list? Since all the recommendations must be done and all are high priority, the common solution is to cut every task by 10%. This avoids making hard decisions. In reality, we should usually eliminate half the tasks that we are doing and more fully fund the rest. Without a prioritization scheme, we have no basis for managing the plan when the real funding, never adequate to implement the whole plan, is provided.

Problem #3: Roles and responsibilities. The last problem with these plans is that often they do not define the roles and responsibilities for implementing each component of the plan. If we are implementing a new student information system, what should the I/T staff be responsible for and for what should the student services community and their management be responsible? When implementing any new I/T initiative, the users must drive the change within their department, not I/T. It is too easy to assume that I/T should be responsible for implementing every change associated with the project. Often decisions will cause significant changes in the way that the institution is run. These decisions can impact policy. If I/T owns the entire project implementation then the user community can argue, disagree, and fight with the changes ("No techie is going to tell us how to register our students..."). If the users own the project and I/T is working with or for them to implement the project, then everyone is part of the team. Everyone has to work together to successfully complete the project. Remember, it is much harder for someone to shoot holes in your boat if they are in the boat with you.

THE PARADOX

Our institutions do lots of I/T plans but rarely execute the plans successfully. They do lots of I/T planning, but the technology on our campuses seems to be getting farther and farther behind. Although there are lots of I/T plans, the users of technology are not listening anymore.

We need to take a fresh start at strategic I/T planning. The strategic alignment framework provides a new planning model that has proven highly effective in both higher education and the private sector. This model, if accepted, can have a significant impact on the value that higher education receives from its technology investments.

STRATEGIC ALIGNMENT: A NEW MODEL FOR INFORMATION TECHNOLOGY PLANNING

Our view of strategic alignment is based on research work done by John Henderson and the IBM Consulting Group (Henderson et al., 1992, 1993, 1994). The results revealed that many strategic planning efforts failed due to a misalignment between the focus of the I/T plan (and subsequently the I/T organizations) with the strategic and tactical needs of the organization. It was found that for I/T planning to be effective it was critical to take a holistic view of the organization's strategic mission and goals as well as to consider the practical realities of the organization's structure and capabilities. In a planning sense, we need to examine the institution's strategy (i.e., its future vision), and the institution's organizational infrastructure and processes (i.e., its current state), then focus on using technology planning as a major tool for helping an institution move toward its goals.

FIGURE 3.1

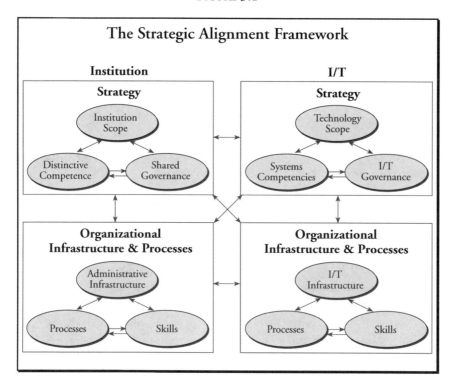

The Strategic Alignment Framework

The principle of strategic alignment recognizes the critical importance of a high degree of integration and consistency between the institutional mission/goals and the technology plan (Figure 3.1). If the technology plan does not align with the strategic goals and direction of the institution as well as address the inadequacies of the organizational structure and processes, it cannot be successful.

A core philosophy of strategic alignment is that any component of a strategic plan must support the fundamental mission of the organization, both in terms of the results that it will achieve and the values that it reflects. If either of these supporting requirements is missing, the integrity of the larger mission may be compromised and/or the success of the larger plan jeopardized.

The strategic alignment framework is a planning tool that helps ensure that the planning process effectively responds to (aligns with, deals with) internal and external forces (drivers) that can have strategic significance (impact) on the institution's future. Internal forces may include:

▶ Institutional mission, goals, strategies

▶ Institutional culture and values

▶ Funding/income capacity

▶ Physical infrastructure opportunities and constraints

▶ Stakeholder socioeconomic profiles

▶ Unique institutional capabilities (differentiators/strengths/niches)

▶ Organizational factors

▶ Political factors

External forces may include:

▶ Regional, national, and/or global socioeconomic conditions, trends, and needs

▶ Competitive forces

▶ Technological changes

▶ Government policies and actions

The cornerstone of the strategic alignment framework is the institutional mission and goals. These represent a formal statement of the purpose and strategies for the institution. The prevailing perceptions, attitudes, and aspirations of the stakeholders form the living, organic expression of the values that drive the mission and goals. It is a statement of how the institution is moving toward the future (its strategic intent) and includes objectives for moving toward that future. Supporting the objectives are goals for measuring the effectiveness of the actions aimed at supporting these objectives. Goals serve as barometers of the success or failure of each objective. A technology plan that fails to align itself with these strategic barometers is on a fast path to failure.

Having made this point, a paradox is often encountered: While the creator of the technology plan must understand the institution's strategic intent, goals, and objectives, these institutional strategic components often do not exist outside of the consciousness of the executive team. How can you do technology planning in this situation? Sadly this is often the rule and not the exception. The answer is that, at least at a high level, major components of the institution's strategy must be defined before you can realistically begin technology planning. The focus of the I/T planning process should be on quickly building the missing institutional strategy components without being sidetracked into doing a complete strategic plan for the institution. It is analogous to building a new house. While your focus is on the design and construction of the house itself, often you discover that your first step is building a road to the job site. To be successful, focus on quickly building these components and return to your I/T planning process. Build a road that can handle your work trucks, not a 12-lane interstate highway. Note: If you find that you cannot quickly define the institution's strategic goals and drivers, then maybe you should shelve the I/T planning effort and get the executive team to begin an effort to build the institution's strategic plan.

While the institution's strategies are a group of ideas, concepts, and goals, the institution's organizational infrastructure and processes are the real organization. It is the people, processes, assets, and organizations that make the institution run. It is where things get done, for better or worse, in the institution. It is in this area that the institution's organizational silos have been built which often appear to value departmental survival over institutional success. These silos have been built up over many years and are heavily fortified. When the institution defines its strategy for moving into the future, it is precipitating change in the organizational infrastructure and processes, i.e., changing the silos.

I/T can be a change agent, but it is not the only or the main change agent in an institutional transformation. In the strategic alignment framework, if you are unwilling to change the organizational infrastructure and processes, then you will be unable to achieve your strategies. Strategic planning is defining goals and strategies and then driving them down into the organization.

STRATEGIC ALIGNMENT PLANNING APPROACH

To build a strategic I/T plan that is aligned with both the institution's strategy and the practical reality of the institution's organizations, a planning process is required that develops:

▶ A thorough assessment of the institution's technology state today

▶ A long-term vision of how technology will support the institution in the future

▶ A plan to move from the current state to the future state

Assessment Phase: Where Are We Today?

It is important to begin by assessing the current state of technology at the institution. We must assess the alignment of current I/T resources and plans with the needs of the institution's strategies and organizations. Based on our consulting studies, we have identified the following assessment criteria that best define the institution's strategic alignment:

▶ Access to resources

▶ Access to information

▶ User support

▶ Cultural issues related to I/T

▶ Communications and expectations management

▶ Governance of IT

▶ Organization of IT

▶ Strategic planning process

▶ IT funding models and strategies

▶ Environmental realities

For the assessment phase to be successful we recommend an approach that includes both quantitative and qualitative analysis. To gather reliable data, we recommend the use of a highly focused survey of stakeholder perceptions and needs. The survey should focus on the strategic alignment criteria, along with any other items that may be appropriate for the campus. The rationale for the survey is to validate your recommendations.

We often hear, "We've surveyed our campus to death! We can't do it again." Upon inspection, we find that most surveys never resurface on the campus or show how their survey input was used to improve the campus environment. To address the campus' concerns, it is critical that the survey be short, focused, and include a feedback process to communicate to the campus stakeholders when the analysis is complete. The I/T plan is designed to help campus stakeholders. Explain how it can help.

While the surveys will provide insights to the current state of technology, they also will raise many new questions. To improve the quality of analysis, we recommend that the planning process include stakeholder focus groups to discuss the survey results, clarify issues, and begin to develop actions for resolving any identified issues. These carefully facilitated sessions should involve all campus communities to ensure that a complete picture of the current state of technology is seen. As one campus executive told us, "We've got over 20,000 students and 5,000 faculty and staff, so it shouldn't be hard to find a few to talk to." The combination of the survey and focus groups will provide a well-documented and understandable assessment of where the campus stands with its current technology.

Vision Phase: What Do We Want to Become?

The I/T vision establishes a view—five to ten years in the future—of how technology will have helped the institution achieve its strategic vision and goals. We need to establish a time horizon that is far enough out to allow for creative, out of the box thinking without being so far removed that it becomes nonimplementable science fiction. We often recommend developing the technology vision after the assessment is completed. This puts a sobering view on the process, often resulting in a more pragmatic and implementable vision.

The first step is to conduct research into new ideas that other institutions (and potentially private sector organizations) have developed for their future. There is nothing wrong with evaluating other good ideas and customizing them to the local environment. These ideas should help you see the possible, but not preclude you from having your own creative ideas.

Along with this research, conduct a series of brainstorming sessions with internal campus stakeholders (students, faculty, staff, and executives) and external stakeholders (alumni, businesses, and if appropriate, government oversight groups). These sessions are conducted with several ground rules:

▶ There are no bad ideas.

▶ Everyone has a good idea.

▶ There's always room for another new idea.

After the initial brainstorming, everyone has the opportunity to describe their ideas and analyze the ideas of others. These ideas are documented, organized, and compared with the institution's overall strategy to filter ideas that are in conflict with the overall strategy.

The next step involves developing a short sentence that describes the role that I/T will play if the brainstorming ideas are implemented. The development of this vision will be an iterative process, involving multiple reviews with several groups across the campus. We recommend that this step include representatives from the major stakeholder groups (students, faculty, staff, and executives) but that it also be completed quickly. While the vision is important, it is critical not to forget that people usually care less about the wording of the vision than they do about how you are going to achieve it.

An additional approach that we have found useful is to write stakeholder-based views of the future states, e.g., "A day in the life of . . ." scenarios showing how the stakeholder has been aided by fulfillment of the I/T vision.

Planning the Journey: How Will We Get There?

The last part of the planning effort involves defining those important projects that should be implemented to most effectively and efficiently move from the current state to the future state. This is where we prioritize and pick the best projects for achieving the future vision.

The most important components of a good strategic plan are:

Project. Document the set of all possible projects (include both ongoing and potential projects) that might help achieve the vision. Each project description should include a high level definition of 1) implementation costs and benefits (tangible and intangible), 2) perceived stakeholder benefits, 3) specific funding issues and opportunities, and 4) an assessment of how each potential project is aligned with the institution's strategies and goals.

Project prioritization. Prioritize each project based on the value that it delivers to the institution and its stakeholders. You can do this through a variety of attributes and measures to prioritize the projects. We've found that using clearly defined stakeholder value attributes is the best way to get campus buy-in and build a plan that can be executed.

Project sequencing. This step involves laying out the prioritized projects on a timeline for implementation, usually not more than five years out. It is best to implement fewer projects well than many projects poorly. If you accept our suggestions for maintaining the currency of the plan, then any recommendations that are more than two years in the future will be reviewed again. This will minimize the level of discourse on which project should be implemented in year four and which in year five.

Implementation strategies. This step involves determining the best path for successfully implementing the sequenced project list. How will the projects be funded? How will their success be measured? How will we manage their implementation to keep them on track and targeted for the desired outcomes? In identifying and addressing these types of issues, your planning process will have the completeness necessary for success.

Governance. This step involves developing the project management oversight groups which will manage the implementation of the plan. The highest level of this governance should involve the institution's executive team. Below them should be user-managed teams with specific responsibilities for each project. The executive team should regularly review (at least once every three months) the progress toward meeting the project timelines and achieving the identified benefits.

Organization. Based on the final plan, this step focuses on developing the optimal way to organize and manage the institution's I/T staffs to implement their portion of the plan. This task focuses on skills, structure, incentives, and measures.

FINAL NOTES: CRITICAL SUCCESS FACTORS

It sounds simple: You assess where you are, decide where you are going, then you build the plan. Experience reveals a variety of factors, often overlooked, that can ruin an elegant planning process. Before you begin, it is important to ask yourself—and anyone else having experience with your institution— what has to occur or be in place for this planning process (and ultimately the final plan) to be executed successfully? The answers to this question are often called the plan's critical success factors. These are the four or five things that can interfere as your institution tries to build and implement the best technology plan. The most common critical success factors are:

Executive support. If your planning effort does not have the support of your institution's top executives, do not waste time in planning. You might as well dust off last year's plan, change the date, and file it away until next year. "Executives" is intentionally plural. A common problem for many planning efforts is that the top executive is enthusiastic about the process and the plan, but the middle tier of campus executives provides only lip service support. While the top executives worry about the school's overall success, the middle level executives run the silos. Top executives must ensure that middle management helps—rather than hinders—the planning process.

Remember the adage "Planning is easy; execution is hard." If you do not have strong executive support from the entire executive team for the planning process, then you will never have support when you need it for implementation.

Leadership. If your institution is not facing tough challenges for which the old approaches no longer work, then you do not need leaders. Why rock the boat? However, for virtually all institutions, the economic and social environment is changing rapidly, and we need to change with it if we are to maintain control over our own destiny.

Successful change requires leadership. Leaders are willing to spend both economic and political capital in order to move in the direction that they feel is right. Leaders push their institutions where they need to go even when the change will cause short term disruption and anxiety. True leadership is a precious commodity—it's not about talk (which is cheap) or emotions (which are unfocused)—it's about passion. True leaders display a burning desire to move to a newer, better future and are the ones who show the way.

Funding. The best way to impede a planning effort is to ask how you're going to pay for all of this. There are always more things that need to be done than there are resources to pay for them.

One of the problems with identifying funding sources for new projects is the typical assumption that any new project should be financed with new funds. While external grants may fund some efforts, they will not pay for the major infrastructure and systems projects that many institutions are considering. When doing a long term I/T plan, look first within the current I/T budget for reallocation opportunities. All projects, both new and ongoing, should be prioritized in the long-term plan. Do not assume that just because the institution has been spending money enhancing and maintaining the X system for five years that you have to continue funding its ongoing maintenance or development. If you identify higher priority projects to fund, you need to begin to sunset these lower priority systems and stop funding them. Demonstrate reallocation before asking others for funds.

There are lessons from the private sector to consider. When the human resources department of a company wants a new human resources system, they must identify a significant level of hard dollar savings to help pay for the system. In higher education, we have been inconsistent in asking the users of our systems to pay for the development and maintenance of systems from their operating budgets. The culture of higher education finds it very difficult to turn potential savings into hard dollar savings. Time will tell whether our oversight governance organizations will continue to support this humanistic but expensive cultural attribute.

Communications and expectations management. You cannot over-communicate the results of the plan or the ongoing status of the plan's implementation. Some institutions call this task marketing, with the idea that we can no longer passively communicate to the campus; rather we must proactively go to stakeholders and show them how the plan will deliver something that they will value. Identify your important stakeholder groups, define the media that they most regularly use to learn about campus activities, and aggressively use these media to keep the stakeholders updated on the plan and how it will benefit them.

The dichotomy of this idea is that we also need to appropriately set expectations. One executive told us, "When you don't set expectations of your users, their expectations are set by their last fast food visit: Anything they want should be delivered in a very short period." If a project is expected to take nine months to deliver, build a safety buffer into your estimates. Broadly communicate that it will be done in 12 months and then hold the developers to getting it out in nine months.

CONCLUSION

Developing plans that cannot or will not be implemented is both frustrating and expensive. With the new realities of ubiquitous technology, technologically aware stakeholders, and an ever growing demand for technology services, effective planning is essential to all higher education institutions. We cannot afford to consume the high level of resources that these new technologies demand without having a clearly defined and pragmatic plan for their implementation. As one campus executive continually reminds us, "This school cannot afford to pay for any mistakes." We have yet to find an institution that can.

The strategic alignment framework provides us with an approach for ensuring that both the long term and short term needs of our campus community are identified, prioritized, and addressed. By working across our campuses we can develop a clear view of our future, our present, and the roadmap in between. It's a journey that we cannot afford to miss.

REFERENCES/SUGGESTED READINGS

Henderson, J. C., & Venkatraman, N. (1992). Strategic alignment: A model for organizational transformation via information technology. In T. A. Koohan & M. Useem (Eds.), *Transforming organizations*. New York, NY: Oxford University Press.

Henderson, J. C., & Venkatraman, N. (1993). Strategic alignment: A process model for integrating information technology and business strategies. *IBM Systems Journal, 32* (1), 4-16.

Henderson, J. C., & Venkatraman, N. (1994). Strategic alignment: A model for organizational transformation via information technology. In T. J. Allen & M. S. Morton (Eds.), *Information technology and the corporation of the 1990s*. New York, NY: Oxford University Press.

Henderson, J. C., Venkatraman, N., & Oldach, S. (1993). Continuous strategic alignment: Exploiting information technology capabilities for competitive success. *European Management Journal, 11* (2), 139-149.

Parker, M., Trainor, H. E., & Benson, R. (1989). *Information, strategy, and economics: Linking information systems strategy to business performance*. Englewood Cliffs, NJ: Prentice Hall.

4

STAGING FOR THE LAUNCH: AN IMPLEMENTATION PLANNING FRAMEWORK

Thomas C. Wunderle

FROM STRATEGY TO IMPLEMENTATION

D eveloping an effective strategy for information technology (I/T) presents its own set of challenges, but advancing to the implementation level can be the ultimate challenge. Implementation planning requires greater detail and more thorough analysis when people, money, time, and other resources must be committed to the project. You can no longer rely on the broad estimates and sweeping generalizations that are more typical of strategic planning. Stakeholders, who in the initial stages of planning may have given only casual attention to their impending role in the project, may now have to deliver on commitments they only vaguely recollect. Furthermore, as the champion of the project, you have given your executive management every reason to believe that the project will deliver on its promises. It is now time to execute, and you are going to have to ask those same executives for significant funds. For most of us, translating strategy into action can be a significant challenge.

THE IMPLEMENTATION PLANNING TEMPLATE

This chapter introduces an alternative approach to implementation planning: the planning template. The template is a planning approach or framework that includes a methodology as well as supporting tools and techniques designed to facilitate the development of a business case plan. The business case approach assumes that the implementation plan is a selling document which should serve as a compelling argument in support of the project. Such a plan would be compelling to the extent that it is based on sound research and analysis, is closely aligned with the project's strategic goals, and was developed through a consensus of stakeholders.

Template Development

The template was designed by IBM consultants to serve the needs of a large university system client. The framework was employed with considerable success to help develop tailored implementation plans for 16 of the system's universities. Early in its use, it became evident that the tool would work equally well in virtually any planning environment—private or public sector, I/T or non-I/T, simple or complex. While the template proved very effective in supporting a wide range of planning requirements, one of the more obvious and immediate benefits was that it provided a solid structure and process that kept everything focused and moving forward. Properly facilitated and effectively managed, we believe the template can be very effective in helping other colleges and universities develop business case plans of enviable quality whatever the specific nature of the project. The template's real strength is that it was designed to support a broad set of requirements and critical success factors that are fundamental to good planning and common in higher education.

In fact, the true formula for success resides not in the methodology itself, but in a solid understanding of the underlying principles that inspired and influenced the design of the methodology. The template was designed to help ensure that the planning process fully supported the development of a compelling business case and major (critical) success factors: stakeholder buy-in, executive sponsorship, and project management competency. Ultimately the methodology employed is a matter of individual choice. If the template approach is not your preference, an understanding of what inspired and influenced the design of the template, plus some of the tips and techniques described in this chapter, may help you as you plan future projects.

Transcending the Narrow View of Planning

Some tend to take a rather narrow view of planning, especially in the I/T context. What if the students are clamoring for e-mail accounts, and the faculty wants more bandwidth for better Internet access? The narrow view would interpret this as an operational and expense challenge. How can we acquire the additional network function, and how can we pay for it? But consider how often projects experience early disaster, not through the lack of operational planning or financial backing, but because critical stakeholders were bypassed in the planning process, or we failed to consider other options that a more integrated view of the challenge might have uncovered. Perhaps if we had taken a more comprehensive view of the planning process; i.e., if we had considered how this requirement might fit into the larger strategy (I/T and/or institutional) and asked the stakeholders (students, faculty, and staff) what additional related requirements they might have, we may have been able to accomplish more at less cost than with the narrow approach. Consequently, the more expanded view of planning will take into account the critical success factors as well as the compelling business case requirement.

Critical Success Factors

Planning's critical success factors are exactly that: Without these certain factors, your project—and perhaps the planning effort itself—is unlikely to succeed. Probably the single most important success factor, at least in higher education, is stakeholder buy-in. As one authority defines the word, a stakeholder is "any person, group, or organization that can place a claim on any organization's attention, resources, or output, or is affected by that output" (Bryson, 1988). Without buy-in from these affected groups you risk a lack of compliance and/or commitment toward the project, if not outright resistance. We have all witnessed those ugly turf battles that often have more to do with slighted feelings than any real fundamental differences in position. Without evidence of stakeholder buy-in you risk losing (or never acquiring) the strong executive support which is itself a critical success factor. In short, your project will need to engage early with the stakeholders. The planning process should incorporate this requirement yesterday.

There is also the need for executive support. However worthwhile the project may appear in your mind, it is unlikely to advance beyond the blueprint stage in the minds of others without the ongoing support of an executive champion or sponsor. This person (or persons) can locate and lobby for funding as well as other critical resources. The executive can marshal his or her peers to support the project at critical moments, such as when you need to borrow the I/T shop's programmers for some initial interface design.

The final critical requirement is for skill competencies within the project management team. While the planning methodology can do little to enhance the native talent of the project team, it can provide tools and techniques that help the team manage a complex process and ensure that equally complex issues get the focus and attention to detail they need.

A Compelling Business Case

We've already suggested that no one will champion your project unless it represents a compelling business case to proceed, including evidence of sound analysis, close alignment with strategic goals, and plan development by way of consensus. All of this, of course, provides credibility and justification for the support of the project by all of the stakeholders—students, faculty, staff, executives, etc. Credibility also is enhanced through good communications and a project evaluation process that is closely linked to the project's primary goals and objectives. Finally, a truly compelling argument will consider how the project will support the effective use of the product(s) and/or service(s) provided by the project. For example, a new network and individual e-mail accounts will do little good without the training, support, and encouragement to use the new tools.

PLANNING DESIGN AND PROCESS REQUIREMENTS

Figure 4.1 illustrates how the planning success factors influenced the template's design and process components.

FIGURE 4.1

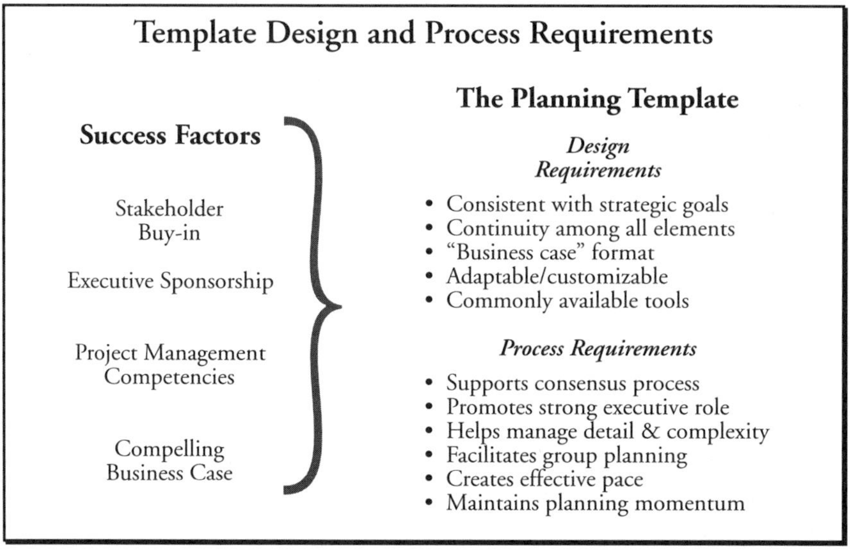

Template Design and Process Requirements

The Planning Template

Success Factors

Stakeholder
Buy-in

Executive Sponsorship

Project Management
Competencies

Compelling
Business Case

Design Requirements
- Consistent with strategic goals
- Continuity among all elements
- "Business case" format
- Adaptable/customizable
- Commonly available tools

Process Requirements
- Supports consensus process
- Promotes strong executive role
- Helps manage detail & complexity
- Facilitates group planning
- Creates effective pace
- Maintains planning momentum

FIGURE 4.2

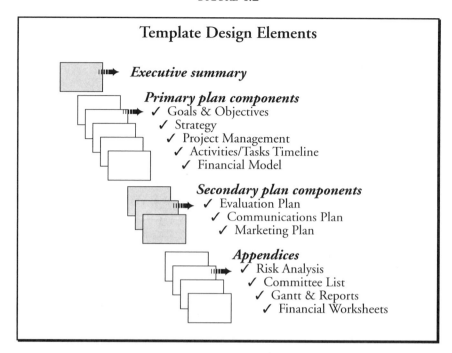

Template Design Elements

Executive summary

Primary plan components
- ✓ Goals & Objectives
- ✓ Strategy
- ✓ Project Management
- ✓ Activities/Tasks Timeline
- ✓ Financial Model

Secondary plan components
- ✓ Evaluation Plan
- ✓ Communications Plan
- ✓ Marketing Plan

Appendices
- ✓ Risk Analysis
- ✓ Committee List
- ✓ Gantt & Reports
- ✓ Financial Worksheets

The template incorporates tools and techniques into a planning structure that supports the full range of requirements described above. On the one hand you have the design structure (Figure 4.2) which ensures that the plan outline includes all of the critical planning components: goals, objectives, strategy, project management, activities and tasks, financial modeling, communications, evaluation, and marketing.

On the other hand you have the process component (Figure 4.3) which ensures that planning occurs in a structured manner so that a consensus process occurs, executive support is prominent, planning proceeds with deliberation and speed, and momentum is sustained throughout the process.

Finally, the template incorporates features and techniques designed to facilitate working through the methodology, managing the planning sessions, and actually developing the final document. These features include popular and widely available software tools which are common in higher education, live data entry during planning sessions using PC projector technology, and use of an action plan template to assign responsibility and track completion of committee tasks.

FIGURE 4.3

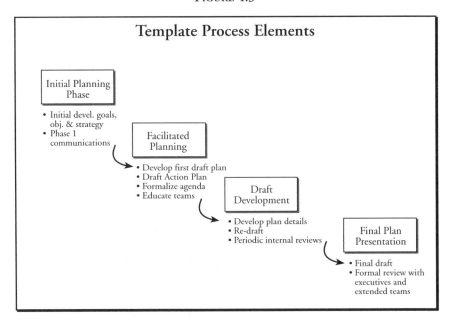

Of course, the integrity and effectiveness of the planning process will depend largely on the planning facilitator's understanding of the methodology and his or her skill at facilitating and managing teams. Each institution should honestly assess whether they have the talent and commitment in any one or two individuals to make this work. If not, the institution might consider an outside consultant. According to Hammer and Stanton (1995) the pros and cons of using outside consultants are:

Pros

▶ The ability to leverage other companies' experiences

▶ Getting access to essential skills

▶ Third-party objectivity

Cons

▶ The risk of outsourcing an important capability

▶ Incurring significant expense

▶ Diffuse accountability

Overall Structure

As illustrated in Figure 4.2, the template is designed around a centerpiece document that includes two major (primary and secondary) sections, an executive summary, and an appendix section. The primary section consists of five topics that follow a general-to-specific flow (deductive process) and address the key components of any project plan: goals, objectives, strategy, activities and tasks, project management, and financial summary. The secondary section addresses the requirement for an evaluation system (measurement plan), communications, and marketing. The appendix section allows for the inclusion of detail that is essential to those on the project committee but probably nonessential to the executive committee or the general public. The executive summary provides a synopsis for the consumption of executives or anyone else who may only be interested in obtaining a general familiarity with the key points of the plan.

FIGURE 4.4

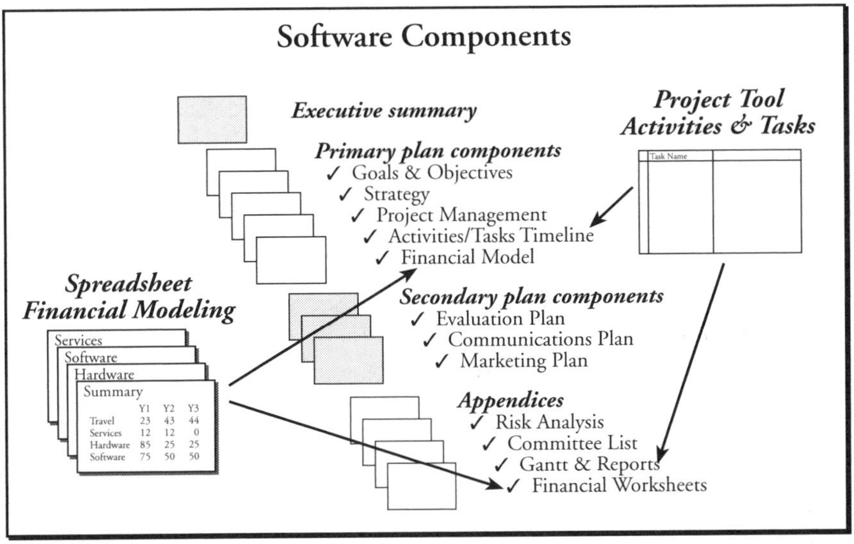

Software Components

The template consists of a centerpiece word processing document (e.g., Lotus AmiPro, Microsoft Word) that is linked directly to a spreadsheet document (e.g., Lotus 1-2-3, Microsoft Excel), plus a project management tool (e.g., Microsoft Project). The word processing document is the collection point for data and/or other documents that are either directly linked to or cut and pasted from the other tools. For example, the spreadsheet document includes detailed spreadsheets for expense related categories (e.g., hardware, software, travel, services, etc.). These detail sheets are linked to a summary document which is itself linked to the central document. This arrangement provides a very flexible way to conduct financial modeling with the development of more than one alternative scenario for the final plan. The project management tool is used to develop a timeline that can include a fairly detailed breakdown of tasks, resource assignments, and cost. Reports and charts generated from the project manager are cut and pasted into the central document as needed, primarily to provide content for the activities and tasks section.

Most of today's general purpose word processing packages support the development of template documents. The consultants made extensive use of tables with their sort and calculating functions (e.g., the sum and average) in the planning document. And use of the template approach in a live data entry environment helped keep the team concentrated on the subject at hand.

In the interest of the business case criteria, the template methodology stresses the maintenance of a strong line of continuity and consistency stretching from the project's goals and objectives through every other component (e.g., tasks, staffing, evaluation criteria, etc.). As we stressed often in the planning sessions, plan content that does not in some way (directly or indirectly) support the project's goals and objectives, or its strategy, should be removed. Occasionally, however, this lack of continuity can also signal that an important goal or objective may have been overlooked. To reinforce this kind of continuity the template forces a linkage between measurable outcomes associated with specific objectives and the evaluation component of the plan. The evaluation component will ensure that success (or failure) will be measured by the ability to achieve the measurable outcomes defined in the goals and objectives section of the template.

The financial model is designed to help planners develop a financial summary from a detailed analysis of revenue and expense categories (e.g., hardware, software, services, travel, etc.). The project management section identifies key management and staffing positions that will be needed (e.g., executive sponsor, project manager, office/clerical, programmer, etc.) and develops an organization chart to illustrate organizational relationships.

Making the Template Work

While the template provides a consistent outline for the design of the implementation plan, it is the management of the process that makes the whole enterprise work (see Figure 4.3). The process supports the consensus planning model through a framework that includes a working committee structure, early participation and regular review with extended stakeholder committees, a highly visible and involved executive sponsor, and periodic reviews with executive management. Planning is led by a project chair who may already have been assigned as interim or perhaps even permanent project manager. He or she will be assisted by a core team composed of a handful (no more than six is recommended) of capable associates. The general body of stakeholders is represented in the extended team. This group should represent all of the key stakeholder groups on campus and may become a sizable group. If properly selected and motivated, these individuals may provide valuable assistance as idea generators and/or participants in subcommittees. The executive sponsor is expected to kick off meetings and otherwise be highly visible in the planning process. He/she is also expected to actively lobby with key management and stakeholder groups (e.g., executive cabinet, student government, faculty senate, etc.) in support of the project.

Initial Planning

As Figure 4.3 illustrates, the planning process consists of four major steps. The first planning phase, which should be completed prior to the arrival of the facilitators for the on-site planning session, has the following objectives:

▶ Appoint, assemble, and familiarize team members with each other, the project, and the process.

▶ Work as a team to develop the goals, objectives, and strategy for the project.

▶ Begin to develop the remaining plan sections in preparation for the facilitated planning.

In preparation for this step, the consultants provide the planning teams with a preliminary set of instructions (Getting Started Kit), and a disk with the template files. The consultant will brief the core committee on the effective use of the template materials and will be available via telephone or e-mail for questions that should arise later. The three-day, on-site planning session is scheduled as early as possible in order to accommodate the schedules of the many participants who will be involved.

Facilitation Sessions

The second step in the process is the actual facilitated planning. Making the template and the process work in the context of a wide cross-section of institutional and individual personalities is a challenge in its own right. In order to be successful, the consultants will have to accomplish a number of key objectives:

▶ Foster an immediate and positive sense of ownership among the planning teams.

▶ Continue to familiarize key participants with the planning concepts and tools.

▶ Create enthusiasm and momentum that will re-energize the project over time.

▶ Set in motion the interpersonal and intergroup dynamics that can promote consensus.

▶ Develop an initial draft document of sufficient (albeit preliminary) substance and integrity that even skeptical observers would buy in to the value of the process.

Prior to the on-site visits, each campus is provided with logistical instructions (meeting rooms, flip charts, overhead projectors, screens, laser printers, etc.) and a preliminary agenda. Figure 4.5 shows a sample three-day agenda. Emphasis is placed on scheduling two one-hour reviews with the extended team during the planning period. The project coordinators are asked to provide a list of names and organizations for all participants to ensure that key stakeholders are represented. Executive sponsors are encouraged to kick off the initial planning session and participate in the two extended team review sessions, as a minimum.

FIGURE 4.5

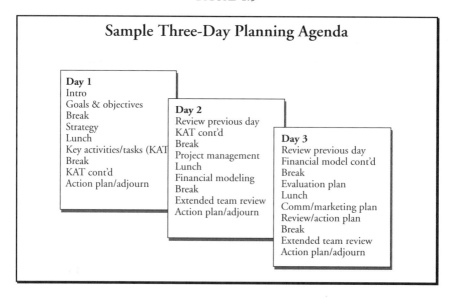

Sample Three-Day Planning Agenda

Day 1
Intro
Goals & objectives
Break
Strategy
Lunch
Key activities/tasks (KAT)
Break
KAT cont'd
Action plan/adjourn

Day 2
Review previous day
KAT cont'd
Break
Project management
Lunch
Financial modeling
Break
Extended team review
Action plan/adjourn

Day 3
Review previous day
Financial model cont'd
Break
Evaluation plan
Lunch
Comm/marketing plan
Review/action plan
Break
Extended team review
Action plan/adjourn

The facilitation team consisted of two consultants, one from IBM and the other from the client. The consultants shared the roles of lead facilitator, notetaker, timekeeper, and data entry person interchangeably during the planning session. The introductory session set an expectation level that emphasized several key points:

▶ The objective of the planning session was to develop an initial substantive document and to familiarize the teams with how to use the planning tools/methodology; the team would be responsible for building content over the length of the planning process.

▶ The major emphasis would be on capturing good ideas and not on wordsmithing or dwelling on unnecessary details (i.e., we will need to stay focused and keep things moving).

▶ The teams, not the consultants, are the owners of this developing plan, and they ultimately will be responsible for defending the information in the plan.

▶ The process should serve the needs of the team and not vice versa, so the process should be adapted or modified if appropriate.

▶ The team should correct the consultants if they are not accurately recording ideas in the template.

LIVE DATA ENTRY

Planning content is entered live via PCs and PC projectors during the core team planning sessions which has proved to be particularly effective for implementation planning. In the appropriate context and if managed correctly, this technique can keep the team very focused on the subject at hand. It also lends a great deal of credibility to the process since you are actually producing a document of meaningful substance and integrity "on the fly." In the context of the university system client referenced earlier, this technique proved particularly effective as a means of providing a fast moving planning process for a project that was inherently complex and involved 16 semi-autonomous institutions.

As the planning team works through the template, articulating goals and objectives, defining critical tasks, and prioritizing measurable outcomes, these ideas are captured in real time via live data entry on a computer whose display is projected onto a large screen. Participants can watch as their ideas are put into words where everyone else can observe and comment on them. This technique keeps all eyes focused on the ideas being articulated and developed on the screen rather than on the individual presenting the idea. While this does not provide the full anonymity that some methods do, it does reduce the level of intimidation sometimes associated with this kind of group dynamics. As planning moves forward, this approach allows the team to easily review, modify, print, and distribute whatever content has been developed up to this point. At the end of the three-day session, the team can have a fairly substantive and well-developed planning document to share with its management.

KEEPING THE PACE

One of the more difficult challenges of group planning is how to keep things moving at a pace that allows time to develop critical content but prevents the tendency to digress into unnecessary detail. The latter is much better left to the time and resources of research teams and subcommittees assigned to specific project areas. The live data entry technique can help by keeping everyone's attention focused on the agenda at hand. Primarily though, it is the job of the lead facilitator to guard against the natural tendency to digress and to keep the group focused. Our recommendation is to capture good ideas rather than worry about grammar, syntax, or style as ideas are articulated in the planning session. In this context, we continually remind our clients that we will be entering ideas and explanatory remarks in parentheses or brackets, and that these can be revised and edited at a later date. The important thing is to capture good ideas and make sure we can recollect what we meant by them when we revisit the plan later. In this way, with the right kind of intervention on the part of the facilitator and the support of the team, a fairly sound plan can be developed within a two- or three-day period.

Cultivating Consensus

One of the most critical of critical success factors is the participation and buy-in from key stakeholders. Defining the key stakeholders depends on the nature of the project, but in higher education this normally includes students and faculty as well as staff. Nonetheless, in an environment where administration and staff usually manage and administer I/T projects, it is all too easy to overlook the need to include students and faculty on planning committees. The facilitated planning agenda can offer a priceless opportunity to begin cultivating committed stakeholders, not just compliant stakeholders. One note of caution: If you have not already informed the stakeholder representatives of the nature and purpose of your planning agenda and assured them that they will have an important consultative and/or decision-making role in the process, you risk an angry reaction at what may be perceived as a fait accompli plan at the review session.

Planning to Act

Any form of communication that intends to persuade someone to act on a message must answer three hypothetical questions (not necessarily in this order) from the audience:

1) What are we are talking about?

2) What's in it for me? (i.e., Convince me I should continue to listen.)

3) What do you want me to do about it?

The last question often gets the least attention in the communication; this is unfortunate because it is the call to action.

There is a very real risk in committee-based planning environments for the group never to get beyond the planning mode. If the planning process is not managed correctly, active planning can devolve into nothing more than a continuum of conversations, where nothing is decided, nothing gets done, and nobody is assigned responsibility for anything. It requires a great deal of attention and work to make sure that ideas are translated into action in any environment, much less one that may require agreement from a large number of participants. The template rises to this challenge by incorporating an action plan component that is designed to avoid the plan-only syndrome and to force an action agenda on responsible participants.

The action plan identifies:

▶ An action category (i.e., budget, organization, staffing, vendor, etc.)

▶ An action item (i.e., activity, task, and objective which identify internal programming resources for the project)

▶ The action item owner (i.e., the person responsible for addressing the action item, not necessarily the one who will perform the action)

▶ The due and completion dates for the action

You may find that the initial planning sessions will identify action items that represent a need to address critical agenda items such as to reaffirm financial backing, identify and assign a project manager, or identify and appoint subcommittees. One parallel exercise that may prove useful is a risk analysis that factors in both the potential negative impact of a risk item and the likelihood of that item occurring. Sorting the resulting numbers from high to low will identify the top five or ten risk items that should be addressed to minimize any future problems in these areas.

MAINTAINING THE MOMENTUM

When the facilitators have left, the continuing challenge is to sustain the planning momentum they created. Step three in the template process includes an interval of time dedicated for further development of the plan details. The length of this time depends, of course, on many factors including the anticipated project launch date, the availability of planning information, and the amount of time your staff has to dedicate to the project. Whatever the limitations, it is critically important that the momentum initially created is sustained throughout the planning process. This may simply be a matter of scheduling periodic planning updates, including action item reviews where key participants are encouraged to play a continuing active role in the project. Executive management can play an important role in keeping the momentum going by attending these sessions, publicizing the progress of the committees at general convocations, and recognizing the contributions of individual participants at these meetings.

THE "FINAL" REPORT

Anyone who has done much planning (or has much experience in life for that matter ...) understands the inherent contradiction in the term "final" when it comes to implementation planning. In fact, the planning process is (or should be) fluid and organic in nature, because planning occurs in an environment that is itself undergoing constant and continuous change. Today's technologies will be obsolete tomorrow. The funding you thought was earmarked for the project may suddenly have to be reallocated to another, more pressing, concern. The reasons for change are almost endless.

Nevertheless, at some point a final report must be presented, normally to an executive committee. If you have done your homework, worked the template, involved the stakeholders at every important step, and if your executive sponsor has been visible, involved and supportive, the final report should be a no-brainer.

This is your opportunity to present, in comprehensive form, a well-rehearsed and finely detailed plan for the project. You will be able to demonstrate a strong line of continuity between the project's goals/objectives and the detailed project plan. The financial model, backed by details for every expense and revenue line, will show how, over three or five years, the project will meet its financial objectives. The evaluation plan will measure success based on how well the project has achieved the objectives and outcomes identified earlier in the template. Phase one of the communications plan will already be underway; in fact, the campus newspaper will have recently run an editorial supporting the project, and plans for a campaign to announce and celebrate the project's launch will have already been worked out. Your executive audience is glowing with satisfaction. You're a success. The business case is compelling and you're ready to move into action with the project.

CONCLUSION

Would that all planning had this kind of happy ending. In reality, the work never ceases, and next year (or next quarter) may present a whole new set of challenges. Just as implementation planning never ceases, neither does strategic planning. The strategic plan that generated the present implementation planning effort will itself need to be revisited, revised, and adapted over time to accommodate new challenges and opportunities.

The initial success of the template makes us optimistic about its use across a wide range of applications and environments. The template works because the developers designed the framework around a critical set of requirements that define the end product (i.e., a business case plan) and the process for getting there. You may choose to follow the process presented here or elect to use another approach. What is important is to have a good understanding of the underlying success factors and techniques that can make or break a project even before it begins. Whatever planning approach you take should promote stakeholder participation and buy-in, create a compelling business case that will encourage executive support, and facilitate creative thinking and interaction among planning participants. With the right kind of implementation planning, you can be assured that the launch will be a success.

REFERENCES/SUGGESTED READINGS

Bryson, J. M. (1988). *Strategic planning for public and nonprofit organizations.* San Francisco, CA: Jossey-Bass.

Hammer, M., & Stanton, S. A. (1995). *The reengineering revolution.* New York, NY: HarperCollins.

5

STUDENT SERVICES FOR THE 21ST CENTURY: CREATING THE STUDENT-CENTERED ENVIRONMENT

Martha A. Beede and Darlene J. Burnett

These are exciting and challenging times for higher education administrators. We are facing unprecedented changes for higher education as we approach the 21st century. Technology, globalization, shifting demographics, declining public confidence, and increasing financial pressures are directly impacting higher education institutions and the way they deliver their services. In this chapter we take a closer look at how these external trends, combined with the limitations of today's student service model, are shaping new models for student service delivery. For the purpose of this chapter, student services is defined as all nonacademic interactions that the student has with a college or university.

Society has undergone a fundamental transformation from the industrial age to the information age. The information age has created a global economy. Whether in business or higher education, global changes will have a direct impact on how we provide services, how we attract students, and how we compete. In the information economy, students are demanding the technological skills they know they will need to survive in a highly changeable society. They are also demanding services that meet their lifestyles. To meet this demand, higher education institutions must evaluate their processes, organizations, and use of technology and implement a student-centered environment. The technology foundation needed for the information age requires a different way of viewing the infrastructure and organization. Providing support services that are accessible, flexible, and innovative will be critical in designing support services for the future.

Changing demographics and expectations of incoming students have also placed a higher demand on institutions to improve the services they offer. In addition to the competitive environment of the early 1990s, public and private ventures such as "virtual universities" are emerging. Computing and telecommunications capabilities allow higher education institutions to offer additional options for learners. This increases competition for students. Those institutions which have designed services to meet this changing environment hold a competitive advantage. Access can be extended beyond the classroom to serve learners who need more flexibility in the time and location of their education, such as adult learners who cannot come to campus because of job or family commitments.

One other change agent for institutions is increased financial pressure. Rising tuition rates and administrative costs are forcing institutions to look for ways to become more cost effective. This has driven the trend toward redesigning administrative services as well as collaborative efforts.

The concern about the cost of a college education is pervasive. Many schools are feeling the crunch of spiraling tuition rates and the resulting financial and public pressures they cause. Since 1980, college tuition has risen at a faster rate than the price of a new car, the Consumer Price Index, and even medical care. According to the Bureau of Labor Statistics, the cost of new cars has risen 54% from 1980 to 1994, while overall inflation is up 80%, and medical care is up 182%. Tuition has risen 253%. Since 1975, administration in higher education grew at more than three times the rate of student enrollment (Heller & Eng, 1996). All of these factors contribute to the need to design a model that works for the 21st century and addresses the pressures that exist today.

Dolence and Norris (1995) outline three questions that must be answered by the stakeholders considering the future of higher education:

1) Is today's industrial age educational model appropriate to the learning needs of the information age—for either traditional learners or learners in the workplace?

2) Is society willing to pay for a 20th century industrial age model in the 21st century information age?

3) Can academe afford to miss the opportunity of reshaping itself to serve the emerging needs of the information age learner?

THE TRADITIONAL STUDENT SERVICE MODEL

The increasing complexity of higher education, administrative requirements, and customer needs has led colleges to add layer upon layer of ad hoc processes and large support infrastructures. To complicate matters further, many of these processes were created when technology was incapable of making the system more user-friendly, effective, or efficient. Future competitiveness will demand that these processes be redesigned to enhance service to the customer and provide more efficient and effective ways of using institutional resources.

In the traditional student services model, each office focuses on a specific area of responsibility. For example, the admissions office focuses on recruiting and enrolling applicants, the office of financial aid concerns itself with providing financial assistance to students, and so on. This model does not meet the needs of students because it artificially segregates the services students require from the institution. This model also presents challenges for administrators in today's environment as they try to be more service oriented. It is difficult to provide a holistic or service oriented environment for the student when the environment is characterized by the following traits:

▶ Major processes are segregated.

▶ Systems are not integrated.

▶ Communication is limited.

▶ Reporting structures vary.

▶ Administrative and academic functions are not linked.

FIGURE 5.1

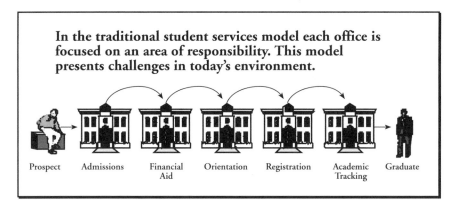

In the traditional student services model each office is focused on an area of responsibility. This model presents challenges in today's environment.

Prospect Admissions Financial Aid Orientation Registration Academic Tracking Graduate

Any individual who has spent time on a campus is familiar with this age old phenomenon of the student being passed from office to office, waiting in line at each office, and growing more and more frustrated as a seemingly simple task takes a great deal of time and energy. Students have always found such treatment frustrating, but today's students will not tolerate this type of service delivery; they are more sophisticated consumers. These students expect simplified processes and may also demand services that are time and location independent. With only a few exceptions, however, today's student services are neither student-centered nor future compatible. If the future compatible institution is to serve residential and distant students whose learning spans a lifetime, then reengineering will be essential.

21ST CENTURY VISION

The combination of these external and internal trends requires transformation to a new model. Higher education must provide services, support, and learning that fit today's lifestyles and the lifelong learner. This means that access to information, services, and learning must become time and location independent. The focus of delivery must be on the student—the customer. Technology should be used to provide the tools to create this student-centered environment, but delivery processes and philosophies will also be transformed to leverage technology and fully implement new service models.

To provide services that are more flexible and responsive to the needs of their customers, colleges and universities need to look at how people, processes, and technology—the key elements of transformation—are structured within their institutions. The use of enabling technologies, organizational designs, and processes allows institutions to enhance service delivery by facilitating change. Those institutions that place a high value on services designed to enhance student success and to meet community and lifestyle needs will become models for other institutions of higher education.

As your institution prepares a 21st century vision, consider asking some of the following questions:

▶ How should we define a student-centered environment that suits the needs of students?

▶ How can student services permeate the entire institution, not just the administrative offices?

▶ Are the changes we are contemplating systemic?

▶ How can we integrate student services functions so they appear seamless to the user?

▶ Are we building the information infrastructure that will allow us to make these changes?

▶ Are we applying principles of reengineering and transformation to student services?

We believe that a student services plan that takes these questions into account will result in an accelerated rate of change yielding more cost effective services, better services to both on-campus and off-campus customers, and an improved image of student services.

When transforming an organization, it is important to focus on the core processes as a starting point. The core processes for student service delivery are highlighted in Figure 5.2.

This model places the student—the customer—at the center. Although students have different wants and needs during their life cycle of interactions with an institution, they should always be at the center of the processes. Another critical element to note is that advising is a key process that extends throughout all of the services. The other areas represent the remaining core processes of a student's interactions with the institution.

If we take a closer look at the major activities within the core student services processes, we can break down how enabling technologies and processes can be used to improve service delivery.

FIGURE 5.2

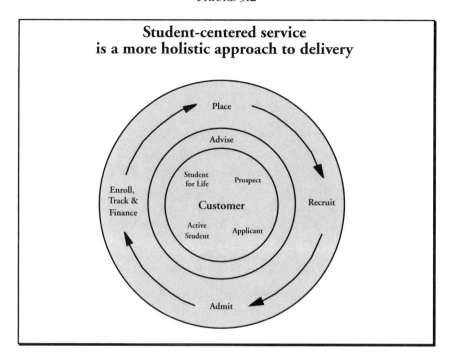

Student-centered service is a more holistic approach to delivery

FIGURE 5.3

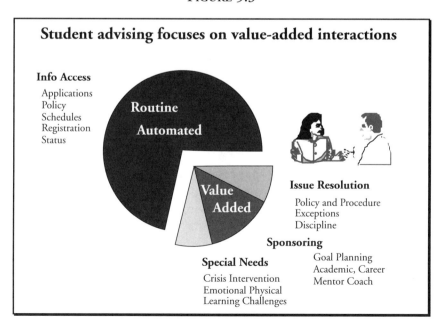

Student advising focuses on value-added interactions

Advising

Student advising should focus on value-added interactions. Routine transactions and requests for information access should be provided through the use of enabling technologies. These routine transactions may include requests for applications, policies, schedules, registration, or current status. The value-added portion should revolve around issue resolution, special needs, sponsoring (e.g., developmental counseling), and activities that assist students in their development and goal attainment.

The fundamental concept to remember in designing a student-centered advising structure is to focus on developmental advising principles. Academic advising is traditionally viewed as providing all students from first semester to senior year with academic information and related assistance with planning. Generally, the focus is on students' progress in fulfilling graduation requirements and on the quality of academic information students receive. The view is prescriptive. The goals of developmental advising are broader:

▶ Growth in the self-awareness of the relationship of education and life

▶ Growth in the ability to identify realistic academic and career goals as well as a program to achieve them

▶ Growth in the awareness of life as extending beyond the college years (Kramer, 1996)

Terry O'Banion (1972) identified these five steps in the developmental advising model:

1) Exploration of life goals (values)

2) Exploration of educational/career goals

3) Selection of educational program

4) Selection of courses

5) Scheduling of classes

The selection of courses and the scheduling of classes are where the majority of advisors spend their time today. Technology can easily facilitate providing those services while the advisor/counselor might spend his or her time facilitating the exploration of life goals (values), the exploration of educational/career goals, and the selection of an educational program. It is through these value-added activities that students will derive the greatest benefits. It is also where they most need the skills of a professional to assist them in their development and goal attainment.

Recruiting

The recruiting process includes developing the marketing image and strategy, market analysis, communications, tracking and ranking contacts, as well as advising. Enablers of change to a student-centered model will include both new processes and technology implementations.

Process enablers

▶ A strategic plan for the institution

▶ An enrollment management plan

▶ Business transformation (redesigned processes)

▶ A marketing shift to target marketing, tracking, and contact or recruitment plan based on tracking

Technology enablers

▶ An information infrastructure (e.g., a robust network)

▶ Interactive applications and communication which allow personnel to access the information they need, communicating internally and externally

▶ Internet access and interactive applications for distribution of information and communication with the institution

▶ An integrated student information system, consolidating all relevant student information in a single system

An example of the use of a technology enabler within recruitment would be using the Internet to reach prospects and applicants, providing them direct access to information about the institution (i.e., programs, activities, courses, requirements) and interactive applications such as building a portfolio, asking questions about programs, and building their admission and financial aid application. Prospects could also use the Internet as a means to transmit their applications, electronically. This saves time for the prospect as well as the staff because they do not have to perform labor intensive paper processing and data entry tasks.

Admissions

Admission is a critical process which includes receiving an application, reviewing the application, monitoring and communicating the applicant status, as well as managing yield. The process can be made more efficient by redesigning workflow and employing technology to shift admissions staff time to value-added activities. For example, technology can enable the admission process through electronic acceptance of the required information (e.g., submitting an application using the World Wide Web), electronic data interchange (EDI) for submission of high school transcripts or college transfers, for application status, and for electronic links to counselors or prospects.

Redesigned workflow, roles, and responsibilities can address the large amount of time spent on multiple reviews and rework. Standard admissions requirements across the institution as well as a clear definition of the population that should be admitted or rejected can allow for some processes to be automated.

Process enablers

▶ Standards and common applications within an institution or system or collaborative employment of standards across institutions

▶ Business transformation which focuses on the shift from administrative to value-add activities, redesigned processes and organization, as well as workflow

▶ An enrollment management plan

▶ Cross-functional service teams

Technology enablers

▶ Electronic acceptance and exchange of information via the Internet (electronic applications, portfolios, EDI transcripts, and communication links)

▶ Integrated student information systems

▶ Auto-decisioning (i.e., predefined base-level criteria for admission which are used by a computer program to admit prospects)

Active Student Process

The active student process includes developing and publishing the course schedule, registering, tracking academic progress, conferring credentials, and advising. It also includes nonacademic registration activities for housing, autos, books, IDs, etc.

Process enablers

▶ Business transformation, such as shifting the focus from personnel handling all transactions, no matter how routine, to handling only those that are nonroutine; and redesigning workflow, roles and responsibilities

▶ Cross-functional service teams which can handle a range of tasks, making information access and problem resolution easier for students (Note that training will likely be required to familiarize individuals with other cross-functional areas)

▶ Direct information access for individual students

Technology enablers

▶ Direct access by students to course information, grades, registration, degree/goal audit, and academic support information via WWW, kiosks, voice response units (VRU), and e-mail

▶ An integrated student information system

▶ Communication links among offices and databases

▶ Electronic data interchange of items such as transcripts

▶ An information infrastructure

Financial Planning and Management

The financial planning and management process includes advising students on the full scope of financial planning and budgeting including charges, aid, loans, payments, and advising. With concerns over the rising cost of education compounded by the increasing student debt load, the concept of financial aid is inadequate. To match the holistic vision of lifelong concern for the student, financial planning is beginning to displace financial aid. The financial planning and management processes include advising students of the full scope of financial planning and budgeting including charges, aid, loans, payment, and advising.

Process enablers

▶ Business transformation; e.g., redesigned processes and organizations

▶ An enrollment management plan

▶ Simplified processes, procedures, and policies

▶ Cross-functional service teams

▶ Training for personnel to allow them to expand their skills into financial planning advisement

Technology enablers

- ▶ Direct access to financial information, available funding, status, profiles, and a counselor

- ▶ Modeling and financial planning support tools

- ▶ Decision support systems which integrate with the institution's core applications for "what ifs" modeling and trend analysis

- ▶ An integrated student information system

- ▶ An information infrastructure

Common Themes

Certain themes emerge in each key process of the student service delivery model.

Information infrastructure. Institutions will need a network infrastructure as well as integrated information systems (infostructure) to provide the foundation for technology applications. Access to intranets and the Internet will be required to serve students of all ages and life circumstances 24 hours a day, seven days per week.

Direct information access. Students, faculty, and other stakeholders will have direct access to the information that they need. The role of the middleman will disappear.

Integration. From a single point of contact, students, administrators, and faculty will be able to reach the information they need rather than being passed from office to office. This concept supports the pervasive notion that is in many redesign projects of "one or none" (describing the number of contacts necessary for a transaction). Design of systems and processes is around self-service. If personal contact is required, then students should only have to go to one place—the first place—to get an answer.

Cross-functional teams. Services will be integrated with teams comprised of professionals who were previously segregated in different offices. This will require reskilling, training, and a shift from specialists to generalists.

Advising as a core. Advising is a key process that extends across all services and should focus on value-added interactions. Technology should be used for automating the routine, freeing staff for value-added interactions. Advising occurs throughout the student life cycle.

Student-centered. This model places the student—the customer—at the center. Services are designed around the needs of the student whether they are a traditional prospect, an active student, or a lifelong learner.

Any time, any place. Technology and global competition will allow institutions to serve students on campus or around the world. Student services will need to be available at any hour of the day from any location, whether on campus, at home, or at work.

Reengineered processes. The goal of reengineering is to alter processes to focus on the students' needs rather than the institution's needs, as well as to enhance effectiveness, efficiency, and cost savings.

As institutions transform themselves, they are able to offer students improved services while reaping cost benefits over traditional approaches, thereby positioning themselves to be more competitive for the future. Campus-wide information access—via Internet, kiosks, laptops, or personal computers—makes the institution more competitive, in part because it provides students with convenient information access. By making information access hassle free, colleges and universities may reap an unexpected cost benefit in improved student recruitment, retention, and enrollment gains. Since the system can facilitate payment of fees electronically, there is another cost advantage in improving the speed with which bills are paid. But the largest cost benefit to an institution may be hidden: an increase in staff productivity when staff are relieved from answering routine questions and can focus their efforts on providing value-added services.

Institutions that seek to improve access to information as a means of achieving a student-centered environment will find that personnel who serve as disseminators and processors of information will become planners and deliverers of value-added services. The result will be a reduction in the amount of time students need to conduct business transactions, and customer services will be improved. We can conclude that the use of technology in providing around-the-clock access to general campus information and the resulting elimination of long lines for class scheduling, fee payments, etc., will go a long way toward improving the student view of higher education services. Additionally, staff time can be refocused whether it be in establishing a financial plan for the cost of a student's education or determining how to incorporate an internship into his or her program of study.

As technology is introduced and used as an enabler, on-campus roles will also be influenced. Specifically, as students and other constituents are provided with direct access to information the routine tasks that were often provided by staff will no longer be necessary. Demand will be focused in nonroutine activities which will require more skill. There will be a shift from routine to nonroutine activities (i.e., from non-value-added activities to value-added activities). Nonroutine activities may include advising and coaching activities such as goal planning and assistance, issue resolution, and special services. Generally, these models require cross-trained generalists rather than the functionally trained specialists that exist in today's environment (e.g., financial aid, student accounting). This shift in roles will require the retraining of staff.

These models also require a technology infrastructure and infostructure that creates an environment of integrated processes. To provide these student-centered services, staff will need access to a greater range of information. As cross-functional teams discuss a range of topics and needs with students, they will also require access to information to support those conversations and advising sessions. The infrastructure and infostructure will require a process view of data rather than one of stand alone applications. For example, a cross-functional advisor may need to access information from transcripts, loans, aid, account balances, as well as enrollment data during a single session. The reengineering of the institution will require not only technology, process, and organization changes, but the supporting process view of data.

The image of the college or university campus may be redefined from a physical location to a "virtual campus," which is globally accessible. Transcripts and other student-related information can be electronically transmitted from one institution to another. Students and faculty from throughout the world can engage in electronic dialogue and have access to services and information. Technology will allow students to access information that is time and location independent. All of these trends greatly influence how institutions create their vision for student services of the future.

EXEMPLARS

The following examples highlight specific examples of how some institutions have already started to improve student services by implementing these practices.

Student Services Center: University of Delaware

The University of Delaware is known for student service improvements that resulted from its student service center project. Dave Hollowell, Senior Vice President, led his team through an effort aimed at improving administrative services. One of the committees that was put in place to address this objective focused on ensuring that students who visited this facility should be served as efficiently as possible, including the novel notion that they might be able to satisfy their questions without talking to a single person. If that was not possible, then they should be served by only one individual, whenever possible. The committee was reminded to take full advantage of technology.

The committee determined that about 20% of the people who visited their offices did so to accomplish simple activities such as to pick up a registration or financial aid form, to get a copy of their class schedule, or to find out the status of their student account. About 60% of the questions were routine and could be answered by a person who was trained to access information in the various components of the student information system. Only about 20% of the questions required the assistance of someone who was a specialist in a particular student service area. Given this information, the committee designed a self-service area with kiosks, phones, and printers for direct information access. Routine activities were handled at a service counter staffed by generalists, and in the 20% of cases where a specialist was needed, staff were behind the service counter. The center has been well-received by students and staff (Hollowell, 1994).

The Seven Steps to a Financial Path to Graduation: Brigham Young University

Brigham Young University (BYU) has a number of innovative projects, including the Financial Path to Graduation project which provides a unique and informative financial plan to students. The objective of the program is to educate and help students build a financial plan to pay for their university education. The program, Creating a Financial Path to Graduation, is a response to the increasing student debt burden. Significant increases in student loan eligibility as a result of the reauthorization of the Higher Education Act in 1992 have had a dramatic effect on student borrowing. Without the benefit of strategic planning, students are borrowing at unprecedented levels. Although the Financial Aid Office maintains a staff and counselors who are qualified in processing the federal programs offered, it has an ongoing concern that the service being provided to students should inform, educate, and assist them in making informed choices about financing their education. To help provide this service, financial aid counselors are becoming certified financial planners. The Seven Steps to a Financial Path to Graduation document has been developed to provide an interactive program that can be adapted to the individual user and educate all students, not just those borrowing federal funds (Peterson,1996).

Pathways Project: University of California

Pathways will allow prospective applicants to explore the University of California (UC) and its campuses, receive timely and up-to-date guidance information, and apply for admission electronically. The goals of the Pathways project are:

▶ Simplify and streamline the application and admission process for applicants, schools, and UC

▶ Improve the accuracy and timeliness of data used during the admission process

▶ Enhance communication with applicants by providing information topics for interest to students

When Pathways is fully implemented, it will consist of four components: 1) discover, 2) contact and advising, 3) application, and 4) admission and preregistration.

Discover. In the discover stage, students will be able to electronically access the same kind of information available in campus catalogs and brochures, including academic programs, housing facilities, financial aid, and extracurricular activities. Students will also be able to electronically tour the University of California's eight undergraduate campuses.

Contact and advising. The contact and advising phase will allow students to begin compiling a record of their classes, extracurricular activities, honors and awards, and other personal achievements as early as the ninth grade. Students will store information in a secure environment that can later be used in the admission application. With Pathways, students also will be able to compare the classes they are taking, or plan to take, with a list of classes that fulfill UC admissions requirements. An interactive feature will allow students to ask questions about the university on-line and receive an answer from an admissions counselor.

Application. When the application phase is fully implemented, Pathways will collect information from the contact and advising stage, including grades, SAT scores, the essay, and other data used to determine admission to the university.

Admission and preregistration. The final stage of admission and preregistration will provide notification of admission, financial aid, and preregistration services to students electronically, reducing the time for exchanging information on these essential services (Ferri, 1996).

Reengineering Student Administrative Services: Babson College

The goals of the reengineering project at Babson College were to significantly increase customer satisfaction and to reduce operating costs by 30%–40%. The focal point of the newly designed student services is the customer service model which assigns an estimated 90% of all routine business transactions to self-directed, on-line services for students. The model then assigns roughly 8% of activity to generalists (one-stop shopping model) and the remaining 2% of transactions are handled by specialists. Self-directed teams have been created to provide more fully integrated specialists. The generalists are to deliver academic advising (supplementing the role of faculty advisors), personal support, and general administrative assistance to undergraduates, integrating what was previously delivered by various offices on campus. They will free up the team members on the specialists teams (i.e., student financial services, academic records, and registration) for more value-added activities (Lewis, 1996).

Networking with Project Agora: Boston College

Agora is a Greek term meaning a gathering place or marketplace. At Boston College, Agora is a communications project that brings voice-mail, e-mail, cable TV, and Internet access to each person in the Boston College community. One of Agora's many goals is to create an electronic community where people can gather to exchange information and ideas. Project Agora brings direct access for exchanging e-mail, registering for courses, and accessing personal information in the residence hall. All academic residence halls are wired with three-part outlets that bring video, voice, and data services into common areas and individual rooms. Over time academic buildings were wired to the campus network, but students living in the dorms had access only if they had a computer equipped with a modem. Eliminating this need, the new service includes voice and e-mail accounts, access to the Internet, and a 51-channel interactive cable TV system. Students plug their telephone, computer, or television into the box next to their beds to activate the services. Students' telephone numbers remain the same throughout their enrollment. The network, called EagleNet, connects the mainframe computers, workstations, and desktop machines of faculty, staff, and students throughout the campus. Service to students for connecting phones and computers has reduced the amount of time and effort needed to initiate or change those services. It has also helped improve access to information and communication with e-mail and the Internet (Lonabocker, 1996).

The projects described here allow resources which were formerly invested in routine functions to be used instead of activities that personalize the student-centered process. Gains in productivity, effectiveness, and efficiency are equated with an improved perception about the institution and the institution's consideration for the needs of the student.

THE ROLE OF TECHNOLOGY

Hammer and Champy (1993) state that, "The fundamental error that most companies commit when they look at technology is to view it through the lens of their existing processes." They ask, "How can we use these new technological capabilities to enhance or streamline or improve what we are already doing?" Instead, they should be asking, "How can we use technology to allow us to do things that we are not already doing? It should be clear . . . that further advances in technology will break more rules about how we conduct business. Rules that still appear inviolate today may become obsolete in a year or less. Consequently, exploiting the potential for technologies to change a company's business process and move it dramatically ahead of its competitor is not a one-time event." Planning for, implementing, and supporting the integration of technology with institutional mission is a complex endeavor that requires careful consideration and change. Change is rarely easy, but the ability to change is critical for those colleges that want to provide the service environment necessary to support the lifelong learner.

To develop a 21st century vision, we must understand what technology will enable us to do. Technology is changing our lives. Predictions are that we will move beyond today's computing model to one of global connectivity—a worldwide, highly distributed computing infostructure. Connectivity enabled by the infostructure will profoundly change access to content, services, and communications. Consider the explosive growth of the Internet in just the past few years. Today, there are approximately 30 million Internet users. This number is expected to grow to 200 million users by the year 2000. The Internet enables individuals to get connected and stay connected (Tuller, 1997).

To use technology as an enabler for change, several elements should be present. The technology chosen should be used as a tool to help the institution fulfill its strategic vision, mission, or goals. Oftentimes technology is implemented for technology's sake rather than as a way to achieve strategic goals. It is also critical to think holistically when considering technology solutions. Focus on integrated solutions and leveraging the information infrastructure.

Critical to any successful change involving technology is ensuring that the infrastructure requirements necessary to support the desired outcomes are in place. To create a truly student-centered environment, institutional leaders must provide access to existing information for a new set of users that includes students, faculty, and the community. It is imperative that an integrated information infrastructure be provided for the network. To do this, leaders must change key paradigms, transform processes, leverage investments in technology, and select technology and process enablers.

Process enablers

▶ Strategic plan

▶ Reengineered student-centered processes, procedures, roles, and workflow

▶ Cross-functional service teams

▶ Time and location independent access

▶ Advising as a core process

▶ Training

Technology enablers

▶ Information infrastructure

▶ Integrated information systems and processes

▶ Direct information access and Internet-based solutions

▶ Network infrastructure

CONCLUSION

With only a few exceptions, today's student services are neither student-centered nor future compatible. If the future compatible institution is to serve both residential and distant students whose educational experience will span a lifetime, reengineering student services will be essential. Student services encompass dozens of activities that can affect student satisfaction, retention, and success. These facts alone would be sufficient to make student services worth attention as colleges and universities move toward the future compatible campus. Students are behaving as consumers—they expect high quality service and will seek out institutions with superior service or shun those whose student services are of poor quality. To remain competitive in the next decade, colleges and universities can differentiate themselves based on how well they create a student-centered environment.

References/Suggested Readings

Dolence, M. G., & Norris, D. M. (1995). *Transforming higher education: A vision for learning in the 21st century.* Ann Arbor, MI: Society for College and University Planning.

Epper, R. (1996, August). *IBM higher education forum: Innovation in student services.* Unpublished.

Ferri, C. (1996, August). *IBM higher education forum: Innovation in student services.* Unpublished.

Hammer, M., & Champy, J. (1993). *Reengineering the corporation.* New York, NY: Harper Business Publishers.

Heller, K., & Eng, L. (1996, March 31). Why college costs so much, pushing many out of the market. *The Philadelphia Inquirer.*

Henry, T. (1996, July 11). College dropout rate hits all time high. *USA Today.*

Hollowell, D. E. (1994, Summer). On becoming a more student-centered campus. *Facilities Manager,* 32-35.

Kramer, G. L. (1996, July). *Developmental academic advising.* National Academic Advising Association, Summer Institute. Unpublished.

Lewis, M. (1996, August). *IBM higher education forum: Innovation in student services.* Unpublished.

Lonabocker, L. (1996, August). *IBM higher education forum: Innovation in student services.* Unpublished.

O'Banion T. (1972, March). An academic advising model. *Junior College Journal, 42* (6), 62-69.

Peterson, E. D. (1996, August). *IBM higher education forum: Innovation in student services.* Unpublished.

Tuller, C. (1997). Another paradigm shift. In D. G. Oblinger & S. C. Rush (Eds.), *The learning revolution: The challenge of information technology in the academy.* Bolton, MA: Anker.

PART 3

MOVING TOWARD THE FUTURE IN TEACHING AND LEARNING

6

STUDENT MOBILE COMPUTING

Diana G. Oblinger, Mark Resmer, and James R. Mingle

"It is time that our institutions give up the industrial age model of personal computers in laboratories and move aggressively to the expectations that every student will come to school prepared with at least a minimally configured personal computer."

Heterick, 1994

"We had a record number of freshman applications this year."

"Our enrollment is up 50% since we started student mobile computing."

"Students are learning more and feeling like they are better prepared for careers."

"Faculty have changed their teaching style: Now they focus more on project-based learning, teamwork, and communication."

"Faculty feel more positive about the quality of their teaching."

"Our institution is more competitive than ever before."

That's just a sample of what colleges and universities who have a strategy of universal student access or student mobile computing are saying. The transformation caused by student mobile computing is about much more than just computers. It is about people, processes, and technology.

Recently, it has been recognized as one of the most powerful strategies for transforming the learning environment.

For several years the number of students purchasing computers for their personal use has been growing, an indication that students are willing to invest in their own learning tools. The strategy of student mobile computing extends this same learning opportunity to all students. Ubiquitous availability of technology acts as a catalyst that changes not only what is taught but how. The result is that student mobile computing changes both the infrastructure as well as student and faculty behavior. This chapter documents the rationale behind student mobile computing, how it is implemented, and the outcomes of the process.

THE NEED

Computers are general purpose tools used in fields ranging from the sciences to the arts, in subject matter that is computationally intensive, word intensive, or graphics intensive. As the applications for computing grow, there is an ever-increasing demand for computing resources and for dedicated lab facilities. Frequent changes in technology almost guarantee that hardware and software are obsolete in less time than it takes a freshman to graduate.

Persons over the age of 25 are approaching majority status, nationwide. Moreover, 70% of all students work full- or part-time (less than 22% of students are 18–22 years old, live in campus housing, and attend full-time). Universal access addresses the new majority of college students and the need for lifelong learning that is driven by the new workplace and economy. The traditional lab model is inadequate for these students who have time commitments elsewhere and often cannot avail themselves of campus computing facilities.

If physical presence is a requirement for communication, both student-to-student and student-to-faculty, then these same students are at a disadvantage for human interchange. Universal access may achieve its greatest value by connecting students to and facilitating direct communication with other students and faculty. In short, the greatest value of the technology stems from human beings. The next greatest value is from the access to information and information resources (e.g., libraries, support services, tutoring, etc.). It is the human and very personal dimensions of the technology and the very practical aspects of it that make for the real added value of an institutional strategy of universal access (Skinner, 1997).

To gain access to computers at their own convenience, a growing number of students (or their parents) purchase computers. Others cannot afford their own computer. As the use of the computer becomes a more integral component of the curriculum, the inequity between the haves and the have-nots becomes more obvious. Many campuses are struggling to cope with expectations, obsolescence, equity, and funding challenges.

DEFINITION

The growing need for students to have access to technology has shifted the emphasis away from institutions providing public labs to an emerging model in which students own a laptop computer and have 24-hour access to the network. The trend is toward universal student access to technology.

Because of the growing importance of networked information and communication, students must be able to communicate and integrate computers into their educational experience. The goal is any place, any time access to information resources.

Characteristics of Student Mobile Computing

Twenty-four hour access. Twenty-four hour access should be provided to a computer, campus network resources, and the Internet. Connectivity is critical to extend the computer from a productivity tool or word processor into a communications tool.

Mobility. Students are nomadic; as they move from class to class or from campus to other locations, a laptop computer can go with them. Mobility enables students to integrate the computer into everyday life. It also fosters social interaction and peer learning. Institutions that have invested in laptop computers report that it is common for students to gather around laptops over lunch or in the quad as they work together solving problems.

Possession. The strategy should allow students to possess their computer even if they do not own it (some student machines are leased, for example). Possession is required to ensure 24-hour access. Students need to be able to personalize the computer and trust it will be in the same condition as they last left it.

Universality. Student mobile computing should be universal and program independent so that a base of functionality is provided to all students regardless of discipline, class standing, residential status, or other characteristics.

Upgrading. Even though it is a requirement that all students possess a computer, some disciplines may require higher levels of performance or greater network capability. Students should be able to avail themselves of these options, if necessary.

Guaranteed service. The program should provide access to shared resources (e.g., dial-up facilities or access ports) with constant, reliable service.

These criteria define the current optimal environment as a laptop computer in the possession of every student, with sufficient network access both on- and off-campus, to permit relatively uninterrupted access to the network at an adequate speed whenever the student needs it (Resmer, Mingle, & Oblinger, 1995).

RATIONALE

Students, parents, employers, and governing bodies are all customers of higher education. They have expectations that higher education will provide learners with the tools, techniques, and content needed for productive careers. Among those expectations is that students will understand and be able to use information technology.

"Students and those already a part of today's workforce need knowledge about technology and skills in its use to remain productive and valued. Among these essential student skills are a basic familiarity and understanding of the role and functions of technology in our present world. Students require a mastery of technological applications that are germane to their professions and disciplines. They need a working knowledge of personal computers and common software tools. They require the ability to search, retrieve, analyze, and use electronic information. Finally, students must develop the capability to use technology independently and collaboratively in their work" (Hall, 1995). These expectations are unlikely to be met without programs of student mobile computing due to issues such as access and equity.

The rationale for student mobile computing emerges from the following factors:

▶ The increasing amount and dynamic nature of knowledge that students must master

▶ Changing models for education

▶ Enhancing the value of the degree

▶ Improving communications

▶ Rapidity of technological change

▶ Improving delivery of student services

Information Access

The body of recorded knowledge is growing at such a rapid rate that it is no longer possible for traditional tools to keep pace. Nor can all information be captured in paper form because of elements beyond text and graphics. Direct access to this body of knowledge is an integral part of a comprehensive educational experience.

The implication for the learning environment is that every student must have access to a networked computer. To be effectively integrated into their educational experience, such access needs to be available within their work environment, whether in the classroom, lab, library, or home. As the availability of electronic information increases—from libraries, museums, and other sources—the amount of time that each student spends using a computer will increase. Personal, continuous access to computers and the network becomes a necessity which will enable the information resources to be intimately linked with other parts of the student's academic experience (Resmer, Mingle, & Oblinger, 1995).

Changing Educational Models

As educational paradigms change from teacher-centered to learner-centered, technology serves as a catalyst for the development of learner-centered approaches to education. Technology can expand opportunities for faculty and students to extend or transform the traditional classroom experience.

When faculty and students can assume a high level of access to technology, more active forms of learning may be encouraged. At the University of Minnesota at Crookston, for example, universal student access has enabled faculty to use new approaches and cover more material than was previously possible. With computers in hand, students can solve science, accounting, math, and statistics problems on their own instead of watching the professor solve them. Students can engage in collaborative writing, expanding the concept of writing-across-the-curriculum to include teamwork, as well. Classes can be structured so students learn by doing and by discovery instead of passively receiving information delivered by faculty.

A psychology professor at the University of Illinois remarked that, "Now it is possible for students, using the computer, to design and run the same experiments that researchers are doing." As such programs proliferate and prove their educational value, the faculty and student demand for computing resources will rise dramatically, a problem that many feel is best solved by each student having a computer (Pinheiro, 1995).

Even in more conventional lecture/seminar settings, institutions that have implemented student mobile computing report a much greater use of presentation tools by students. One of the best ways to learn is to teach. The enhanced focus on the students as presenters places them in the role of a "teacher" and can allay the concern that faculty will have to spend too much of their time preparing presentations for class. Although presentations have a place in the high-tech classroom, they are more likely to be the work of students than of faculty (Resmer, Mingle, & Oblinger, 1995).

Enhancing the Value of the Degree

Technological competency is becoming a requirement in the workplace. "There is no question that technology skills will be essential in ever-increasing portions of the labor market of the 21st century; the use of computer and other information technologies is becoming prevalent across all fields and occupations" (Green & Gilbert, 1995).

Communication

Communication between faculty and students can be enhanced by access to networked computers. For example, a student can post a question to the professor at the time the problem arises (perhaps late at night), instead of taking class time or seeking the professor out during office hours. By the next day the student has often forgotten the question so it is never asked or answered. Similarly, the professor can post significant questions and answers on the network so the entire class, not just a single student, can benefit from the interaction.

In spite of the obvious importance of communication, little effort is made in the average undergraduate course to develop students' communication skills. The common instructional model still features a teacher-centered environment which puts a premium on presentation skills for the teacher but requires little in the way of communication capability from the students. Success in many careers depends on communication, collaboration, and cooperation, all of which can potentially be enhanced through the use of networked communications. Cooperative learning techniques have also shown success in encouraging the success of minority students (Wilson & Mosher, 1994).

Technological Change

Technology changes rapidly. New products enter the market on six to nine month cycles. Educational institutions cannot keep pace with these changes. Institutions with universal access strategies are better able to match the pace of technological development with technology deployment. At the University of Minnesota-Crookston, for example, computers are "refreshed" annually through a leasing program.

Student Services

The implementation of mobile computing may allow the institution to provide more efficient and cost effective services to students. Student and faculty directories, class rosters, course schedules, event notices, and institutional policies may all be made available over a network, now easily accessible by all students. Students may register and sign up for campus jobs or for placement office interviews electronically. Campuses which have implemented such programs report a reduction in the paper used to print course catalogs, student directories, and class schedules. With student mobile computing, students may obtain course materials in electronic form, thus increasing the availability of information.

Each institution will have its own rationale that is consistent with the student body, institutional image, and goals. Clayton State College in Morrow, Georgia has established notebook computers as one component of a three-part plan (the other components being a universal campus card and financing as auxiliary services). Their rationale includes several benefits:

▶ Enhance learning productivity; i.e., find ways for students to learn more and faster in the face of the increasing amount and dynamic nature of knowledge that students must master.

▶ Improve career readiness. In an age when preparing someone for a job is dangerous, we must find ways to ensure a graduate's readiness for a career. Information technology is a pervasive part of the workplace now and in the future.

▶ Accommodate the needs and circumstances of the new majority of students in higher education who are over age 25, working full- or part-time while rearing a family, and are committed or resigned to lifelong learning but unable to avail themselves of congregate learning formats.

▶ Make lifelong learning practical. A graduate can continue to be provided a notebook computer and support from the college and participate in learning without having to "stop out" from employment to acquire additional education or training.

▶ Expand and improve services on- and off-campus to all students.

▶ As a result of Clayton's financing approach, seek to reduce dependence on state funding but still create and maintain state-of-the-art technology (Skinner, 1997).

As you begin, consider asking questions such as the following:

▶ Is the emphasis on student access appropriate, or should faculty access or institutional capacity be emphasized first?

- What are the goals we seek to accomplish through enhancing student access?

- How should we define optimal student access?

- What incentives are needed to achieve this goal?

- What methods of financing should be used?

- How should we define and implement universal connectivity?

- What are the constraints/barriers to a universal student access strategy?

- What kinds of assessment and evaluation need to be part of such a strategy?

EDUCATIONAL IMPACT

There is growing evidence that the use of computers can have a positive impact on teaching and learning (Berge & Collins, 1995; Cartwright, 1993; Ehrmann, 1995; Green, 1995; Tynan, 1993). Emphasizing learning is the single greatest benefit universal access seeks to facilitate. Universal access to information technology can enhance learning in several ways. For example, "The computer makes it possible for the learner to make choices that determine both the kind of material presented and the rate of information flow. Hypertext or hypermedia documents open up the ability to follow relationships among ideas. The timely access to relevant information is intellectually arousing for the student and assists in discovery learning. The interactive format makes it possible for the presentation of information to occur under natural conditions of inquiry; that is, when the learner has framed a question and is receptive to the answer" (Noblitt, 1995).

Retention may be improved, as well. "Many have noticed improved retention from interactive instruction. Students seem to remember when they are actively involved in absorbing data, and it appears that a combination of media, including visual and audio cues, tends to make a stronger impression" (Tynan, 1993).

By providing universal access, education will be improved by 1) promoting student adaptability and encouraging lifelong learning; 2) increasing the relevance of higher education to students and society; and 3) enhancing equity of access to information and education.

Promoting Student Adaptability

For many disciplines, it is estimated that the volume of information doubles every five years or in about the amount of time it takes to complete a degree

(Molnar, 1988). Because of the volume of information, it is becoming more important for students to develop processes for acquiring information, thinking critically, and making decisions, and less on memorizing facts. The expectation that professionals will change careers several times during their lifetime makes the memorization of facts less important and mastering processes more valuable.

"The important thing in education is to distinguish between what the student must internalize and what may be safely relegated to storage in information technology" (Noblitt, 1995). This implies that information must remain extremely accessible. This is only possible with access to both computers and networks that permit students to integrate electronically-stored information into their work in an intuitive, convenient manner. Student mobile computing offers the only viable approach to providing this level of access.

Increasing the Relevance of Higher Education

Institutions that have announced student mobile computing programs have elicited enthusiasm and support from parents, employers, and the media. The perception is that such programs are highly relevant to the needs of the institutions' "customers" and make colleges and universities more responsive to the "real world." Students, who are increasingly motivated by career considerations, see student mobile computing programs as having direct relevance to them. Institutions that have implemented such programs have seen the number of applicants for admission rise and transfer rates increase (Resmer, Mingle, & Oblinger, 1995).

Enhancing Equity

There is an increasing centrality of technology to the educational process. Student mobile computing can help ensure that all students have equal access to technology. The disadvantaged student should not be excluded because the more affluent student can afford a computer. Without an institutional commitment to student mobile computing, we risk building a society of haves and have-nots. There is evidence that this is already happening. Students with the means to purchase computers are doing so (national estimates are 40%-50%). These students have a significant advantage over students who must rely on computer labs.

For those who cannot afford to purchase a computer, public lab facilities are the only option. These labs often have outdated equipment, are only available during limited hours, and are often overcrowded. As demand for access to technology grows, this situation can only get worse. While the issue frequently raised is that imposing the additional financial burden of a computer purchase on students with limited means is unfair, it is precisely these individuals who will be disenfranchised without a strategy which guarantees access to technology. If this strategy is implemented with due attention to equity issues, it offers an opportunity to bridge the existing gap between the haves and have-nots.

MODELS

There are as many models for student mobile computing as there are institutions which have implemented it. To illustrate some of the major options, the University of Minnesota at Crookston, Wake Forest University, and Sonoma State University are used as examples. Major differences exist for ownership of the computer, funding, phasing of implementation, and uniformity of hardware.

University of Minnesota at Crookston
The University of Minnesota at Crookston implemented a program for universal student access in 1993. In its model, the computers are leased by the institution. Those students who pay the full-time student technology fee (approximately $950) receive a computer for full-time use. Part-time students may elect to pay the full-time fee (thus being entitled to a computer full-time) or a part-time fee which allows them to check out a computer for 24-hours at a time. Classrooms, residence halls, and other student facilities have been modified to accommodate network access and power. All students are required to complete a course in the fundamentals of operating the computer. All faculty and students have the same computer and software.

Wake Forest University
Wake Forest University (WFU) began phasing in student mobile computing with the freshman class in 1996. All freshmen are given a laptop computer with preloaded software (students all have the same computer and software). An increase in tuition financed the program and covered not only computers and the associated infrastructure, but additional faculty and staff. During the spring semester of 1996, a pilot group of students and faculty began using technology in their courses. At the same time, the infrastructure was being enhanced to accommodate additional users (additional network capacity, file servers, print servers, printers, etc.). Hardware will be replaced/upgraded every two years, with returned equipment being refurbished and provided to public school districts. All students participating in the program receive training in the use of the technology. Faculty were provided with some options on hardware configurations (e.g., a desktop model

could be chosen instead of a laptop); thus not all faculty and students use the same system.

Sonoma State University

Sonoma State University's policy on universal student access requires possession of a computer but does not mandate that the student own it. A minimum configuration is stipulated. Students may choose their own vendor and configuration provided it meets the minimum requirements. Software with cross-platform capabilities was chosen. A loaner pool was established for students who might not be able to afford to purchase their own computer. The program began with the freshman class of 1996, being phased in over four years. All students receive training in the use of technology.

IMPLEMENTATION

Infrastructure

For student mobile computing to have the desired impact, more than computers for students and faculty will be required. Significant changes should be made in an institution's infrastructure.

▶ Expanded network capacity
  Network extended to all buildings and classrooms
  Provision of network connections in convenient student locations
    (e.g., student union)
  Internet access service for remote access
  Provision of e-mail, uploading, and downloading services
  Additional servers, if required

▶ Classrooms that can accommodate the use of student computers
  Network connections at student seats
  Power at student seats
  Larger desk space
  Lighting controls, control panel, projection systems, and computer for
    the instructor

▶ Hardware
  Determination of how many standard configurations will be supported
  Determination of where printing will be done and how it will be paid
    for
  Provision of special carrying cases or backpacks

▶ Software

Determination of the supported operating system(s)

Determination of a standard application suite

Determination of where software resides (e.g., individual machines vs. a server)

Virus protection scheme

Security

Project Management

Strong project management is required in the implementation of student mobile computing initiatives. At Wake Forest University, for example, over 200 project teams were established. A full-time project manager was designated by WFU and the technology vendor. Adjacent offices were established to promote rapid communication.

Not only is project management required because of the scope and complexity of student mobile computing, but it can be used as a mechanism to create buy-in from faculty and student groups, as well. Those who participate in defining and solving the problems are more likely to be satisfied than those who only observe.

At the University of Minnesota at Crookston, three major categories of projects were defined: academic affairs, student services, and finance/operations. Within each group, unit-level project management (i.e., subcategories) were defined:

▶ Academic affairs: curriculum, computer services, faculty development

▶ Student services: financial aid, student government, residential life

▶ Finance and operations: redirection of resources, infrastructure

(For more on project management, see Chapter 15.)

Funding Models

There are different funding models for student mobile computing. Two consistent components are student ownership and technology fees.

Student ownership. While the details vary, programs require the student to possess a computer. Each institution must decide between purchase and possession. Options, such as loans of institutionally-owned leased machines are possible. There appear to be advantages to having a student make a personal financial investment in possession, whether it be through outright purchase, a monthly fee, or a work-study commitment.

While student ownership increases the cost of a student's education, it is not disproportionate with other expenses accepted as reasonable educational costs. Students typically spend around $200 per semester on textbooks. Purchasing a $1,600 computer, paid for over four years, represents a similar level of investment (Heterick, 1994). The potential benefits are at least as great. However, adding a cost of this magnitude to existing educational expenses may price some students out of the market. For this reason, any program must recognize and provide for the special needs of these individuals (Resmer, Mingle, & Oblinger, 1995).

Technology fees. Many institutions assess a student technology fee to support the additional infrastructure required by today's technology. In fact, these fees exist at institutions without student mobile computing programs. Fees range from under $50 per semester to over $300 and cover very different levels of service—from basic connectivity and computer labs at one extreme to the provision of loaner laptop computers at the other. Some institutions have elected to embed the technology fee in their tuition; others assess a separate fee. The University of Minnesota at Crookston and Sonoma State University have both elected to keep tuition constant and impose technology fees. Wake Forest University increased tuition to include the cost of a computer with a two-year replacement cycle as well as additional faculty and support staff (Resmer, Mingle, & Oblinger, 1995).

Public/private partnerships. Clayton State College in Morrow, Georgia recently adopted a "universal personal information technology access" initiative which includes leased notebook computers for all students and faculty. The initiative will be run as an auxiliary enterprise financed through a combination of technology fees and revenue sharing arrangements with for-profit companies. By combining their "computers for all students" approach with a universal campus "smart" card, they can provide vendors, such as Internet service providers and on-line banking operations, with exclusive opportunities to market and sell goods. While the basic technology fee will include a specified number of hours per month for remote access, the successful bidder to their planned request for proposal (RFP) would be expected to market additional services to students and "either pay the institution a percentage of the resulting gross revenues as commission or provide in-kind goods and services" (Clayton State College, 1996).

Challenges and Prerequisites for Success

Introduction of student mobile computing represents a major shift in the way that an institution operates: It impacts many aspects of institutional culture and thus requires significant planning. Extensive dialog with students, the faculty, the administration, executive management, and governing bodies is necessary to engage their support.

Policy issues. Development of clear policy statements regarding student mobile computing should be established. Among the policies to be considered are:

▶ Theft

▶ Insurance

▶ Replacement of machines

▶ Costs for repair

▶ Availability and eligibility for loaner machines

▶ Inventory control

▶ Ownership vs. leasing

▶ Policies for part-time students and students who drop out

▶ Technology fees

Recognition and rewards. The institutional recognition and reward system should be modified to recognize contributions of faculty and staff to reengineering courses, developing electronic media, and mastering a new set of skills.

Change in roles and responsibilities. As technology is adopted and courses are modified to accommodate the use of technology in the curriculum, faculty roles will change from content providers to managers and designers of learning environments. Students will also be required to adopt a more proactive and responsible role in their own education. In fact, students will assume more of the role of the "instructor," guiding their own learning.

Reengineering the curriculum. Anticipate that the curriculum will undergo a gradual reengineering as technology becomes more prevalent. Courses will focus less on content and more on processes. Because technology allows the use of techniques that are difficult to use in a lecture setting (e.g., simulation), the character of many courses often changes. Tests may be taken electronically. Assignments may be submitted over the network. Helping students anticipate how their courses will use technology is an important part of this transition. At Sonoma State University the technology used in courses is advertised in the course catalog. The categories are:

▶ Communications

▶ Distance learning

▶ Technology-centered

▶ Discipline specific

▶ Information based

▶ Presentations

▶ Computer-based learning

▶ Other

Critical mass of adopters. Student mobile computing is an institutional initiative. As such, its success depends on having a critical mass of adopters. If students have computers, but only a few faculty make use of the capability, the initiative will fall short of its potential. Therefore, the institution must facilitate the development of a critical mass of adopters among faculty, staff, and administrators.

Access to information. The success of universal student access is contingent on having access to valuable sources of information. Among those sources an institution might consider are library access, access to the Internet and World Wide Web, access to administrative systems, e-mail, course syllabi, class notes, etc. Helping individuals find valuable sources of information will become an important support function.

Support structure. Few campuses indicate that their current support for technology is adequate. Student mobile computing will increase demands for support, both from faculty and students. Functions range from help desk support to training for faculty and students to classroom assistance and repairs. To maximize the value of the infrastructure and information available, an adequate support structure must be in place.

Training. A prerequisite to successfully implementing student mobile computing is the provision of training for faculty, staff, and students. In most cases, training is provided to each group independently. For example, if the expectation is that faculty will use technology in classes, faculty training may need to precede student access to machines. Note that faculty training often goes well beyond hardware/software use to include pedagogy and learning theory. An institutional policy should be established for several variables, such as whether student training is mandatory or voluntary, credit-bearing or not-for-credit, as well as the topics included.

ASSESSMENT

For any initiative as significant as student mobile computing, it is important to assess the value and perceptions of the program. Wake Forest University began its assessment with attitude surveys. WFU students responded to a survey shortly after they completed their computer training. Some of the results include the following:

- ▶ 80% indicated that they welcomed increasing use of computer technology
- ▶ 83% said they believed the technology should make learning easier
- ▶ 65% felt that the computers were not being introduced into the classroom too rapidly
- ▶ Only 19% feared that the computers would make the teaching process too impersonal

At Sonoma State, there was controversy before student mobile computing was implemented; there has been none since the program began. Sonoma State University has seen a record number of freshman applications since their program was announced. Faculty report noticeably greater freshman engagement in courses and feel there have been positive effects on faculty development. Much less financial resistance was encountered than was anticipated. For example, the average purchase price of student computers was $1,700 rather than the minimal configuration of approximately $1,000. Forty percent of the students purchased a computer outright; 50% used some type of loan; 9% used a computer from the loaner pool; and 1% paid for the computer through a work-study program. Other positive results have accrued:

- ▶ A 50% increase in admission inquiries
- ▶ A record number of freshman applications
- ▶ An 8% increase in "show rate"
- ▶ Improved freshman/sophomore retention
- ▶ An increase in the average semester course load per student

The University of Minnesota at Crookston has seen student numbers increase from 800 when the program was begun to 1,350 in 1996. During the 1996 academic year, 83% of courses incorporated technology. Faculty feel they have changed their teaching approach to one that focuses on projects, communication, and team building. In surveys of students, 93% report that they are building technology skills that will be needed for their careers. Eighty-five percent feel they have improved their research and information gathering skills. Eighty percent of the faculty feel there is increased communication between faculty and students.

The University of Minnesota at Crookston has identified several requirements for successful implementation of the student mobile computing program:

- ▶ Cabinet level planning

- ▶ Unit-level project management

- ▶ Faculty and staff training

- ▶ Curriculum revision

- ▶ Financial creativity

- ▶ Redesign of facilities and expansion of the local area network

- ▶ Standardization on a single computer model and software

- ▶ Adjustment to software trends

- ▶ Additional support services (e.g., student help desk and faculty/staff instructional technology center)

- ▶ Adjustment to change

QUESTIONS TO ASK

If your institution is considering student mobile computing, the following questions will help you begin the planning.

Financing

- ▶ Will the institution finance the computers or will it be done by an external agency?

- ▶ Will the machines be leased or purchased?

- ▶ Is a student technology fee required? How was the fee determined?

- ▶ What input have students had into the financing decisions?

Ownership

- ▶ Do the students buy the computers or lease them?

- ▶ Who owns the computers, the institution or the student?

- ▶ How often will the equipment be "refreshed"?

- ▶ At the end of the life cycle, what happens to the machines?

Rules and Regulations

▶ Is there a penalty for a lost or stolen institutionally-owned machine?

▶ Must students who already own a machine purchase the campus model?

▶ If the computer is institutionally owned, can students take the machines off-campus over the summer? during semester break?

▶ What is the policy for part-time students?

▶ Will student mobile computing implementation occur all at once or in a phased process?

▶ Who insures the machines? Are they self-insured? What does the vendor policy cover?

Configuration

▶ What are the students' hardware needs (modem speeds, hard disk space, RAM, CD-ROM)?

▶ What are the faculty hardware needs?

▶ What are the hardware needs for staff?

Software

▶ What software will be used?

▶ Will the software be preloaded on all machines?

▶ Who will own the software, the institution or the student?

▶ Is the faculty software load the same or different as the students?

▶ Is there a software library for unique software?

Network

▶ Is the network capacity adequate to handle the anticipated increase in use?

▶ How will students with laptops connect to the network?

▶ How will off-campus students and faculty connect to the network?

▶ Which classrooms will be wired for network connections?

▶ Can the network handle multimedia, such as video and audio?

Classrooms

▶ What kind of network access will be provided?

▶ What kind of projection equipment will faculty need?

▶ Will extra power outlets be required?

▶ Are room configuration changes needed to promote more collaborative learning?

▶ Will desk surfaces accommodate a computer?

Faculty Support

▶ Will the faculty have the same machine as the students?

▶ What kind of support do the faculty feel they will need?

▶ Is there an instructional technology support center?

▶ Does faculty development include technology training as well as pedagogy?

▶ Is there a baseline of training required for all faculty?

▶ How will support be provided within individual divisions/departments?

Curricula

▶ Is there a plan to enhance the curriculum to take advantage of the availability of the machines?

▶ What technical competencies will students need to be competitive?

▶ Are there opportunities for internships and job-related experiences that will enhance the curriculum?

Students

▶ What skills do incoming students have in computer use?

▶ Is a baseline of training required for all students?

▶ How will the students carry the machines?

CONCLUSION

The interest in student mobile computing is growing. Those institutions with established programs have seen applications increase, enrollments climb, and the competitiveness of their students improve. Support from students has been strong. Student mobile computing is not a panacea for all instructional or financial challenges, but it creates a climate for change that revitalizes colleges and universities.

References/Suggested Readings

Berge, Z., & Collins, M. (1995). *Computer mediated communications and the on-line classroom: Overview and perspectives.* Cresskill, NJ: Hampton Press.

Cartwright, G. P. (1993). Do computers help students learn? *The Edutech Report, 9* (9), 1.

Clayton State College & Floyd College. (1996, October). A proposal to the chancellor of the University System of Georgia: The Information Technology Project.

Ehrmann, S. C. (1995). Asking the right questions: What does research tell us about technology and higher learning? *Change, 27* (2).

Green, K. C. (1995). *Campus computing survey.* Los Angeles, CA: University of Southern California.

Green, K. C., & Gilbert, S. W. (1995, March/April). Great expectations: Content, communications, productivity, and the role of information technology in higher education. *Change, 27* (2), 8-18.

Hall, J. W. (1995). Educational technology initiative: Greeting the dawn of a new millennium. *Empire State College: CLT News, 1,* 1.

Heterick, R. C., Jr. (1994). The shoemaker's children. *Educom Review, 29* (3), 60.

Molnar, A. (1988, October 27). *Information and communications technology: Today and in the future.* Presentation to the Lifelong Engineering Symposium, Royal Swedish Academy of Engineering Sciences, Stockholm, Sweden.

Noblitt, J. S. (1995). *Redefining the boundaries of language study.* In C. Kramsch (Ed.), *Issues in language program direction.* Boston, MA: Heinle and Heinle.

Pinheiro, E. (1995). *Introducing mobile computing to the college campus.* White Plains, NY: IBM.

Resmer, M., Mingle, J. R., & Oblinger, D. G. (1995). *Computers for all students: A strategy for universal access to information resources.* State Higher Education Executive Officers (SHEEO).

Skinner, R.A. (1997). Personal communication.

Tynan, D. (1993). Multimedia goes on the job just in time. *New Media*, 3.

Wilson, J. M., & Mosher, D. N. (1994, Summer). The prototype of the virtual classroom. *Journal of Instructional Delivery Systems,* 28-33.

This chapter draws on an earlier publication:

Resmer, M., Mingle, J. R., & Oblinger, D. G. (1995). *Computers for all students: A strategy for universal access to information resources.* State Higher Education Officers (SHEEO).

7

Wake Forest University's Strategic Plan for Technology

David G. Brown

A Theory of Learning

A strategic plan rests upon a clear theory of learning and an understandable set of basic concepts. The theory and concepts undergirding Wake Forest's adoption of Thinkpads for everyone are presented, not as a prescription for all, but as a catalyst for thinking about the relevance of technology for learning.

College is about student learning. Students learn most when motivated by expert professors, by the ideas of scholars of different centuries and different cultures, and by fellow students. The special challenge for a college or a university is to create a communications environment with the people, policies, and traditions that motivate and facilitate learning.

Summary of Plan

Bold and complex, Wake Forest's Plan for the Class of 2000 aspires in 37 specific ways to strengthen community, communication, and therefore, student learning. At the heart of the plan is the addition of 40 new tenure-track faculty, a 15% increase. A newly required first year seminar assures each freshman an in-depth intellectual encounter in a class no larger than 15 students. Twenty percent of each class receives a scholarship to study abroad. Another 20% receives a fellowship to join with a faculty member in research. More books, more faculty leaves, more technicians, more start-up and matching funds, more grants, more laboratories and classrooms, more endowed professors, more faculty salary dollars, more emphasis upon intellectual climate, more study options in the summer, more emphasis upon the fine arts and ethnic studies—these are all parts of the plan. Fifteen million new dollars have been added to a $130 million annual budget. In addition to the increase in the annual budget, approximately $100 million is being devoted to new buildings and new instrumentation.

This plan emerged from the deliberations of a routinely constituted triennial faculty-student strategic planning group. After collecting ideas from retreats, questionnaires, interviews, and reactions to a full-scale interim report, the committee advanced 37 recommendations which were endorsed and/or approved as a package in a series of five votes over an eight-week period in the spring of 1995 by the college faculty, the student legislature, and the board of trustees.

Among the 37 recommendations was a statement, "By the fall of 1996, all teaching should proceed from the premise that students have personal access to and routinely use computers. The university should consider the possibility of requiring all incoming students of the class of 2000 to buy a personal computer and should investigate means for making this possible for all of our students." This article focuses upon the what, the why, and the how of this single, most notable recommendation.

The university now leases a standardized Thinkpad 380D computer to every freshman. Students receive a second new computer at the beginning of their junior year and take that computer with them upon graduation. The Thinkpad for the class of 2000 includes 32 mb RAM, a 1.35 gb hard drive, a 150 mhz Pentium processor, Ethernet/fax/modem connections, 4X CD-ROM, and a built-in floppy drive. All faculty and staff have been placed on a similar two-year cycle, and may link from home or abroad to the campus network via unlimited IBM Global Network (IGN) access. Software includes Windows 95, Microsoft Office 97 (Word, Excel, and PowerPoint), Lotus Notes, Netscape, etc. All computers have a custom designed Notes-based course and project filing system. Lotus Notes Mail is becoming the campus standard. Nearly 200 computer based training (CBT) modules are available upon call.

Virtually all offices, residence hall rooms, and classroom seats are directly linked to an Ethernet network. A robust network has been built upon SP2

RCSC 6000 servers and ATM switches. Special laboratories have been equipped in music, writing, business, physics, chemistry, the languages, and elsewhere. Remote access is made available to our students, faculty, and staff wherever they are.

Twenty academic computer specialists have been hired by department chairs and the library to assist students and faculty in their disciplines. Student computer technicians have been hired for each residence hall, and a corps of student designers aid faculty in the use of the computer for teaching.

A 25-point strategy for faculty exposure and usage is being implemented. Many courses emphasize electronic access to library materials and distant experts as well as within class collaboration. Some courses are paperless.

Configuration and policy decisions are made by an elected faculty committee. Network and hardware decisions are made from a centralized computer center. Adoption and usage decisions are made by departments and individual faculty.

WHY LAPTOP COMPUTERS FOR ALL?

Often I am asked, why would a selective, private liberal arts college such as Wake Forest invest in so much technology? Aren't you emphasizing the wrong thing?

Clearly, there are dangers. Much like a group of teenagers first learning how to drive or a group of octogenarians sharing information on ailments, we are currently spending too much time evolving new strategies and learning new programs. The means to learning is temporarily too prominent. The substance of learning must soon, and once again, become primary. The infatuation with our new utility will end soon. Our willingness to endure the learning curve is explained by the following five benefits.

First Benefit: Personal and Individual

Wake Forest's comparative advantage rests with providing education that is both personal and individual. Before the computer revolution, the way to personalize education was to focus vast quantities of faculty time upon teaching and students. Individualization and customization was achieved by the same means. Suddenly, with the advent of computers, a student's education can be individualized and customized through computer access. Corps of graduate students can answer individual e-mails, even when students are in very large organic chemistry classes. Assignments can be individualized, even when large numbers are involved.

If Wake Forest is to maintain its comparative advantage in both personal and individual education, it must strengthen its means to personalize (which means more faculty) and strengthen its capacity to individualize (which means more computers). A few well-funded universities will have an opportunity to be both personal and individual. We are not computerizing for the age of distance learning. We are computerizing for the sake of individualization while preserving personalization.

Second Benefit: Technological Transformation

Suddenly the computer has become a basic tool of scholarship in every discipline. Like the newly powerful telescopes, which are drawing many research programs to reanalyze earlier hypotheses with never-before-available evidence, and like new scholarly theories about the relevance of gender and ethnicity of the authors and readers when analyzing literature, the ability of the computer to dig more deeply and to analyze larger and more complex data sets means that most of the dissertations over the next decade or so, in virtually all disciplines, will draw heavily upon possibilities presented by the computer. Old hypotheses will be retested using new powerful techniques of analysis.

In turn, this means that prospective faculty seeking first jobs will cherish those positions accompanied by adequate computer facilities and computer literate colleagues and students. Our capacity to attract the best and brightest faculty over the next decade is dependent upon our capacity to provide for them a computer environment where they may practice their profession.

Third Benefit: Nomadic Learners

Students are a privileged class in our society, yet they are without home or office. They are intellectual nomads, spending part of each year in a residence hall, a family bedroom, traveling abroad, and visiting friends. Wherever they are, students need access to the instruments of learning and scholarship. The instruments they learned to use while in school need to continue to be available to them upon graduation. The solution is a personally owned mobile computer.

Fourth Benefit: Access Information

Much like the telephone and the public library, the computer has become a common utility for communication and the access highway to information. In the information age our graduates will be greatly disadvantaged if they do not have access to a primary means of communication.

Fifth Benefit: Level Playing Field

We sensed that we were rapidly moving toward a two-class society, those students with computers and those who could not afford them. To level the playing field, we felt we could not deny computer access to students who could afford them, and yet, we could not afford to support this disparity. Universal ownership of computers seemed to be the only solution.

GUIDING PRINCIPLES

In the computer world, decision options multiply to baffling proportions. In order to make many decisions quickly and consistently, 14 fundamental concepts emerged.

Students First

Students were likely to be the most eager, and in many cases, the most knowledgeable computer users. Students will introduce faculty to the advantages of electronic communication, a role reversal. If we expect students to use computers, they must be available when students are in the classroom, studying abroad, home for vacation, and researching in off-campus libraries and laboratories. Students must feel that they have full access to the best computing facilities on campus. Faculty computing power is a second priority. Staff computing power is a distant third.

Academic Freedom

Copyright, security, and privacy are elements in our decision to adopt a system with heavy encryption. We believe that the communications between and among students and faculty must be private. We must avoid establishing open records that haunt individual students and scholars for the rest of their career. The desire for commercial-level security in order to assure academic freedom was a major reason for our Lotus Notes acquisition.

Communication and Community

We identified four uses of the computer: for communication, for access to databases and experts, for analysis, and for presentation. Our system is designed to maximize the possibilities of communication and interaction within the community and with the outside world. Communication and access were our emphasis. Analysis, the use stressed by early adopters within the faculty, will take care of itself. The use of the computer for presentation has been judged to be of marginal value, when compared with the investment required to prepare such presentations.

Standardization

Early on we decided to standardize the computer provided to all students, the software load, the campus-wide introductory instruction, and the possibility of a filing system. Clearly there are cost savings and maintenance advantages to standardization. The driving force in our decision, however, was educational.

Our community must have a common language, "tracks with common gauge." With common systems, professors and students can write comments on each other's papers. With common systems, the underlining and bolding associated with e-mail messages can be transmitted in the format and aesthetics that were intended. Standardization means that students can help each other learn, that it is no longer necessary to take two early class periods to explain how the computer will be used in each particular course (class periods that can be devoted to teaching English literature, instead of how to use the computer to learn English literature). Standardization means that how-to classes on computer usage can be taught more frequently and in greater depth. Standardization means that computer consultants who are trained in the applications within a single system can be hired more readily than more broadly based consultants. Standardization means that when a computer breaks down in the middle of a class, a loaner computer can be checked out from the departmental secretary with minimal disruption to the class. Standardization means that a student who is having problems with her computer can submit an assignment through her roommate's computer.

After College

Decisions concerning hardware and software were made more easily when we emphasized the criterion: What will students most likely have access to upon graduation? Once we identified the market leader, we sought that standard. Although most of our students used Macs in high school and brought Macs for college, most of our graduates were using PCs in their life beyond college. In software, Windows 95 and the Microsoft Office Suite are dominant, so that's what we adopted.

Basic Service

Our emphasis has been upon providing a basic level of service to every member of the community. Hardware, software, and educational programming has been designed so that every user can achieve a basic level of proficiency and use. The system is designed first to serve every student, with the presumption that the experts will be able to build upon that base. As shown in Figure 7.1, this is a reversal from the normal way that systems evolve with the experts building the base of the system which then eventually is extended to serve the novice users (but often in a fairly contorted and complicated way).

FIGURE 7.1

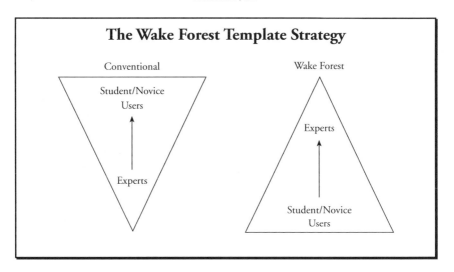

The Wake Forest Template Strategy

Self-Financed Extensions

The university's central computer system provides basic services. Specialized services, for example, for physics majors or computer science majors, are paid for by the departments. Individual students wishing the capacity to print more than 150 copies per year, wanting to place their own Web page on a server (instead of on their own computer), wanting to establish more than three project file cabinets on servers (not counting courses or recognized campus organizations) are able to purchase these extensions from our newly opened computer store. Faculty wishing to avoid long waits for modem connections can access the campus computer network from home and are furnished remote access services for free.

Empowerment of Existing Units

For both political and operational reasons, many faculty and many offices are involved in our community commitment to technology. An elected committee of the faculty determines the standard load on student computers and sets myriad policies. The computer center decides upon networks, distributes and maintains computers, and advises administrative offices. Academic computer specialists formally report to the dean and are assigned to clusters of departments (defined by academic buildings) to assist faculty and student adoption and use of technology with particular educational emphases. The bookstore operates the computer store which sells add-on capacities. The library, which has traditionally provided access to information, is responsible for choosing the supplier of electronic information, for coordinating presentational equipment used in the classroom, and most of all, for the basic training of both students and faculty in computer usage. Individual faculty members are responsible for actually adopting technology in their teaching and in their classrooms. The whole campus is consequently invested in making the transition in technology.

Exposure, Not Mandated Adoption

With time, the power of the technology itself will sell the use of technology. Faculty are curious about the possibilities provided by computers. Students reared on computers will, with time, push faculty to usage. It is neither wise nor necessary to insist that any faculty member adopt computer methodologies for his or her instruction. Our obligation is to enable faculty, without risk or extraordinary inconvenience, to explore uses of the technology and to experiment with it. Our corps of student designers is part of this strategy. Other parts include delegations visiting other campuses, on-campus symposia featuring specific uses in other universities, subsidized trips to workshops, a special fund for purchasing software for a particular purpose, another special fund for equipping laboratories in special purpose classrooms, and the customized development of a Notes-based filing system that can be universal.

Lesser Dependence on the Internet

Much has been written about the possible browning of the Internet, a breakdown created by overuse. We believe we must have local control over an alternate system of communication if such clogging occurs. We have therefore avoided using Web pages on the Internet as the primary storage location. Instead, we are emphasizing local use of groupware and the use of local servers.

Rapid Change

Information technology is a fast moving field. Obsolescence of both equipment and knowledge is great. Our system, with its complete turnover of hardware every two years, is built to anticipate this rapid change. There may be a time in the distant future when things settle, but for now, our policy committees and our computer staff and individual faculty members will each year reevaluate what we are doing and make changes as necessary.

Pilot Year

Virtually every system on campus was to be changed. Never before have we had so much discussion about how one should teach toward what goals and in which ways. This ferment needed time to work. Many false starts would be made. For all these reasons, it seemed essential to involve roughly 20% of our students from the class of 1999 in a piloting of our various programs. In retrospect that decision was absolutely essential.

Marketable Difference

Our early adoption of ubiquitous, mobile computing provided an opportunity for us to market the difference among high school seniors and others. Financing this bold move required a tuition increase, to be paid at first only by the incoming freshmen, of $3,000 per year. The benefits from this much higher tuition needed to be visible in order to be credible. The computer, although it was only one component of the total plan, provided such visibility for the plan. We now know that applications for the class of 2000 are the highest in the university's history, and that the students are coming to us with the highest ever test scores and class ranks.

Partnership

A university of our size has a limited amount of expertise. When implementing a change of this magnitude, it has been essential for us to have immediate and ready access to consulting expertise. We also needed a relationship with a vendor that would allow for modifications of the equipment available on the market and of the systems relating to delivery and maintenance. Our long-term partnership with IBM provided that depth of capacity. On several occasions when IBM would have liked us to adopt its software and operating systems, we said, "No, there's a better way for us." At the same time, there have been many times when IBM has said, "At least try this." And we have found that it works well. While retaining the independence and autonomy and academic freedom of the university, partnerships are absolutely essential in business ventures of this magnitude.

CONCLUSION

Time will judge the efficacy and wisdom of decisions made. So far they seem to be wise ones.

8

Collaborative Learning

Edwin J. Pinheiro

Much has been written on the potential of technology to revolutionize education. Often technology has been used to mimic or replace an existing process. For example, word processors have replaced typewriters, and presentation software has replaced the overhead transparency or classroom blackboard. In such cases, technology can enhance the process and can be introduced without too much disruption, but the benefits are correspondingly modest. Technology's true potential is realized when it is employed in innovative ways which do not necessarily correspond to traditional classroom practices. One such innovation is the use of the computer and appropriate software to enhance collaborative learning. Collaboration is not new; however, computers allow collaboration to take place independent of time and place.

WHAT IS COLLABORATIVE LEARNING?

We define collaborative learning as the process of students working in teams to pursue knowledge and learning. In collaborative learning, information, ideas, and problem solving are actively shared among the team. It can be synchronous, where students meet together either face-to-face or via audio or video conferencing tools that bring them together when they are geographically dispersed. Collaboration can also be asynchronous, where students log onto a network at different times and locations leaving their contributions for others to see and discuss.

How Do Students Learn?

Most higher education is based on individual learning. Assignments are completed by individuals, and collaboration on tests and exams is forbidden. Some learning occurs in the lecture setting, some through working homework assignments. Despite the dominance of the individual learning approach, we know that students learn in a variety of ways suited to their specific learning styles.

Learning also occurs through informal collaboration. Students might study together for a test, solicit explanations from classmates on unclear topics, or discuss topics covered in class. However, collaborative learning can play a much more formal and significant role in education. Many traditional courses can be modified to become collaborative learning courses and, if wisely constructed, can enhance student learning.

Does Collaborative Learning Work?

D. A. Bligh (1972), in a review of 100 studies of student learning at the college level, concluded that students who interact with other students and are engaged in the discussion of their ideas are less likely to have irrelevant or distracting thoughts and spend more time in synthesizing and integrating ideas and concepts compared with students who listen to lectures. Kulik and Kulik (1979) concluded that student discussion groups (a form of collaborative learning) were more effective than the lecture method in promoting student problem solving skills. In fact, collaborative procedures (student-student interactions) are related to higher levels of critical and active thinking and lower levels of rote memorization (Smith, 1977). Although these studies were conducted before the computer revolution, they validate the effectiveness of collaborative learning independent of the influence of technology. In addition to its value in learning, collaboration is a skill which is increasingly required in today's work environment. People in business and industry work in teams because the amount of knowledge and skill required in today's workplace is beyond the capabilities of a single individual. This collaboration is not limited to individuals within a firm. Companies often form external partnerships where collaboration is required to achieve objectives, such as to develop a new product, to solve problems, or to complement each other's place in the market.

How Does Collaboration Work?

While there is not a single theory on how learning occurs, several researchers (e.g., Piaget, Vygotsky) have developed learning theories which emphasize that "learning is a social (group) process that occurs more effectively in a cooperative context" (Alavi, 1994). In a collaborative environment a person can test his or her understanding (learning) against that of others (feedback), correcting, reinforcing, or refining their knowledge. In collaboration, learning is active: Each member of the team contributes ideas and thoughts. We know that active learning (i.e., learning by doing) is more effective than passive learning (e.g., sitting in a lecture) (Miller, 1995). Even casual observation provides us with evidence that learning requires doing, whether learning a mechanical skill (a pilot, a surgeon, a pianist), problem solving (a chess player), or even creating (a composer learns by composing, and a writer by writing).

Won't Technology Impede Collaboration?

Some fear the depersonalization of the education if technology is used in teaching and learning. However, numerous studies show just the opposite, especially where computers facilitate collaborative learning. Students report they have more interaction with faculty and with other students in such courses than in traditional lecture courses. For example, Drexel University converted some existing courses to an asynchronous collaborative learning format, using Lotus Notes. They report (Andriole & Lytle, 1995) that 85% of the students felt they had more access to the instructor than in a conventional course, and 75% felt they had more communication with fellow students than in conventional courses. As Mayadas (1997) explains, although the face-to-face method may be the most efficient form of communication, these meetings do not occur very often. Said another way, the communication bandwidth peaks during face-to-face sessions and drops to zero in between. Averaged over several hours, the effective bandwidth for asynchronous communication can be much higher than face-to-face communication.

Studies have shown that electronic facilitation, in which collaboration takes place through the computer, enhances rather than inhibits, participation (Harasim et al., 1995). There are several reasons for this:

▶ Students participate at a time and place that is convenient to them.

▶ Participants have time to compose questions, comments, or answers before typing them in.

▶ Even after input is typed, it can be studied and revised before being submitted.

▶ Student comments are not interrupted by others.

▶ Inhibiting factors, such as shyness, stuttering, physical appearance, or lack of confidence in oral skills are not present.

▶ The discussion cannot be dominated by individuals.

Computer collaboration improves group performance over individual performance. This occurs because computer mediation minimizes the inhibitors to communication while optimizing the facilitators (Alavi, 1994).

How Does Collaboration Apply to Higher Education?

Collaboration is more than an in-class tool; collaborative techniques can be used outside of the classroom. For example, when a group assignment is made it is often difficult to find a time when all members of a team can meet. A problem on residential campuses, it is aggravated when you mix in commuting students and part-time students. In addition, traditional collaboration can be nearly impossible in distance learning situations. Technology can solve the problem by allowing members of the team to sign onto a common discussion forum at their own convenience, pick up the thread of the discussion, and create their own comments. Students might join the discussion from a computer lab, from the dorm, from home, or even from the workplace. Students have time to digest the substance of the discussion and to think before they write. Studies have shown that computer-mediated discussions increase not only participation by students, but also the quality of the student's contribution. The real value of collaborative learning emerges when the professor, instead of treating it simply as an adjunct to the class, integrates the concept into the pedagogy of the course.

There are advantages for faculty as well. At their convenience they can monitor the team discussions and redirect them if they are off course. There is a written record of the contributions of each student which faculty might use for grading or research purposes. In addition, there is an opportunity for private communication between student and professor. The student can formulate a question for the professor at the time the question arises (perhaps when the student is tackling a homework assignment) and will receive an answer when the professor has an opportunity to reply. This has proven to be an effective query system since students are shy about asking questions in class, questions are forgotten by the time the next class session meets, and often there is not an opportunity to answer questions. This private communication between a professor and individual students also gives the faculty insight on how well students are learning the material and over which topics they seem to be stumbling. Often students go directly to other students in search of answers, relieving the professor from dozens of electronic mail messages.

WHAT DO I NEED IN ORDER
TO ENABLE COMPUTER COLLABORATION?

Computer facilitated collaboration requires three elements.

Computers

In order to collaborate with computers, computers must be available to students. Collaboration outside of the classroom can occur when students have access to computer labs, to computers in the residence halls, or at home. Increasingly, students have their own machines, whether as a personal purchase or furnished through the university (e.g., the University of Minnesota at Crookston or Wake Forest University). Collaboration inside the classroom requires that computers be available to those attending the class. This can be accomplished by holding the class in a computer lab or by having students bring their laptops into the class.

Networking

An isolated computer cannot facilitate collaboration. The computer must have a connection to a network that will exchange information and messages with the computers of other students in the group. Collaboration within the classroom can be accomplished when all of the computers are connected to a local area network in the classroom. Collaboration outside of the classroom generally occurs over the campus network, with students who are off-campus dialing into the campus network.

The Internet has greatly facilitated collaboration at a distance: Its evolution has resulted in platform-independent tools and protocols. Students can communicate using a basic format, such as SMTP, without having any knowledge of what computer or software another student might be using.

Software

There is great flexibility in the software tools that can be used for collaboration. In its simplest form, collaboration can take place through electronic mail where students send each other messages. However, there are a number of specialized software packages available that facilitate collaboration, such as First Class, Collabra Share, Groupwise, and Lotus Notes.

Each of these three items can be complex. Their implementation requires support from the executive administration on campus, investment by students (e.g., purchasing a computer or paying a technology fee), and the availability of capable support for training, maintenance, and problem resolution. Implementation is similar to the issues raised in Chapter 6 on student mobile computing.

How Do I Foster Collaboration Among My Students?

There are many ways to encourage collaboration in courses.

Review of Journal Articles

Students in class might be given the assignment to review a journal article and to post their contribution in a forum. In this way the whole class benefits by being exposed to a greater variety of articles than they would have been able to read on their own. Consider allowing students to start discussion threads from the reviews so that other students can expand on the interpretation of the article or voice agreement or disagreement with the conclusions of the reviewer.

Electronic Forum Discussions

Students might be given a reading assignment followed by discussion in an electronic forum. The electronic forum is likely to attract greater student participation than the in-class discussion. For example, several students might be contributing at the same time while in class only one student can talk at a time. One student contribution might stimulate a new insight by another student who will think about it and contribute his insight later. Finally, the contents of electronic forums can be preserved so the professor is able to gauge the amount and quality of each student's participation in the discussions which might contribute to the student's grade.

Team Questions

The professor might pose a question to the class and have teams of students work together on the answer. If the professor poses separate questions for each team, each team will become expert on the assigned topic which the team will then explain to the rest of the class. In this way students are involved in active learning—instead of trying simply to absorb information, they are actually discovering it. The process of having to teach the rest of the class and handle questions also helps each team cement its knowledge of the assigned topic.

Workplace Simulations

Teams might be engaged in competition simulating the workplace. Each team might manage a separate simulated firm, or teams might compete in different roles in a market (for example, farmers, brokers, and corporations that purchase commodities, such as a cereal company). The competition might illustrate market principles, military strategy, social, or psychological principles. The software used for collaboration might be programmed to reinforce certain rules of the market, or to introduce variations in the simulation which are generally not under the control of players in the real world situation (e.g., drought in the commodities simulation).

Collaborative Writing

Students can engage in collaborative writing. For example, students might write a short paper for class which is then shared with a small number of peers who will comment on it. The student then revises the paper and submits it. The professor annotates and grades the assignments making the graded papers available to the entire class. One advantage of this approach is that students can see examples of good and poor papers (in the professor's opinion) by examining the graded papers. They can learn from each other's experiences. Students might also be motivated to write better papers since their work will be made public.

One-Minute Papers

If there are computers in the classroom, additional approaches are possible. One such approach is the one-minute paper. Students are assigned a topic with preparatory readings for class. The professor might lecture on the topic after which the students compose a one-minute paper (two to three sentences) summarizing the topic. Once they complete the papers, all students are given access to everyone else's submission. The professor can choose some for class discussion.

Professors incorporating collaborative strategies into a course may need to revise their approach to teaching. The structure of the course can no longer be planned around a sequence of lectures. Instead, responsibility for learning shifts to the student, and the role of the professor changes from that of lecturer to a guide and mentor. For example, as a result of studying the electronic forum the professor might be prepared to spend more time on topics with which students are having some difficulty. While this demands a change in teaching approach, many professors find this method more stimulating, rewarding, and effective.

WHAT ABOUT AN ASYNCHRONOUS COURSE?

Technology has enabled a new form of teaching which transcends the classroom, either totally or partially. In an asynchronous course the professor and the students are connected, not by a physical encounter in the classroom, but by computer and networking technology. Asynchronous courses differ from correspondence or video courses: The link is not only between professor and individual student but also among the students in the course. Planning and teaching an asynchronous, collaborative course demands more of a change on the part of the professor than using collaboration in conjunction with regular class meetings. However, experience with in-class collaboration might help the transition to asynchronous collaboration.

Some of the questions to ask yourself as you plan an asynchronous course include:

▶ Is the course for credit? Is it available to students off-campus as well as students not enrolled in the hosting university? If so, how are charges and credits handled?

▶ Will all materials be available on-line or does the student have to procure other materials, such as a textbook?

▶ How are assignments made, submitted, and returned?

▶ How are exams managed? How will the professor ensure that the actual student is taking the exam instead of a proxy? (One solution is to have students come to a proctor facility for tests and exams. These facilities are available on some campuses as well as through outside companies.)

▶ Does the course have a definite start and end date or is it ongoing? If new students can sign up and start on any date, is there a time limit on how long the student has to complete the course?

▶ What are the enrollment limitations? How many students can be handled by the professor?

▶ What technology requirements must students meet in order to take the course? Do they need their own computers and specialized software, or can they take the course from any computer with Internet access?

▶ How will the course be structured so that the student knows how to follow the material, knows what is expected and where to go for help? How will the professor monitor individual student progress or prompt students who are neglecting the course?

Asynchronous courses have been implemented in many institutions, and some institutions mix synchronous and asynchronous activities. One example is the Fuqua School of Business (Duke University) Global Executive MBA (GEMBA) program. Participants in the program meet on campuses around the world for two-week periods of traditional classroom instruction. For the remainder of the program students are at their home locations, pursuing all of their courses asynchronously. Collaboration is interwoven in the synchronous and asynchronous portions of the program. This program has the advantage that students do not have to leave their country or employment for long periods, yet the two-week on-campus periods give students a chance to meet each other as well as the faculty.

CAN COLLABORATION ENHANCE VIDEO DISTANCE EDUCATION?

The technology of delivering education at a distance via video is well-established. For example, the University of Minnesota ran a program in the mid-1970s called UNITE (University and Industry Television for Education), which consisted of a one-way microwave video link from the Twin Cities campus to the participating companies with a two-way audio link so that students could ask questions of the instructor during class. This form of distance learning is relatively common today, except the microwave link has often been replaced with a satellite link, enabling delivery of the course to a wider geography. Variations of this approach exist, including the broadcast of previously recorded classes, or the mailing of videotapes of recorded classes. In these variations, however, the ability of the students to ask questions during class is lost.

What these classes lack compared with the traditional classroom is the opportunity for teaming or collaboration. However, they can become more effective with the addition of computer-mediated collaboration (described earlier in the chapter). Given the existence of the three technology elements—access to computers, networking, and software—video education can be more interactive and vibrant. It is not even necessary that the original instructor—the one appearing on the screen—be available: The course interactions and electronic discussions can be facilitated or moderated by another person knowledgeable in the content of the course.

ARE THERE TOOLS AVAILABLE TO HELP?

There are many tools that faculty use to facilitate collaborative learning using computers. Some have created courses using Internet tools, such as word processors or Web page authoring software to create the course content, electronic mail packages to communicate with students, and newsgroup tools to implement discussion forums or computer conferences. Others have chosen to start with software designed for collaboration, such as First Class or Lotus Notes. Because these tools were designed to be general purpose collaboration tools, a certain amount of development has to be undertaken to adapt them for instruction.

Newer collaborative tools are appearing that add other functions necessary for the delivery and management of instruction (e.g., Lotus LearningSpace, an application developed in Lotus Notes). LearningSpace includes facilities to manage discussions, teams, the course roster, test generation and administration, a grade book, as well as the organization and delivery of course content. It uses either a Lotus Notes network or the Internet, where the students only need access to a Web browser in order to be able to take the course. Such tools allow faculty to concentrate on course content and delivery instead of tool creation.

ANY PRACTICAL HINTS FOR GETTING STARTED?

First and foremost, the physical infrastructure and technical support must be in place to allow collaboration via computers. Once a decision is made to teach collaboratively using computers, it is necessary to examine the learning objectives and the course content. What needs to be changed? Where can collaboration significantly enhance learning in the course? How can students become more actively involved?

Some specific suggestions may help you get started and enhance the learning experience for both faculty and students.

▶ On-line teaching materials should be well-divided and short. Computer screens are still not as easy to read nor as convenient as printed materials. The objective should not be to deliver a 50-minute lecture in text but to provide the highlights, definitions, and explanations, enabling students to synthesize the material.

▶ Because the use of collaborative learning is relatively new, the instructor should devote some time—up front—to explain how the course functions, how to get help, and what is expected of the student.

▶ The course should start with a short assignment or two to get the student involved in collaboration and familiar with the technology.

▶ The instructor should encourage participation and discourage silence. Since electronic discussion forums (or computer conferences) retain a record of each student's contributions, it is practical and desirable to make some percentage of the student's grade dependent on the degree and quality of participation.

▶ The professor should discuss with students some rules regarding discussions, such as keeping entries short, avoiding insults, providing constructive and not destructive criticism, etc.

▶ It is critical that the instructor keep a close watch on participation of each student, especially during the first two weeks. In this way any problems with the student's understanding, access, use, and comfort level with the technology can be identified and resolved, clearing the way for the students to focus on the course content.

▶ The instructor should moderate the electronic discussions to steer discussion threads that might be getting lost or off the subject. In addition, once specific threads (or discussions) reach a certain point, it is probably not productive to let them continue. The instructor should summarize the discussion and terminate it.

DO I HAVE TIME FOR ALL THIS?

A very real fear for professors embarking on collaborative learning is that they will be overwhelmed by the demands of the technology, putting in much more time than they would in a traditional course. There are some ways of preventing overload, but keep in mind that converting to any new style of teaching and learning will require more work, at least initially. It is similar to creating a course from scratch—it requires more work than one which the instructor has already taught several times. Here are some suggestions.

▶ Encourage students to answer questions and participate; give them credit for doing so. Nothing says that only the instructor has the right answer to questions. You might assign student leaders to handle questions in different parts of the course. The professor would be responsible only for answering those questions that the designated student could not handle.

▶ Get your colleagues (even at different institutions) involved. It might be a refreshing experience for them to interact with students in your class, without constraints of being physically present during the class period.

▶ Teaching assistants might be assigned to conduct recitation sessions, tutor, or to grade homework and tests. If you have such assistants available, they can participate as on-line discussion moderators.

▶ Involve professionals. Every professor knows people in their field who are outside the university environment. Invite them to participate as a content expert or discussion moderator or in some other appropriate role. A law professor at Wake Forest University involved colleagues who are state Supreme Court justices. Not only was his work load shared, but the students had a unique experience in their first year of law school. They made arguments to Supreme Court justices which were listened to and "judgments" rendered—all through asynchronous computer conferencing.

▶ Post electronic office hours so that students know when you will (and will not) be signed onto the class discussions. In this way a delay in a reply will be expected and acceptable to the student and will limit the amount of time you are engaged. If you are not available to answer a question, students may take the initiative and answer it for you.

CONCLUSION

The trend is for institutions of higher education to reach out to students who might not be able to come to campus and to change the mode of instruction for those who do come. Collaborative learning will play an important role in enabling these changes while the quality of the teaching and learning experience is enhanced for both faculty and student by lowering the barriers to communication and allowing collaboration to occur independent of time and place. Implementation of collaboration through technology is essential in order for institutions to provide quality education at a distance for the increasing numbers of nontraditional students.

REFERENCES/SUGGESTED READINGS

Alavi, M. (1994, June). Computer-mediated collaborative learning: An empirical evaluation. *MIS Quarterly*, 159-174.

Andriole, S. J., & Lytle, R. H. (1995, October). Asynchronous learning networks: Drexel's experience. *T.H.E. Journal*, 97-101.

Bligh, D. A. (1972). *What's the use of lectures?* London, England: Penguin.

Harasim, L., Hiltz, S. R., Teles, L., & Turoff, M. (1995). *Learning networks: A field guide to teaching and learning on-line.* Cambridge, MA: MIT Press.

Kulik, J. A., & Kulik, C. L. C. (1979). College teaching. In P. L. Peterson & H. J. Welberg (Eds.), *Research on teaching: Concepts, findings, and implications.* Berkeley, CA: McCutcheon.

Mayadas, A. F. (1997). Asynchronous learning networks: New possibilities. In D. G. Oblinger & S. C. Rush (Eds.), *The learning revolution: The challenge of information technology in the academy.* Bolton, MA: Anker.

Miller, M. A. (1995). Technoliteracy and the new professor. *New Literary History, 26* (3), 601-612.

Piaget, J. (1926). *The language and thought of the child.* London, England: Routledge & Kegan Paul.

Smith, D. G. (1977, April). College classroom interactions and critical thinking. *Journal of Educational Psychology, 69* (2), 180-190.

Vygotsky, L. S. (1978). *Mind in society: The development of higher psychological processes.* Cambridge, MA: Harvard University Press.

9

Instructional Technology and the Mainstream: The Risks of Success

William H. Geoghegan

One cannot go to an academic conference—especially one that deals with instruction—without facing an agenda dominated by the issue of change. We hear about institutional change, reengineering (a form of directed change), paradigm change and paradigm shift, cultural change, technological change, and the pace of change. Some of these changes hold great promise; some inspire great trepidation; some do both. In this chapter we focus on the last of these—the promising scary sort of change that has started to surface in the realm of instructional technology, in the use of information and communication technology to support teaching and learning.

Vannevar Bush, both former vice president of MIT and former president of the Carnegie Institution, wrote an amazingly prophetic article toward the end of the Second World War in which he reflected on the implications of the many electronic technologies that the war effort had spawned. In it he noted that, "The world has arrived at an age of cheap complex devices of great reliability, and something is bound to come of it" (Bush, 1945). Bush's words are just as valid today as they were in 1945. The computer age is one of "cheap complex devices of great reliability," and something is starting to come of it, though occasionally from unexpected directions and with some unanticipated side effects.

We will begin with a quick review of the instructional technology revolution that has been a constant topic of prediction over the last few decades—a revolution that received a strong boost from the spread of desktop computing in the early 1980s but went into apparent hibernation toward the end of the decade. Secondly, we will review recent signs of a dramatic reawakening and renewed movement in this erstwhile revolution, as well as some of the reasons for renewed growth and for the unexpected direction it has been taking. Finally, we will turn to the implications of rapid expansion in the demand for instructional technology and how this is contributing to a steadily growing support crisis. We will conclude with several suggestions about how the risks of renewed growth can be managed, and its more serious consequences averted.

A Brief History of the "Revolution"

It has become painfully obvious over the last several years that the long-promised revolution in education that was to be propelled by information technology—especially by desktop computing—is still a long way from being realized. This is true despite constant promises that the revolution was "just around the corner," that its impact on instruction was imminent. Predictions of a technology-based revolution in teaching and learning have been with us throughout most of the 50-year history of the modern computer. Consider this 1966 statement by Patrick Suppes of Stanford University, one of the pioneers in educational technology:

> Both the processing and the uses of information are undergoing an unprecedented technological revolution. . . . This is perhaps nowhere truer than in the field of education. One can predict that in a few more years millions of schoolchildren will have access to what Philip of Macedon's son Alexander enjoyed as a royal prerogative: The services of a tutor as well-informed and as responsive as Aristotle.

The revolution has failed to take hold despite major financial investments in instructional technology by our colleges and universities. Accurate figures are hard to obtain, but the best estimates today suggest that well over $20 billion has been spent on hardware and software for instructional technology over the last decade and a half. Given the fact that raw technology typically accounts for less than half of the academic computing budget (the rest going to personnel, supplies, communications support, etc.), total costs over the last 15 years have very likely exceeded $50 billion, or more than

$2,000 for every two- and four-year college degree awarded in the United States since 1980. In the 1996-97 academic year, the academic computing budget averaged about $1,000,000 among our 3,700 colleges and universities (Green, 1996)—between three and four billion dollars in total, or about two percent of all current fund expenditures in higher education.

This figure does not begin to take into account other institutional resources that have gone into supporting instructional technology: space (the rarest commodity in higher education), utilities, administrative support, and even parking permits to accommodate vendor service personnel. Nor does it include the hundreds of millions that business and industry have poured into support for instructional technology development efforts in higher education.

The revolution has failed to catch hold despite many excellent examples of instructional applications, uses of information technology that clearly demonstrate its promise for enabling significant improvements in the quality of teaching and in the learning experience. There are many examples of what can be done. Unfortunately, these examples tend not to be adopted for classroom use by anyone other than the original developer. Very few have been commercially successful, or even successful as noncommercial shareware.

Despite all the positive indicators—a strong belief in the benefits of instructional technology, extensive financial support, solid examples of positive educational benefits, a strong start and fairly rapid growth during most of the 1980s—progress nevertheless slowed down during the latter part of the decade. It came to a halt just at the point where all the signs—lower personal computer prices, increasing power and ease of use in desktop machines—would suggest that growth should have been picking up rather than slowing down.

As recently as 1994, the penetration of information technology into instruction was extremely limited. Apart from the use of word processing and presentation graphics, which for the most part had developed into functional replacements for typewriter and blackboard, the proportion of faculty actively using various information technologies in their classes tended to fall within the five to 15% range. This is not far from where it was in well-equipped colleges and universities in the latter part of the 1980s. In fact, growth in the use of instructional technology during that decade seems to have progressed to the point of saturation among the so-called early adopters of the faculty. Further progress ceased at that point, and instructional technology failed to reach and engage the much larger mainstream of potential but as yet uncommitted faculty users.

As to why this occurred, I believe the answer can be found in the field of diffusion studies, a body of social science theory and research that seeks to describe and understand the processes that underlie the acceptance and spread (or "diffusion") of innovations—new methods, new products, new ideas, etc.—among the members of a community. In what has come to be regarded as the classic work in diffusion theory, Rogers (1995) pointed out the existence of a well-defined pattern in the way any innovation is adopted by the members of a community. This pattern has two aspects:

1) An approximately normal (bell-shaped) distribution in the rate of new adoptions over time

2) An adoption process in which the innovation moves through a predictable sequence of well-defined adopter categories or groups, each of which differs from its predecessors (and successors) in important social and psychological characteristics

Consider the pattern that underlies the rate of adoption over time (Figure 9.1). The process begins relatively slowly, attracting small, though increasing numbers of new adopters during the early stages. The pace of adoption grows steadily as awareness increases and the force of numbers drives additional members of the community to make a positive decision. At the halfway point, when the rate of adoption peaks, the pattern reverses and the number of new adopters in each subsequent time period declines and eventually tails off as the pool of uncommitted candidates decreases and eventually disappears. The result is a distribution that can be approximated reasonably well by the familiar bell-shaped (or normal) curve shown in Figure 9.1.

FIGURE 9.1

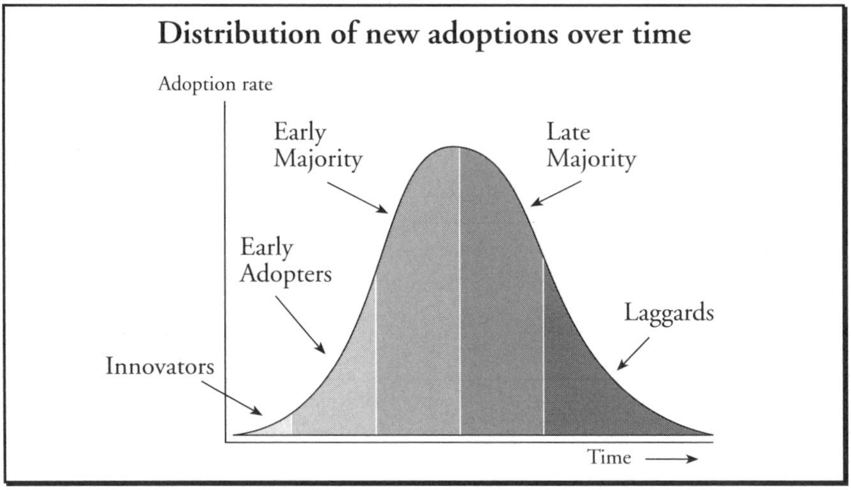

Distribution of new adoptions over time

In addition to the pattern of adoption rates over time, Rogers pointed out that as the adoption process moves forward, it engages and spreads through a series of distinct adopter categories that differ from one another in important social and psychological dimensions. Figure 9.1 also shows Rogers' adopter groups, their relative sizes, and where they fall in the adoption life cycle. Rogers refers to these groups as:

Innovators. Venturesome experimentalists who are willing to work with almost any new idea to see what it can do. They amount to about two or three percent of the total population.

Early adopters. Those who look for ways to use the innovation to make major, though possibly risky breakthrough improvements in core processes. They constitute 10% to 15% of the total.

Early majority. A more conservative and deliberate group, less interested in breakthrough improvements than in nondisruptive incremental change and the net value that an innovation brings to the process it addresses.

Late majority. A more skeptical group who begin to adopt during the latter stages of the process. The early and late majority each represent about one-third of the total population.

Laggards. A group that is highly resistant to change, and who will adopt the innovation only toward the very end of the cycle, if at all. They form the final 15% to 16% of the population.

Although these adopter groups are relatively homogeneous internally, there are significant differences among them. This means that an innovation can encounter difficulty spreading from one adopter group to the next. Geoffrey Moore (1991), building on Rogers' earlier work, noted that in the area of high technology innovations the differences between the early adopter population and what he called the mainstream (a combination of Rogers' early and late majority) are so great as to create a metaphorical chasm between them (see Figure 9.2). According to Moore, one high technology innovation after another has foundered in the gulf between the early adopters and the mainstream. It is a transition that for technology innovations appears extremely difficult to accomplish.

The differences among the adopter groups, and especially between the early adopters and the mainstream, are not really differences in technology skills or affinity for technology in general. After all, the vast majority of faculty, including the mainstream, are already active users of some type of personal computing. The differences are much more a matter of focus and of one's overall approach to change and process improvement. Early adopters are willing to experiment with intriguing new technologies, and to undertake risky technology-based projects that they believe have the potential for

FIGURE 9.2

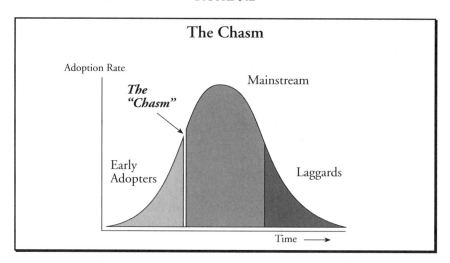

breakthrough improvements in core processes (such as instruction), while the mainstream are more concerned with sustaining and improving those same processes in an incremental, nondisruptive fashion.

Early adopters participate in wide, cross-disciplinary and cross-functional social networks that give them access to a broader range of technical resources and experience than the mainstream has access to. The latter rely more on vertical, or peer-based networks, united more by an interest in discipline-oriented matters than in technical or methodological ones. Among the mainstream there is a certain aversion to unproved, difficult, or disruptive innovations of any type that might risk successful performance of core tasks, in this case, the core tasks of the instructional process. Early adopters are much more tolerant of the risks and potential disruption that may accompany revolutionary, breakthrough improvements.

Finally, innovators and early adopters tend to be relatively self-sufficient from a support standpoint, especially in instructional technology. They may need deep technical support on occasion, vendor contacts (for access to the latest technologies), etc., but their cross-functional networks give them good access to informal sources of support that they can use when needed. Mainstream adopters, on the other hand, usually require strong technical support, as well as assistance in the effective use of technology. This is due not so much to an inherent lack of technical skill as to a focus on the process rather than on the tools that will be used to improve that process.

So why did the progress of instructional technology stall at the end of the 1980s? Why couldn't it jump the chasm? The problem can be attributed to two basic sources.

1) Advocates for instructional technology failed to recognize the social and psychological differences that separate early adopters from the mainstream; e.g., their respective approaches to change and process improvement, the networks they use for information and support, their willingness to tolerate risky and potentially disruptive changes to the instructional process, etc.

2) Ignorance of these differences led, in turn, to failure in responding to the mainstream's needs, and to the eventual institutionalization of an instructional technology support model that was developed in large part by and for the early adopters themselves. The support model's overriding technology focus, its concentration on supporting high-tech breakthroughs in instructional technology, and what was effectively a one-size-fits-all approach to support may have been major contributors to the mainstream's alienation.

The rapid expansion of instructional technology in the early and mid-1980s, starting from square one at most institutions, seems in retrospect to have been an expansion almost completely internal to the innovator and early adopter categories. Its growth among these groups was strong during the 1980s, but the saturation point (about 15% of the total faculty population) seems to have been reached toward the end of the decade. At that point, continued growth ran up against our metaphorical chasm, where matters came to a halt for perhaps half a decade.

SIGNS OF CHANGE

After years of apparent stagnation, however, something has started to happen; we are seeing unmistakable signs of change in the instructional technology landscape. Consider the findings of Green's *Campus Computing* surveys for 1994, 1995, and 1996. Among a number of other topics, Green's survey asks about faculty use of information technology in support of teaching and learning. The survey is addressed to chief information officers (CIOs) and academic computing directors at U.S. colleges and universities. Among other things, it asks for an assessment of the proportion of courses in which each of several different kinds of information technology are used. The technologies that Green surveyed include:

❱ Computer-based classrooms or labs

❱ Computer-based simulations or exercises

❱ Presentation handouts

❱ CD-ROM-based materials

❱ Electronic mail

❱ Commercial courseware

❱ Multimedia

❱ Internet resources (from off-campus sources)

❱ World Wide Web (WWW) pages for class materials and resources

If we use the proportion of courses as a surrogate for the proportion of faculty using these technologies, then Green's data should provide a good indicator of recent changes in faculty use of instructional technology.

FIGURE 9.3

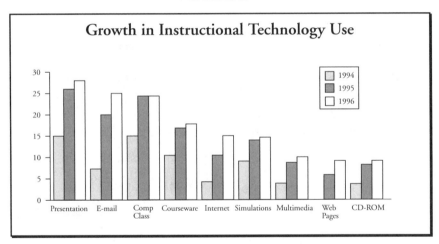

Looking at the changes over this two-year period, growth is visible across the board, ranging from a low of 23% annually in the use of computerized classrooms and labs (which can probably be attributed more to scheduling problems than to demand), to highs in the vicinity of 100% or more per year (and better than 200% over the full two years). Apart from these unexpectedly high rates of expansion, it is also worth noting where the most rapid growth is occurring, and the fact that adoption rates have already exceeded the critical 15% level in a number of areas.

Consider for a moment the kinds of applications that are exhibiting the most rapid growth. These include use of the World Wide Web as a vehicle for distributing class materials and student work and for helping students to obtain access to relevant information sources on the Internet in general and via the Web in particular. Usage in this area has gone from almost zero in 1994 (when Web browsers for the personal computer were just becoming widely available) to about 10% today. It is happening in the overall use of Internet resources for instruction, an application that has almost quadrupled in the space of two years. It is happening in the use of e-mail as a vehicle for student-to-student and student-to-faculty communication, for distribution of course materials and assignments, for receipt of student work, and for other forms of collaboration. The use of instructional e-mail has more than tripled in two years.

These technologies are not the ones that were generally predicted to be the major drivers of change, even as recently as two or three years ago. At that time multimedia and CD-ROMs were commonly seen as the technologies most likely to foster improvements in teaching and learning. Although the use of these technologies is still growing, their growth and adoption rates have been outstripped by instructional use of the Internet (including the Web) and class-related e-mail.

This does raise a few questions: Why e-mail? Why the Internet? Why these technologies instead of the applications (such as multimedia) that were so recently held to be the wave of the future in instruction? Why is the use of e-mail and the Internet increasing so rapidly in instruction, while other technologies once touted for their educational potential have a relatively low level of adoption? In short, what differentiates the winners from the losers in this race for adoption?

WHAT MAKES FOR A SUCCESSFUL INNOVATION?

At least part of the answer can be found, once again, in the field of diffusion studies. We have already discussed the characteristics of adopters and how they play a role in the process. But we also need to take into consideration the nature of the innovation itself, the characteristics of a new idea or product that make it attractive or unattractive to potential adopters. It is this aspect of the instructional technology story, I believe, that helps us understand why the adoption process was restarted, and why growth is concentrated where it is.

Rogers pointed out five characteristics of innovations that influence their rate of adoption as well as their eventual success or failure in a community (Rogers, 1995). These include:

1) The relative advantage of the innovation over what it replaces or supplements (in time, cost, effectiveness, quality of results, etc.)

2) The innovation's compatibility with existing practices, values, needs, culture, etc. or, conversely, its disruptiveness to existing practices, values, and other cultural factors

3) The complexity of the innovation: how difficult it is to learn, to understand, and to use effectively

4) The innovation's trialability: how easy or difficult it is to experiment with the new way of doing things before making an adoption decision

5) The observability or visibility to other potential adopters of the results achieved by using the innovation

An innovation that performs well on these attributes—with good relative advantage, excellent compatibility with existing practices and norms, a low level of complexity, ease of use on a trial basis, and easily observed results—would be susceptible to rapid adoption. Another innovation, one that does poorly on some or all of these characteristics, would be adopted much more slowly, or would fail to achieve any significant penetration into the community.

In reviewing the results of Green's 1995 survey, it appeared as though an analysis using Rogers' adoption attributes might help to explain the unexpected pattern of growth that had become apparent. The uses of instructional technology that intuition suggested might score well on the five adoption characteristics were precisely those that were growing at a more rapid pace, while those that might not do so well were the ones lagging behind.

This is the thinking that lay behind a brief survey that I carried out among participants in the Teaching, Learning, and Technology Roundtable (TLTR) meeting at the AAHE convention in 1996. I asked attendees at the first TLTR session to score eight different uses of instructional technology on the five attributes just described, collected the results, and analyzed them for use in a presentation at the closing session (Geoghegan, 1996). The applications covered in the survey were:

▶ CD-ROM-based materials for student use

▶ Building a Web page to organize and present materials for a course

▶ Student use of the Web to access external sources of information

▶ E-mail for faculty-student communication and to foster student teamwork

▶ Multimedia for lecture or lab

▶ Interactive presentation software

▶ Commercial self-paced courseware

▶ Using a word processor for overheads and class materials

Each application was scored on each of the five attributes using a five-point scale (where a five corresponded to high adoptability). The scores for each application were averaged without weighting to obtain an overall adoptability measure for each. Although the number of responses to this simple survey was too small for statistical reliability, the pattern that emerged was nevertheless very informative.

At the top of the list (Figure 9.4) is use of a word processor to prepare class materials, overheads, handouts, and so forth. It outscored the other applications on every dimension except observability, where Web-related applications were slightly higher. This was the first, and continues to be the most widespread use of information technology to support instruction, albeit one that has relatively little potential impact on instructional effectiveness. It does, however, provide an excellent baseline against which to judge the adoptability of other applications.

FIGURE 9.4

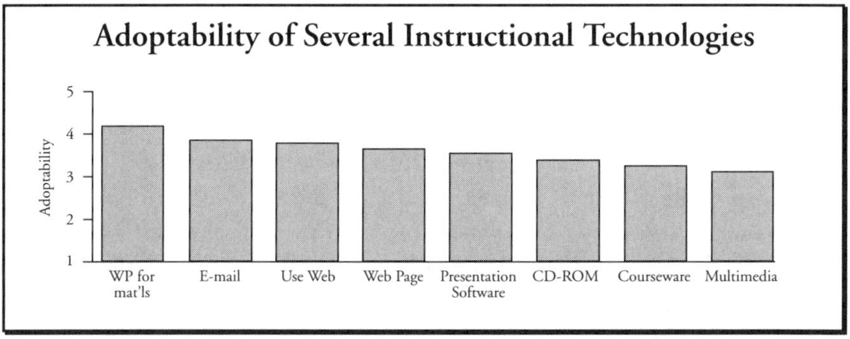

Adoptability of Several Instructional Technologies

The next three items in rank are especially intriguing:

▶ The use of e-mail to facilitate interaction and teamwork

▶ The use of the Web as a learning resource

▶ The use of a class Web page (or Web site) as a means of presenting class material and organizing external Internet resources

These are, for all practical purposes, the same ones that exhibited the greatest two-year growth in Green's *Campus Computing* survey. At the bottom of the list, on the other hand, are the development and use of multimedia materials for instruction and the use of commercial instructional software (or courseware). But it was the latter that served as the primary target for higher education and information technology industry investments of time, effort, and money during the 1980s, and where additional investments (most notably by the publishing industry) continue today.

It would be risky to expect too much from this limited set of data, but it is instructive to note that while the use of multimedia is high on relative advantage—ahead of e-mail and Web-based applications, for example—it fares poorly on complexity, trialability, and compatibility. This suggests that among the five adoption factors cited by Rogers, relative advantage may play the most important role in early adopter acceptance. It is certainly consistent with the early adopter's interest in revolutionary, breakthrough improvements in core processes and functions. Complexity, compatibility, and trialability, on the other hand, would seem to have a much stronger influence on potential mainstream adoption.

This suggests that innovations with high relative advantage—those that show promise of significant improvements in key areas—will be the ones that first attract the innovators and early adopters. This clearly occurred with the use of multimedia during the 1980s and, more recently, with class-related e-mail and use of the World Wide Web. But when it comes to bridging the chasm between early adopters and the mainstream, the mainstream's concerns with compatibility, complexity, and trialability hold the key to ultimate success. As a group, e-mail and Web usage score high on these characteristics. It is not difficult to begin using them; they are easy to try out (and to give up if the effort is unsuccessful); and they are certainly compatible with academic values that emphasize communication and teamwork, active exploratory learning, and so forth. Multimedia, on the other hand, lies near the bottom on all three of these characteristics despite its generally accepted pedagogical potential. The result: Instructional e-mail and World Wide Web use obtain mainstream acceptance, while traditional multimedia does not, at least at the present time.

This helps us to understand why we have had so little success until recently with the adoption of instructional technology. We tended to focus on demonstration projects using complex technologies, such as self-paced instructional software or multimedia-based instructional materials that could be integrated into the instructional process with positive benefit. Our strategy was to demonstrate what could be done with information technology in teaching and learning, its positive benefits, and its power to transform education. We hoped that others would recognize the benefits, and then use such applications as models for their own instructional technology efforts. We aimed for depth of integration into the instructional process, with an expectation that breadth—that is, diffusion outward to the rest of the faculty—would naturally follow once the benefits were observed. Unfortunately, applications that are high on relative advantage often turn out to be poor candidates for widespread diffusion until matters of compatibility, complexity, and trialability can be resolved. The more complex applications progressed as far as the early adopters, but failed to catch hold among the mainstream.

The changes visible today point to a very different and far more effective model. E-mail and various uses of the Internet (via the Web) all display good relative advantage over what they replace or supplement. This ensures rapid acceptance by innovators and early adopters. But they also perform well with respect to the characteristics that seem to be of major concern to the mainstream. This generates a pattern of very rapid adoption, initially at a rather shallow level of integration (e.g., e-mail as a supplement to office hours and as a distribution channel for assignments, or the Web as a supplement to library resources). But as time goes on, and as faculty have an opportunity to experiment with relatively simple uses of these technologies and to gain familiarity with them, the level of integration becomes deeper, and the real impact on learning can be felt. This model aims at breadth—the widespread adoption of an innovation—before depth of integration. This appears to be precisely what is happening with the use of e-mail and the Web today, and why we are seeing such rapid growth in these areas.

THE SUPPORT CRISIS

Whatever lies behind the renewed growth, increases in the instructional technology adoption rate of the magnitude we see today have serious negative implications that accompany the positive ones. The most disturbing of these is what has come to be called the support crisis in instructional technology: a collection of seemingly intractable problems in faculty development and support services that is being driven by the increasing demand for instructional technology. The source of the problem is not hard to find.

Look again at the diffusion curve discussed earlier, but this time in its cumulative form, where it describes the total, or cumulative, proportion of the population that has actually adopted the innovation at any particular point in time (Figure 9.5). The chasm in the adoption process occurs at the point where an innovation would normally pass from the early adopters to the mainstream, after it has been accepted by about 15% of the total population. It is that point where the spread of instructional technology seemed to drop off at the end of the 1980s.

FIGURE 9.5

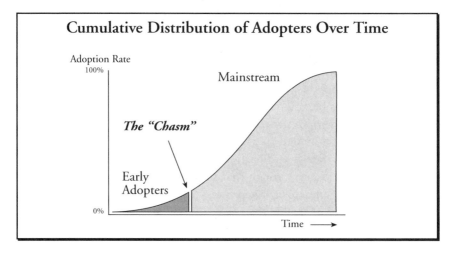

Note that this so-called chasm lies near the foot of the curve, just at the point where the process would normally begin to take off, where the total number of adopters would begin to grow at a rapidly increasing pace within a very short period of time. What lies on the other side of this chasm is growth both in the number of adopters and in the rate of adoption as well. Almost 85% of the total population waits on the other side.

Green's data clearly suggest that we have already started to bridge the chasm, not just in one or two application areas, but in the majority of those his survey covers (Green 1995, 1996). Growth of the kind we have been seeing—not to mention what lies just around the corner—puts immense strain on the service organizations that support instructional technology in our colleges and universities in terms of money, personnel resources, the availability and distribution of critical skills, etc. The sheer number of new users, which has already doubled in the brief space of two years, places major demands on campus support services, which are already stretched to the limit.

As if the increase in numbers were not enough, growth has been concentrated in application areas that were not well-anticipated nor adequately planned for. Just a few years ago, CIOs at some of our large research universities began to comment on the negative impact of growing faculty and student interest in educational uses of the Internet. They began noting how increasing demand was beginning to require the diversion of resources originally earmarked for support in other areas of academic computing. The segments of most intense growth (e-mail, instructional use of the Web, and so on) are not well-aligned with the support services that were put in place in the 1980s. The latter frequently emphasized support for faculty who wanted to create multimedia materials or to develop specialized instructional software for classroom use. It was not well-attuned to the support requirements that accompany growing instructional use of e-mail and the Internet which include increased demand for connectivity and e-mail access by faculty and students, additional network bandwidth to handle increased traffic and Web-based multimedia, and Web page design skills, among other things.

The crisis is becoming particularly acute in support for instructional uses of technology. Just a year ago the consensus that developed in several Internet discussion groups focusing on faculty support issues was that the ratio of faculty to instructional technology design staff—that is, the people who work with faculty to help develop instructional technology applications—was somewhere in the vicinity of 200 to one. That might have been adequate when less than 10% or 15% of the faculty were using anything more complex than word processing to support their teaching, and when that group was dominated by self-sufficient early adopters. It is completely inadequate to meet the demand created by rapid increases in the number of mainstream users.

As an indicator of how quickly these changes are leading to crisis, I would point to the fact that the single most important information technology issue over the next two to three years, according to those who responded to Green's 1996 survey, is assisting faculty to integrate technology into instruction. Close behind it in the ranking of important issues is the need to provide adequate user support (Green, 1996). As for the source of this concern, the use of Internet resources for instruction was cited for the first time as the highest technology priority for the responding institutions, edging out CD-ROM libraries (which actually fell in importance), instructional software, and other traditional areas of concern.

ADOPTION AND SUPPORT STRATEGIES

How does one manage this situation? How can a college or university continue to build faculty interest in technology to improve teaching and student learning and match that growing interest with increased support for effective technology use?

In addressing this question, keep in mind that our institutions are dealing with two distinct faculty populations that have quite different interests and needs. The early adopters need leading edge technology, direct contacts with technology vendors, deep technical assistance, funding for new projects, etc. The mainstream needs peer-to-peer, discipline-focused support, seamless and nondisruptive integration of technology, and instructional design assistance. Supporting not only greater numbers of users, but also new types of users, means additional costs. It certainly calls for some very innovative ideas about information technology support if it is to be provided within the budgetary constraints under which most colleges and universities labor today.

Let us consider how we might go about meeting these two objectives. We will first take up strategies for encouraging continued growth in the effective use of instructional technology, and then turn to strategies for successfully addressing the support needs that such growth engenders.

Involve the Mainstream

This is especially important in planning and decision-making activities that set the direction for instructional technology, and in the composition of academic computing committees, task forces, advisory boards, strategic planning committees, etc., that are usually assigned this responsibility. The traditional model for staffing such groups has been to seek out faculty who are already knowledgeable about technology use and who have a strong personal interest in technology—in other words, individuals fairly typical of the innovator and early adopter categories. Let me suggest that such committees also be given a healthy dose of mainstream faculty, of individuals strongly committed to the improvement of teaching and learning who have an open mind about the use of information technology where and when it makes good pedagogical sense.

Accommodate the Mainstream's Need for Peer-Based Support

In contrast with early adopters, whose support networks often extend well outside their immediate fields, mainstream faculty tend to look within their own or a closely related discipline or profession to meet their support needs. The support model for information technology developed in the 1980s was not intended nor well-designed to provide peer support. The focus was too often on technology *per se* rather than on the needs of the discipline or profession in which that technology was to be used.

Put the Focus on Teaching and Learning
Rather than on Technology

It is entirely too easy to leave instructional technology completely in the hands of the technologists. A technology focus may work for the innovators and early adopters, but it will not work for the mainstream. Why not consider incentives and rewards that focus on concrete instructional improvements rather than on clever applications of technology? Acknowledge and reward successful uses of instructional technology, but let success be defined in terms of the improvements gained in teaching and learning.

Put the Initial Focus on Highly Adoptable Uses of Technology

Look for applications of compelling value, ones that combine high relative advantage (in Rogers' terms) with real strength in such factors as compatibility, lack of complexity, ease of experimentation, and visibility of results.

Nurture the Innovators and the Early Adopters

The innovators and early adopters provide much of the innovation and creativity in technology use that can help to attract the mainstream and provide models for effective instructional technology use.

All this, of course, serves to increase the number of faculty users, not to mention the support needed by them and by the students in their classes. How do we address that demand without breaking the budget, compromising the quality of service, or defaulting on service commitments and alienating the very faculty we want to encourage? The following are a few strategies that should help to avoid or address the more negative aspects of the support crisis.

Use Peer-to-Peer Support

The mainstream prefers discipline-oriented support in any event; this provides an opportunity to build support on the basis of a few academic units at a time, as described below.

Try to Achieve Critical Mass

Aim to bring enough faculty into the fold to permit development of an informal support structure within the unit, and to generate the pressure needed to enable institutionalization in terms of budgeting priorities, staff support, etc.

Locate Support Where It Is Needed

Put discipline-oriented instructional technology support within academic units, while keeping general technical support (hardware, generic software, networking, etc.) within the central information technology organization.

Use a Team Approach to Instructional Design

Let faculty serve as the content experts for the courses that are being addressed. Use an instructional design specialist to handle the pedagogical aspects of the application. Employ a technologist from the information technology organization to address issues related to hardware requirements, software, and networking. The team approach is becoming increasingly popular as an effective way to address the support and development requirements of mainstream faculty.

Move Instructional Support into Individual Departments

Select a few pilot departments or divisions very carefully, perhaps through a competitive request for proposal (RFP) process, and then provide seed money to permit the successful applicants to bring in people with good disciplinary knowledge and the technical skills needed to work directly with faculty in developing effective uses of instructional technology. Try to achieve a critical mass of adopters within the unit, so that continued progress can become self-sustaining. After two or three years of seed money support, move on to the next unit or cohort of units. As individual successes become more apparent, it should become increasingly easier to find new takers. Unless one has an information technology budget that can keep pace with the kind of increases in demand we have been seeing, the alternative to an approach such as the one outlined above means spreading already limited resources ever more thinly, never developing the self-sustaining critical mass that is vitally important to long-term success. It also leaves more and more neophyte users frustrated with their initial efforts and with the potential of instructional technology in general.

Consider Outsourcing

Consider bringing in a reliable Internet access provider to serve student (and even faculty) needs. Fees today are reasonable (less than $15 a month for unlimited access via local dial-up connections), and the cost can be borne by students, perhaps with an institutional subsidy or need-based assistance. Consider outsourcing at least some of the required technology to students where feasible. Growing numbers of institutions (or individual academic units) are beginning to require student ownership (or at least possession) of a computer, whether through outright purchase, through institutional lease-purchase arrangements, or through some other means. It is worth noting that the cost of a full-function slide rule, a common requirement in science and engineering programs in the early 1960s, was between five and 10% of annual tuition—not much different from what a good desktop personal computer costs today.

None of this will be easy, but all of it is at least doable. At the very minimum, it is worthy of debate. Of one thing we can be certain: The situation that we see developing today cannot be left to run its course without direction.

Conclusion

What lies ahead of us? In a nutshell, it is the other side of the chasm. Now that we seem to have bridged the gap, the challenge before all of us— faculty, students, trustees, administrators, parents, all stakeholders with a concern for the quality and effectiveness of our higher education institutions in this time of profound change—is to insure that instructional technology is wisely and effectively used and that faculty willing to take such steps to improve the quality of their teaching and the effectiveness of student learning are acknowledged, supported, and rewarded for their efforts.

What lies ahead of us? It is the other 85%, the majority who constitute the mainstream and their successors, those who are just beginning to engage the instructional technology revolution after all these years. They are the ones who hold the key to bringing about the kinds of improvements to teaching and learning for which all of us have been searching. How to address their requirements to the ultimate benefit of our students will continue to be the big issue in the years just ahead.

A slightly different version of this chapter was originally presented as the first Maytum Distinguished Lecture at the State University of New York College at Fredonia on October 23, 1996.

References/Suggested Readings

Bush, V. (1945, July). As we may think. *The Atlantic Monthly*, 101-108.

DeVry, J. R., Greene, J. A., Millard, S., & Sine, P. (1996, Fall). Teaming up to develop a faculty institute on teaching, learning, and technology. *CAUSE/EFFECT*, 22-27.

Geoghegan, W. H. (1994a, September). Stuck at the barricades. *AAHE Bulletin*, 13-16.

Geoghegan, W. H. (1994b). What ever happened to instructional technology? In S. Bapna, A. Emdad, & J. Zaveri (Eds.), *Proceedings of the 22nd Annual Conference of the International Business Schools Computing Association*. Baltimore, MD: IBSCA, 438-447.

Geoghegan, W. H. (1996, March). *E-mail and beyond.* Paper presented to the AAHE 1996 National Conference on Higher Education. Chicago, IL.

Green, K. C. (1994). *Campus computing 1994.* Encino, CA: Campus Computing Project.

Green, K. C. (1995). *Campus computing 1995.* Encino, CA: The Campus Computing Project.

Green, K. C. (1996). *Campus computing 1996.* Encino, CA: The Campus Computing Project.

Moore, G. A. (1991). *Crossing the chasm.* New York, NY: Harper Business Press.

Rogers, E. M. (1995). *Diffusion of innovations* (4th ed.). New York, NY: Free Press.

Suppes, P. (1996, September). The uses of computers in education. *Scientific American,* 206-208.

10

Making Ends Meet: A Faculty Perspective on Computing and Scholarship

James S. Noblitt

Top-Down Meets Bottom-Up

The dialogue between faculty and administration concerning the use of information technology (I/T) for teaching and research is not always civil. The top-down folks (usually charged with administrative or institutional duties) seem to want to spend all available funds on infrastructure, sometimes neglecting to explain to the academic community just why the new technology is needed. The bottom-up people (usually charged with instructional or research duties) seem to pose endless demands for resources and released time to get their projects underway, but never quite out the door. They show little interest in working through all the detailed planning for implementation within institutional budget guidelines.

In reality, these adversaries have a deep mutual dependency. The top-down program advocate needs convincing exemplars to justify large investments in technology at a moment when funds are scarce. The bottom-up project advocate needs a well-conceived and reliable working environment for successful implementation of innovative concepts. It is simply an accident of history that the realities of the new technology are upon us before we have had a chance to evolve an effective forum for discussing these procedural matters. It is unlikely that such a forum will be in place and working smoothly until there is more widespread agreement on technological standards, and standards will not be in place until the rate of innovation in the computing industry cools off a bit.

In the meantime, mutual understanding and communication will be needed to see us through. The following comments are offered in this spirit and represent a faculty perspective. The point of view is unabashedly bottom-up, that is, reflecting a focus on scholarly problems that need technological support for their solutions. It's not that faculty members don't understand the need for infrastructure; it's just that technology *per se* is not the point of the academic enterprise. It is impressive, for example, that the Internet can put a world of information at one's fingertips. But that resource alone does not deliver an education or create new knowledge, any more so than does having a wonderful library on campus. The books are there to support learning and research, the complex processes at the heart of the business of education. Electronic information technology is likewise a means for achieving an outcome, not an end in itself. That having been said, the bottom-up people still have to make their case with the top-down people in a way that is professionally responsible, about which more anon.

THE CASE FOR DOING NOTHING

Quite apart from the engaged bottom-up and top-down innovators in the use of information technology for scholarship, there are a number of academic onlookers who simply are not ready to participate. It is not hard to see why many hesitate to become involved, given the state of the art in the evolution of instructional technology. Some are scholars who want to see evidence of added value in research and teaching before adopting technology. They wait for assessment studies. Some are technology vendors who want to see a market for their goods and services before adapting their products to the demands of the educational marketplace. They wait for the solid business case. And some are publishers who want to see evidence of demand before investing in the production of quality products. They wait for a sign that the educational establishment is ready to use the digital medium for research and teaching. Let it be noted, these are not unreasonable concerns. Those who propose wide scale adoption of a technology-based curriculum must find a way to combine innovation with a responsible plan for implementation. This means providing for the contingencies that invariably arise with the uncertainties of transition.

Even the technological enthusiast must admit that the institutional implications of the changes brought by the information age are difficult to assess at this moment. Print has historically been the medium of choice for the creation, transmission, and archiving of knowledge. That is, print supports scholarship by providing the researcher with analytical tools, a means of communication with peers and students, and a vast knowledge base of primary and secondary materials. These functions are vital to the interests of a number of interested onlookers: academic institutions, professional societies, discipline-based departments, publishers, and libraries. The digital medium—with its ability to link images and sound with text, and with its support of inexpensive reproduction and communication—represents a change agent with complex and far-reaching implications. The individual scholar-teacher is faced with uncertain outcomes as normal standards of productivity are called into question. The issues of quality, access, and cost for research and learning are just beginning to be posed, let alone understood. Even advocates for the scholarly uses of information technology can rarely point to a graduate program that combines disciplinary expertise with technical training in the new media.

Resistance to change, which may take various forms, is usually not as perverse as it may appear to the bottom-up and top-down innovators. Academics are trained to be critical (in the best sense of the word) and may be expected to make demands for justification of resource allocation. They are not well-prepared for the debate, however, unless they have had an opportunity to sort out for themselves what is simply old wine in new bottles and what is a difference that makes a difference. The wait-and-see onlookers should not be viewed as necessarily inimical to change. They simply need convincing evidence of the value of innovation. Satisfactory experiences with the following issues figure heavily in gaining the support of opinion leaders in the ranks of the onlookers.

Providing Functional Examples

Acceptance of new technology depends critically on seeing an exemplar of new functionality for disciplinary interests, such as multimedia coordinated with text for language learners, or interactive simulations that improve visualization for scientific concepts. Because of their interest in creating knowledge from information, scholars are particularly interested in tools of the trade that increase productivity, such as word processing, e-mail, bibliographic databases, and the like. These applications often produce a natural bridge to more innovative uses of computing.

Demonstrating Feasibility

It is essential to find ways to bring together faculty, administrators, and computer services personnel to discuss problems in implementation. The idea is to insure that educational innovations are not divorced from strategic planning and technical support. It is important to coordinate system design with efforts to solve actual educational problems.

Defending the Value System

The incorporation of information technology must not be seen as diverting of resources from worthwhile educational institutions (such as libraries), or displacing humanistic values (such as critical thinking), or replacing mentoring faculty (with impersonal information-dispensing machines). Internal education becomes an essential counterpart to technological innovation.

Maintaining Quality

Technology—by promoting an explosive growth of connectivity with worldwide information sources of text, image, and sound—can introduce serious problems of quality control. Scholars are socialized to believe in the value of their various disciplines as guardians of the reliability of published research. The digital medium must demonstrate its ability to provide peer review, bibliographic accuracy, and the instruments for editorial refinement that lead to scholarly reliability.

THE CASE FOR GETTING INVOLVED

The discussion to this point has offered some reasons why one might reasonably expect a prolonged institutional debate on the educational uses of information technology. John Holt reported that a colleague once said to him that there were really only two questions of importance for the educator: What are we trying to do? Are we doing it? Similarly, two tough questions need to be asked concerning the use of information technology for educational purposes:

1) Are there problems critical to mission that are intractable or poorly resolved under current practices in our educational institutions?

2) Can modern information technology play a role in providing solutions to these problems?

If one answers these questions in the negative—assuming the response is well-informed—there is no reason to pursue technological solutions. An affirmative answer, on the other hand, suggests that one cannot afford not to be involved.

The reasoning is simple. If educators do not define the educational uses of information technology, others will. For example, a few specialized educational software publishers are engaged in producing courseware, but the market is not particularly profitable. Textbook publishers attempting to make a transition to interactive multimedia report that they are having difficulty locating scholars qualified and willing to assist with the requisite technical and subject matter expertise. Note that there are very few research scholars engaged in creating textbooks or multimedia for general education, primarily because the scholarly reward system has not operated to reward this function. As a consequence, candidates for interactive educational materials are often produced by those who have devised a business case for their software, including the gaming and entertainment industries. Surely the educational resources of the not-for-profit sector, with vital input from philanthropic and governmental agencies, can transcend the limitations of a strictly commercial approach to the problem.

The information age presents a new frame of reference for discussing old epistemological concerns: What is knowledge? Where does it come from? What is its value? The attendant philosophical discussion is familiar: How do scholars share their learning with their students? What is the scope of their responsibility for creating governance systems that insure institutional success? Solutions to such broad issues will take time, and the top-down people have to give the bottom-up people a chance to advance their thinking about scholarship in the new media. It took many years for the print medium to mature to the point that scholars could be expected to understand indexing, concordances, style manuals, and cataloguing systems. The analogous systems are not yet in place for the scholarly uses of information technology, although much progress has been made in defining the issues, chiefly through the labor of interested scholars and administrators, working through professional societies interested in educational reform.

GETTING STARTED

Bottom-up innovators are most successful when they begin by addressing a real problem with the current way of doing things. That is, they do not simply transfer current curricular materials to electronic form. Rather, they leave alone what is working well and innovate where it will do the most good. To take an example in my area of concern, foreign languages, we have a difficult time providing enough meaningful practice in listening comprehension. Group classroom instruction is not very sensitive to individual variation, and audio tapes don't provide efficient random access, interactivity, or access to visual cues (Noblitt, 1995). Interactive multimedia can do wonders for creating a productive learning environment for this kind of learning. Of course, it is up to the discipline specialist to identify the problem and work on the design of effective and affordable technology-based remedies. Assuming that a legitimate education problem has been identified, the following procedural tests for innovation should apply:

▶ Does the problem affect a broad population of students? If not, its solution may not be worth the effort or be justified as a top priority for innovation.

▶ Does information technology provide real added value, educationally? There is no point in digitizing a novel for the computer when a printed version is more portable, easier to read, and already available at a reasonable price. If an indexed version is needed, with key word in context information, that is a different matter.

▶ Can the innovation be implemented within the support resources available? There is no point in wasting effort on programs that will fail as soon as the innovator's interest or energy flags.

It is possible to have measurable impact, even with modest resources, if one is careful to think in terms of optimizing rather than maximizing the use of information technology for educational purposes. It is important, whenever possible, to rely on already developed software resources. (I encourage bottom-up educators to think of themselves as pioneers on the trailing edge of technology.) It is a mistake to lead one's institution to rely on technologies that are not broadly supported in the commercial sector, simply because unsupported programs cannot be maintained. The innovator will quickly be overwhelmed with work, particularly if successful. This is why the top-down people are persistent in asking whether a solution will scale before they lend support.

It follows from the preceding discussion that understanding the sociology of change is likely to be more difficult than the technology of change. Technological challenges amount to a kind of puzzle that will be solved with the application of good thinking and appropriate resources. The attendant sociological challenges should be thought of as a kind of ongoing problem that is never wholly resolved. One may explore endlessly the fractal dimensions of human learning. That is what makes scholarship so interesting. Even so, there are moments when decisions are needed about resource allocation, which is another matter. As difficult as the problem may appear, we may surely set aside the argument that the safest strategy is to wait and see what happens. Information has always been a primary concern of the educator; its technology simply cannot be ignored. The use of information resources must be actively brought in line with the economic realities facing the business of education. As Oberlin (1996) puts it, "Part of the mythology dominating information technology management is that it is all about technical issues. It can be argued, instead, that it's actually all about managing change—technical, social, pedagogical, political, and financial."

I agree. Bottom-up people are fond of waving their hands over difficulties in educational management. Focused on problems of effective teaching and scholarship, they define success in terms of how well they accomplish their educational mission or research agenda. But, especially because the new information technology is making such serious demands on our limited resources, we cannot afford to shun responsibility for intelligent decision-making. We face a number of critical strategic decisions about the business of higher education. What appears to be a discussion about technology is, in reality, a discussion about curriculum. Resource allocation will determine what is done and what is not done for our students.

The dialogue between the private and public sectors has only begun to address the serious issues in curriculum reform raised by the new information technology. But even here there are surprises. Individuals in both the publishing and computing industries are highly sensitive to the qualitative issues facing education. After all, our business leaders have all been through the system and hold opinions based on direct experience. Given opportunity and encouragement, they participate fully in the intellectual debate concerning the role of education in our culture. Publishers seek opportunities for leadership in quality control and distribution of educational materials; technologists seek opportunities for leadership in innovative design of hardware and software. We simply have not found the means to bring their collective knowledge and expertise to bear on the educational problems confronting our society.

DEFINING QUALITY

The digital medium appears to create an appetite among learners for exposure to the primary matter of the various scholarly disciplines. That is, image and sound, in addition to text, have become a part of the interactive educational environment. This comes as welcome news to scholars who require sound and image for the proper visualization of the subject matter, such as language studies, art, music, biology, and astronomy. Virtually any subject matter is made more immediate by providing access to authentic samples of the real stuff of knowledge.

Educators are generally pleased to see the spectrum of available instructional materials broadened to include visual and acoustic elements as an important supplement to the familiar textbook that has characterized education in the past. Multimedia documents are not only rich in educational content, they also introduce new elements of composition and graphic design for instruction. Elements of both content (image, sound, and text) and process (tools for analysis and recombination) are readily available in digital form for both instructor and student. Particularly attractive is the fact that the computer makes it possible for the learner to make choices that determine both the kind of material presented and the rate of information flow. Hypermedia links open up the ability to follow relationships among ideas. Timely access to relevant information is not only engaging for the learner, it creates possibilities for task-focused instruction; i.e., instruction that is motivated by the posing of significant problems for the learner.

At the same time, the use of highly complex authentic materials in the learning environment presents new challenges for educational design. Students will need new tools and new strategies for learning with information technology. Scholars who participate in creating solutions for interactive learning face a host of new problems:

▶ What is the best way to represent the essence of my discipline in the new media? An interface designed for meaningful access to raw data will be essential.

▶ How do I connect with models of instruction that are theory-driven? Many disciplines do not incorporate training for their graduate students in the developmental aspects of human learning.

▶ How do I handle the cross-disciplinary aspects of the use of primary data? Scholars are trained not to offer comment on areas outside of their specialty.

▶ Where do I turn for training and technological assistance? Scholars in some disciplines are socialized to work independently and are not in the habit of forming teams for materials development.

Everyone is for quality, of course. The real issue is, quality at what cost? Viewed in this light, quality means different things to different people. Administrators are likely to focus on the issues of effectiveness and productivity. Does the digital learning environment improve the quality of the educational outcomes? What are the costs of implementation? Computer support personnel are likely to focus on the feasibility of maintaining a learning environment based on high technology. Does the digital medium rest on a solid basis of industry support? How can adequate support services be provided under current funding? Faculty are concerned about educational content. Does the digital format provide an enriched learning environment? Will innovation divert resources from the existing program of research and learning?

Quite apart from the differing points of view on what to do about implementing educational technology, there is a more subtle issue about when innovation is likely to be successful. The issue of timing involves bottom-up and top-down educators in another intricate dance of mutual dependence. If the economy requires consolidation, the cost of innovation can disrupt the ongoing and productive activities of an institution. If innovation is needed, moneys spent on continuing the status quo are a waste, regardless of the quality metric applied. The focus must be on what reform is needed and when productive change can take place. As my top-down colleagues have observed, we cannot afford educational innovation that is ahead of the industry. Like it or not, academics need to understand how the process of commercialization of information technology serves the educational mission by attending to things that scholars cannot (and should not) control, like distribution, user support, and code maintenance.

The success of the familiar print textbook was based in part on well-defined roles for author and publisher in its development, and for teacher and student in its use. As interest now focuses on the digital interactive learning environment, developers and users are facing interesting new issues of production, distribution, and quality assurance. The educator has little concern with what form the educational materials take as long as they are effective. The current interest in interactive learning comes from its promise for inexpensive access to general education coupled with effective training in the tools of an information society. High quality materials that demonstrate effective scholarly use of the expanded media (images, sound, and hypertext) meet little or no resistance, even from conservative scholars.

INFORMATION TECHNOLOGY AND AUTHENTICITY

The quality features of the digital medium create a learning environment where the student can interact with more authentic learning material. Again, everyone is for authenticity, but the innovator must be prepared to demonstrate how information technology assists in achieving it. The following questions may be useful for the bottom-up innovator in attempting to gain support for the use of technology to solve a particular educational problem.

Does I/T Help to Put the Students in Touch with the Primary Observed Data of the Discipline?

Educators value interactive learning environments that allow them to share primary observed data with their students and provide the tools for performing operations on that data. Textbooks that offer primarily decontextualized knowledge can be nicely complemented with interactive multimedia that provide a sense of reality about the abstractions learned in class. A successful demonstration of the methodology of the discipline also lessens the tension that is felt between teaching and research.

Does I/T Help to Relate a Narrow Specialty to the Larger Concerns of Society?

Instructors who are pressed to cover even the essentials of their discipline in the classroom environment are pleased to have a learning environment that attends to the possibilities for general education offered by their specialty. It is possible to assemble reference materials, links to Web sites, and foster threaded discussion groups for one's students without having to water down the curriculum.

Does I/T Help to Place the Instructor in a Legitimate Position of Expertise in Relationship to Students and Subject Matter?

Students can benefit from a wide range of teaching skills in the learning environment, from novice to expert. Novices often have insight into the developmental stages of students, but they need support for their own stage of professional development. I/T provides excellent support for the facilitator who assists students in dealing with primary data and the appropriate tools for analysis. Experts who have lost sight of, or interest in, the developmental problems of their students may use I/T for tutorial or peer support purposes.

Information technology has always had an impact on educational innovation, but cause and effect for actual reform is mediated through all sorts of societal complexities. It is helpful to think of technological innovation as having its own dynamic, just as educational innovation has its own dynamic. The interest for the innovator comes from observing how the two intersect. Educators can modulate the interaction of these forces through successful innovation and technological implementation. Conscious reform efforts serve chiefly to modify curriculum. Technology, with all its economic implications, determines what curriculum is feasible.

The challenge for top-down and bottom-up innovators is basically one of design. Educators need to be a part of the process that creates technology designed to provide both access to information and tools for creating useful knowledge from it. The changes brought by I/T will not be so much a difference in mission as a difference in the relationship of general education to professional development. Granted, there is a danger that the extended learning and research community will be seen as simply an enlargement of the scholar's scope of work without increased resources. But the unprecedented amount of information now at the disposal of the learner should place a high premium on those who can synthesize complex material and communicate a coherent view of it. As long as faculty perform this role in society, information technology will serve them well.

The issue can be transposed as follows: Is the faculty member to function as an expert consultant, of greatest value to those who are already knowledgeable enough to articulate their need for information? Or is the faculty member a knowledge broker, operating with expert understanding of both a field of specialization and the developmental attributes of learners? The consultant model predicts weak institutional commitment and direct marketing to students as clients. The broker model predicts a broader social role with strong institutional commitments that mediate contact with students.

THE BOTTOM LINE

The bottom-up and top-down folks need to talk with one another about which model will serve the future needs of their educational institution. Stratified discussions of faculty with faculty and administration with administration only serve to harden rehearsed positions and create converts to the legions of the chronically aggrieved. It is easy to understand why internal education is often neglected. Governance structures that encourage arbitration rather than adversarial debate are in disrepair; and the economics of disintermediation and disaggregation appear to be so compelling as to make discussion beside the point. This line of reasoning needs to be examined carefully, as it undermines effective leadership and leads to easy fatalism among those who could benefit most from change.

Bottom-up people, in my experience, really enjoy talking with an educational champion (i.e., someone with a vision and a budget) who is willing to accept input on defining objectives and allocating resources. For what it's worth, here is some advice for the top-down people who want to open a dialogue leading to operational definitions for the use of information technology in education.

Establish Communication Channels

Establish communication channels concerning the curricular implications of information technology for your institution. Internal education is a serious concern when the rate of change accelerates, and the educational community needs to focus on the best uses of faculty time and effort in the emerging information environment. Don't let the system view of things eclipse the user view in discussions between innovators, administrators, and onlookers.

Use Open Management Approaches

Use open management approaches (to the extent financial disclosure is reasonable and practical) when discussing resource allocation. Recognize that educational technology consists of classrooms and books as well as computers and networks, all of which serve to support research and learning.

Establish a Timetable

Manage expectations concerning the rate of change by establishing a timetable with realizable milestones of achievement. Allow a decent amount of time for receiving input, then adopt a plan that insures that measurable progress can be observed.

Create a Shared Sense of Reality

Make sure that faculty, administration, and computer support have a shared sense of reality about implementing the institutional strategic plan. A discussion of the tradeoffs between centralized and distributed computing services is usually not meaningful in the abstract.

In short, a context-sensitive implementation plan is needed, and this means that top-down and bottom-up people must work together on setting priorities. I was amused to hear to a colleague complain that modern information technology—voice-mail, surface mail, fax messages, e-mail, campus mail, and the Internet—didn't leave any time for communication with his colleagues. I can sympathize with the complaint—the information age has us awash with messages representing a multitude of points of view. On the other hand, the educator's job is precisely to search for coherence amidst multiple perspectives. The technology is what it is, nothing more or less, and its significance lies in the use we make of it. And as for time, we have all there is.

REFERENCES/SUGGESTED READINGS

Holt, J. C. (1995). *How children fail.* Reading, MA: Addison-Wesley.

Noblitt, J. S. (1995). The electronic language learning environment. In C. Kramsch (Ed.), *Redefining the boundaries of language study.* Boston, MA: Heinle & Heinle.

Oberlin, J. (1996). The financial mythology of information technology: Developing a new game plan. *CAUSE/EFFECT, 19* (2), 10-17.

PART 4

DEVELOPING
THE
INFRASTRUCTURE

THE IMPORTANCE OF THE CAMPUS NETWORK INFRASTRUCTURE

Richard Nichols

Network infrastructure is a term many of us added to our vocabulary in the mid-1990s. Every organization needs one. But what is a network infrastructure? As used in this chapter, it defines the collection of interoperable elements that form the institution's network foundation. Included are the wiring, hubs, bridges, routers, gateways, switches, network interface cards (NICs), patch panels, patch cords, wall jacks, and other elements which form the underlying network structure. Although some definitions include additional components such as the servers, workstations, network operating system (NOS), and machine operating systems, as well as the applications, it seems most appropriate to define the infrastructure as the lower layer of elements which needs to be in place within all buildings and throughout the entire campus.

DEFINING INFRASTRUCTURE

Let's begin with the definition of infrastructures found in the *American Heritage Dictionary:* "The basic facilities, services and installations needed for the functioning of a community or society, such as transportation and communications systems, water and power lines, and public institutions including schools, post offices, and prisons."

Next, update the definition to use a more inclusive word for "communications systems" which would cover video distribution systems and data (computer) networks as well as the commonly assumed telephone systems. If this broader definition were adopted, everyone—from architects to university presidents—would begin to understand that these communications infrastructure elements must be included in all budgets, plans, designs, and construction. Unfortunately, the most common omission within new building and renovation plans is the network infrastructure. When a building construction budget is being scrubbed, often one of the first things to be removed is the network wiring. In the long-term, this is a costly decision. The costs to retrofit a building with appropriate network wiring after the building has been constructed is often many times the cost of the same wiring had it been installed during construction.

Common Expectations for Campus Computer Networks

It is generally accepted that technological improvements will continue at a rate of about 20% each year through this decade, continually opening up new computing and operational possibilities. Most institutions share a vision of a universal communications network connecting networks together and enabling scholars anywhere in the world to communicate. Administrative and academic networks are being integrated into a single network configuration that gives all users access to university computing resources. Expectations vary from campus to campus, but certain elements emerge consistently:

▶ Networks should support classrooms, computer labs, public access, faculty and administrative offices, libraries, and student housing. Access should be extended to any campus-related person who has a computer and a modem.

▶ Networks should handle information in multiple forms simultaneously, including text, graphics, video, and audio.

▶ Networks should facilitate e-mail and electronic conferences, campus access to external sources, such as the Internet, as well as the sharing of storage, printing, and communications elements.

Building a networking infrastructure would be an easy task if there were only one network architecture for higher education institutions. However, diversity is the rule rather than the exception. All network designs are an amalgam of user needs, the physical campus arrangement, existing related systems (e.g., voice, video, and data), and budgetary concerns. Rarely is an institution allowed the luxury of creating a network design from scratch; almost never for an entire campus. Another issue is future compatibility. Fortunately, we understand much more about computer networking and the integration of voice, data, and video than we did a decade ago, allowing us to arrange network structures, wiring, and operational strategies to more adequately take advantage of the latest technologies.

Many existing network designs are evolutions which resulted in a force fit of LAN architectures and campus backbone structures. LAN architectures, when expanded to their theoretical maximums, rarely performed adequately or did not function at all. Backbone architectures were not cost-effective in small sizes. Campuses forced to deal with different architectures saw their networks become more and more interconnected and interoperable until they ceased to perform effectively. Colleges and universities, pressured to keep the cost of education down while enhancing delivery services, have a new tool available through the use of today's scalable, hybrid systems.

The key to longevity in network architecture is scalability. There will continue to be pressures for incorporating new technology, expanding user requirements, and containing costs. For a network design to survive, it must be scalable. This means that one can increase the amount of bandwidth of the network without changing the architectural structure. A scalable network design allows the incorporation of new technologies even if some aspects of the prior architecture are eliminated or expanded.

The current trend is to migrate to switched networks. Switched networks use switching devices in the architecture to provide a full capacity network segment or ring connection to each server or workstation connected to the switch. The aggregate capacity within the backplane of the switching device is many times greater than the individual connections to network devices. In layman's terms, the total capacity of a switch network is measured in gigabits rather than megabits. This switching capability, when introduced into a campus network architecture, allows the network to scale upward, providing many more connections while retaining the same basic topology. Many network experts feel that switching will extend Ethernet, for example, indefinitely.

Benefits of Campus-Wide Networks

Ironically, the primary benefit of networking—increased access to information—has also been cited as contributing to a modern problem of information overload. Let's take a look at how the problems can be addressed if anticipated in the long-range technology plan.

College libraries. Networks provide single point access to enormous resources. On campuses where there are multiple libraries, students can use electronic card catalogs and hypertext-oriented search engines which allow them to conduct their research in hours instead of days. They do not have to wait in line at multiple reference desks anymore. However, not all information is legitimate, valuable, or applicable. Along with easy access to information, students must be taught to discriminate much more carefully between available data and relevant information. To work efficiently, users must learn to define their objectives rigorously. And remember, data is not necessarily information.

Student records. From registration to grades, students are able to use the network to access pertinent information without requiring administrative assistance. The major concerns regarding security and privacy, which typically have been handled procedurally, now must be incorporated into the technology. Continual improvements have been made in security as we progress toward full client/server networking.

Faculty collaboration. Finding time in faculty schedules for meetings often presented a roadblock to the sharing of ideas and joint projects. With the use of networks, groupware, and e-mail, faculty can collaborate easily with others on their own campus or with colleagues anywhere in the world.

Access to outside experts. On campuses where the Internet is accessible, for example, students and faculty have been pleasantly surprised to find that, on occasion, one of the commentators on a given topic is a Nobel laureate. Today, the Internet links thousands of computer networks spanning North America, Europe, Australia, and Asia.

Multimedia. Using high speed networks, multimedia applications have the potential to transform student learning environments. As an emerging technology, multimedia must be woven into the technology plan, taking care to incorporate relevant pedagogy while avoiding deadend developments.

Specialized networks. Various disciplines have their own highly specialized networks, such as COGNET, a distributed network for the field of cognitive science.

Electronic conferencing. Today, geography ceases to be a factor in connecting the scholarly community. When we consider faculty and students from diverse backgrounds and countries communicating on topics of common interest, the potential is enormous. The store-and-forward concept of data communications also removes the time-based problem of interactive communications.

STRATEGIC PLANNING

To bring their technological expectations into focus and to ensure results which will adequately integrate technology into all aspects of their campus activities, leadership institutions often use a long-range technology plan. These plans provide a road map for technology implementation over the next three to five years. By using a plan, these institutions minimize short-term, deadend situations resulting from the rapid obsolescence of networking elements.

A long-range technology plan should provide a technology-based vision that describes where the institution will be—academically and administratively—in the near future (usually about five years). The plan should anticipate the needs of academic and administrative users and provide for the eventual sharing of technology between the two groups, including the use of the same infrastructure. When developing the plan, it is important to document the expectations that campus users have and to separate the needs from the wishes.

A long-range technology plan is an attempt to distill and coordinate the complexity of the technological changes occurring throughout the network infrastructure so that institutional goals are met. This is a difficult task because various segments of the network evolve at different rates. For instance, network hardware such as switches or hubs may evolve faster than the network management software needed for their support. In addition, competing new hardware technologies, with varying technical implications, further complicate the development of the plan. Therefore, the plan should include a generic description of the use and need for computers, networks, and related technology support issues. Recommended components of a technology plan include technical opportunities, academic requirements, administrative requirements, network, staffing, and management (Figure 11.1). It is not advisable to develop a plan that includes models and specific equipment descriptions because of rapid changes.

This plan should be viewed as a dynamic document that is updated as the environment, financial status, or technology changes. Once written and agreed to, the plan should be updated every year. A plan that has not been revised in as much as three years is probably outdated; the technology available at the time it was written may not support today's needs. If the plan is implemented properly, the college or university will have the basis for a network infrastructure that will last well into the future.

FIGURE 11.1

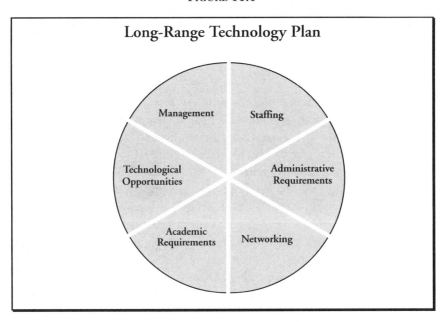

FIGURE 11.1

INTEGRATION OF VOICE, VIDEO, AND DATA

The 1990s have seen the beginnings of the integration of data, voice, and video within the same network structure. Technology planners are beginning to realize the benefits of building one network infrastructure which will support all modes of communications, especially as digital video becomes more cost-effective. With computer communications inherently digital, most modern telephone systems digital, and the emerging digital video, digital information will allow the true integration of all modes of communication. When these modes of communication are merged, the true integration of technologies will be a practical solution to the historic need for multiple networks. The long-range technology plan should include consideration for future network integration, including the selection of a backbone architecture and topology such as asynchronous transfer mode (ATM) which will handle all three communications technologies.

WIRING IS THE GLUE THAT HOLDS IT ALL TOGETHER

One of the most important parts of the network infrastructure is the wiring of the network. Wiring is used here as a generic term that includes the actual wire—including fiber optics and/or coaxial cable—the connectors, plugs, jacks, and physical terminations. Prior to the early 1980s, building wiring was always done by the telephone company. The telephone company provided the information for the building wiring design, conduit runs, wiring closet locations and dimensions. Architectural firms did not need to have specialists in wiring design. When building wiring was deregulated, there was a simultaneous explosion of interest in LANs, building networks, multiple inter-exchange carriers requiring points-of-presence (POPs) in the buildings, fiber optics, and the installation of powered equipment in wiring closets. Simultaneously, the design became significantly more complicated, which meant that architects weren't always prepared to handle these complexities. For a few years, it seemed that nobody was responsible for wiring infrastructure design. Many buildings were designed with virtually no consideration given to the installation of conduits, wiring closets, underfloor ductwork, or other features necessary to support the network infrastructure. Consultants have appeared to handle this design and architectural firms have begun accepting the responsibility for network infrastructure design. Institutions learned—sometimes the hard way—that they had to be watchdogs about wiring issues which they had never worried about before. Today, an institution must be vigilant to make sure that voice and data wiring needs have been included just like other parts of the utility infrastructure.

One example illustrates the importance of wiring. Approximately 80% of the communication errors that can occur on a network are the result of faulty wiring connections. The two key components to pay attention to are the design and selection of the actual wire and the connecting components used to terminate the wire. There is not a specific type or method of wiring which is optimum for all situations. In determining the optimum wiring, a number of questions should be asked:

▶ How large is the building?

▶ What is the existing wiring?

▶ If the building is old, is it possible to install wiring and ensure its physical integrity?

▶ What are the technical requirements for bandwidth, crosstalk, and distance limitations?

Regardless of the building structure and the networks to be interconnected, decisions must be made regarding the capabilities of the actual wire and the electronics used in conjunction with it. It is not adequate to consider the wire alone; it must be chosen in conjunction with the architecture, topology, and structure of the network(s) to be interconnected. There are trade-offs to be made related to the cost-effectiveness of available wire. In all cases, the associated cost of the termination and attachment devices must be considered when making the evaluation. The trend today is to favor the purchase of more intelligent electronics, anticipating that they will provide the flexibility for growth. A properly constructed wiring design, for example, should include the provision for expansion without major retrofit.

UPGRADING NETWORKS

Many of the campus networks currently in use were installed prior to the existence of the majority of today's products. Multimedia, including audio and video over a network, high performance computing, Internet access, and high resolution graphics are standard requirements today. Many of these requirements did not exist a few years ago. The increased network demands for support of graphic intensive applications and other sophisticated user requirements have not merely doubled or tripled from the 1980s; they have increased by several orders of magnitude. Many of the original networks, while acceptable for character-based computing, will not handle today's graphics-based world. Even if we could have envisioned such a future years ago, it would have been a rare institution that had planned for the current network demands or had the budget to implement such a network. To support the high demands that will be placed on future networks requires a thorough analysis of current and projected network requirements and a migration plan to move to a new design within a few years.

If an existing network is based upon old, noncategorized wiring or coaxial cable, and used one of the original topologies or network architectures which are not currently viable nor popular, there is no easy way to convert to the latest scalable architectures. The products needed to implement cost-effective, scalable architectures are available, but the changes in the old networks are simply too difficult and certainly not cost-effective. It is much more efficient to simply overbuild the old wiring with a new fiber optic/Category 5 wiring infrastructure which will meet the latest end-to-end performance specifications, use a new switched architecture and either Ethernet or Token-Ring topology for building/departmental networks, and a scalable campus backbone capable of carrying voice, data, or video, such as ATM. The institution should be able to migrate all the old functions and applications to the new scalable network architecture with minimal changes.

The secret of success in network architectures today is the use of centralized switching technologies. A modern, scalable network architecture may be implemented more easily if the network wiring has been installed as a centralized wiring structure. Often, existing building wiring is star-wired but the campus is ring-wired from building to building. Token-Ring and 10BaseT Ethernet systems, for example, are wired in a star arrangement typical of what is needed for scalable architecture networks. A star arrangement provides a separate wire from the hub to each workstation, server, printer, and other network-connected device. Campuses with a ring-wired backbone are often difficult to convert to a centralized switching architecture unless many spare fiber strands or wire pairs were installed.

The older workstation and server hardware—a major investment on the part of the university—should be put to best use within the plan. It can be trickled down to be used in one of the simpler functions such as print servers or for use in electronic laboratories gathering and processing data, if equipped with some additional adapter cards. This trickle down philosophy can be very functional and cost-effective.

MANAGING THE NETWORK

The adoption of decentralized, multivendor, heterogeneous, open architecture networks places not only a new burden on the institution and personnel for support; it also raises the awareness of the entire campus to the successes and failures of the network systems. This atmosphere demands the very best from support organizations. They must have a clear understanding of their roles as outlined in the technology plan. Proactive management is a must to minimize downtime. Thorough record keeping and performance baselines are necessary to prevent wasted effort. Some years ago, a report was prepared by a consulting firm which attempted to identify the long-range costs of hardware, software, and staffing needed to support local area networks. This was the first time anyone tried to identify the actual costs of operating a local area network, and it indicated that the long-range costs were actually more than those required to support the old centralized mainframe. In addition, it is now known that the long-term (three to five years) support costs for networking greatly exceed the initial hardware and software expenditures. Of course, the networked workstations and applications provided many more technology-based applications, flexibility, and opportunities than were available with the old mainframe. As the institution grows more and more dependent upon the network infrastructure to support its day-to-day activities, the statement, "The network is the system," will become a truism.

THE POWER OF THE PLAN

Properly implemented, an institution's long-range technology plan can be a powerful and cost-effective way to build a communications infrastructure that will accommodate change in a dynamic environment. The long-range technology plan not only provides the road map for development and implementation, but also the criteria for assessment. Continuous review and updating of the plan helps to ensure that the plan remains viable. Review of the plan also emphasizes the complexity of the tasks and interdependent nature of all elements of the institution.

Many campuses have successfully installed communications networks that enhance their ability to meet their academic expectations. Their long-range technology plans will ensure that the resulting networks support the quality programs they expect.

DETERMINING VALUE

A question to consider: Has the institution received value for the money spent in network infrastructure as well as networking hardware and software? If you answered yes, next question how you will measure such value.

Value can be defined as the benefits justifying the costs. In other words, that the investment of time, money, and effort in technology provides measurable results, especially when the long-term commitments and expenditures are considered. Over the past ten years, technology plans and implementations were selected and executed with little or no consideration given to whether or not the organization received the results desired. In many cases, the technology was implemented with little or no identification of the expected results and no identifiable way to measure improvements. It is no longer sufficient to assume that the implementation of technology of any sort will result in improvements in something. Long-range planning should incorporate results measurements to identify the value of the technology to the institution. The value measurements can encompass many aspects of the institution:

▶ Administrative efficiency

▶ Increased output with existing staff/faculty

▶ Staff/faculty increase avoidance

▶ Staff and/or faculty redeployment or reduction

▶ Increased student success

▶ Increased faculty retention

▶ Additional faculty release time available

▶ Improved community relations

In many of these cases, specific measurements are a challenge, especially if there are no baselines. Many organizations have no baseline data with the exception of historic records of staff, faculty, and student complaints. Therefore, one of the first things that is done during the implementation of an institution's long-range plan should be to identify what needs to be measured and how the measurements will be made. In order to do the final analysis, the actual technology costs over the next X years (fairly long time to be valid) must be identified and included in the calculation. Once the actual costs of technology are known and all items are calculated, the institution will have some idea of the value of the technology in quantifiable terms.

Intangible elements should also be considered. While the intangible elements are difficult to reduce to monetary terms, the institution is encouraged to equate them in sufficient detail to something that does have measurable terms, assigning an identifiable aspect of value to the intangible item. How does one assign value to loyalty, for example? Although not quantitative, these intangible elements have qualitative value, especially in areas such as influencing students to attend or retaining high caliber faculty.

Once an institution adopts the networking paradigm, it quickly becomes apparent that adequate technical support staff, plus hardware and software upgrades, are absolutely imperative to keep the voice, data, and video networks up-to-date and useful. When the entire campus depends upon the adequate functioning of the network(s), then the institution must identify and accept the true long-term costs of this technology. Unfortunately, most vendors and users admit that these true costs are not well-known or understood and often not discussed during the planning stages. To ignore these costs is a mistake: Their magnitude is always greater than anyone initially thought. Some of the long-term cost elements of technology include:

- Network management
- Staffing
- Training
- Hardware upgrades and replacements
- Software upgrades
- Technology integration (e.g., the time required to reengineer business processes to take advantage of the networked technologies)
- Inefficiencies while implementing a new technology

When creating an institution's long-range technology plan, these elements should be discussed, planned, and the related costs identified. These recurring costs should be added to the initial costs and amortized over time. Only then can the value calculation begin. The easiest place to begin is with administrative procedures. If measured prior to implementing networked computing solutions, these processes can be measured again after the networks, computers, and new applications are operational to determine if time and money has been well spent. Academic measurements are more difficult, often requiring the assignment of value to intangibles.

CONCLUSION

While some of this planning sounds unnecessary, institutions which are successful in moving to the network-centric paradigm all use a long-range technology plan which considers all aspects of the institution's needs. To attempt to implement technology piecemeal without a plan will lead to poor performance, wasted money, reworking, and perhaps total disaster. Planning pays.

12

PLANNING FOR SUCCESS: ARE YOU READY FOR CLIENT/SERVER?

David L. Bellamy and Danuta C. McCall

CLIENT/SERVER: TECHNOLOGY PLATFORM OR CHANGE AGENT?

"Why are we doing this project?" The question is a simple one. Many institutions that embark on an enterprise-wide client/server (C/S) project move to C/S because everyone else seems to be doing it. Client/server is used to champion a variety of causes. Some enterprises move to client/server because the common wisdom is that client/server is less expensive than mainframe computing. Other information technology providers do so because their users demand the look and feel of client/server. If not provided, the users will attempt to implement it themselves, making user support and standards enforcement a Herculean task.

We have helped many clients implement client/server technology in the private and public sectors. As a corporation, we have made our own transition to a networked application environment, as well. These experiences have taught us that there is only one good reason to adopt client/server: fundamental change in business processes. Changes in business processes that are implemented in a distributed environment often demand client/server as an enabling technology.

USING TECHNOLOGY TO DRIVE BUSINESS VALUE

Before proceeding with a client/server project, identify and quantify its value to the institution. Value, while not limited to financial measures, should always be measurable with specific goals. General objectives, such as improved student services or reduced administrative cost, do not provide a measure of the contribution made by the project. For example, to support the institutional goal of improved efficiency in enrollment management, one specific objective might be to reduce the number of drop/adds by 50% through on-line registration, providing access to section, instructor, and prerequisite information. The assumption is that the percentage of drop/adds is inversely related to students obtaining their preferred course and section. Once the cost of the drop/add process is estimated, we can quantify the cost savings of the 50% reduction. In addition, we can use satisfaction surveys to measure less tangible benefits such as increased student satisfaction and decreased loss of class time during the drop/add period.

A larger, more comprehensive project is, for example, a move to technology-enabled self-advisement. This requires the institution to redesign the entire advising process, including the roles of faculty advisors as well as institutional policy. While certainly more complex, this project has greater potential impact by allowing the institution to create a competitive advantage, such as a four-year graduation guarantee. In this case, benefits to the institution expand to include increased enrollment and retention as well as reduced cost. For such projects, quantified business value is critical when seeking funding and organizational support. Technology upgrade projects proposed without a well-defined business case rarely obtain funding. In studies of the derivation of business value in client/server applications, we have found that it is "directly related to the degree to which underlying business processes have been reengineered" (IBM Consulting Group, 1994).

What constitutes reengineering? Process reengineering, as defined by Hammer, is "the fundamental rethinking and radical redesign of business processes to bring about dramatic improvements in performance" (Hammer & Stanton, 1995). The advisement case illustrates reengineering while the on-line registration project would be better termed automation. Automation can reduce the cost of labor intensive operations, but dramatic improvements are only achieved by rethinking the underlying process. Ideally, reengineering should be well underway before technology decisions are made. However, in many cases, the platform and application selection are made early and are used to drive the project forward and motivate the organization.

To understand the business value of a potential project, ask two questions: 1) What is the problem we are trying to solve? and 2) What is the result if we solve that problem? Keep asking until you and every stakeholder in the project agree on a basic purpose and value statement for the project.

BALANCING PEOPLE, PROCESS, AND TECHNOLOGY

Three critical factors affect the success of an enterprise-wide, client/server implementation strategy: people, process, and technology. You cannot achieve successful delivery of expected business value to the institution by focusing on technology alone.

FIGURE 12.1

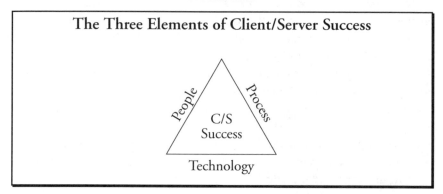

The Three Elements of Client/Server Success

Technology

Technology is clearly an important element of successful client/server projects. Be aware of three potential problems as you address the technology.

1) The application software, the workstations, servers, and the database system, often the focal point of technology discussions, represent only about 15% of the technology cost of the project (The Gartner Group, 1994).

2) The supporting infrastructure which includes the most expensive component—the local-, campus-, and wide-area networks, systems management, and user support—carries hidden costs. In real cost terms, each time you place a PC on the desktop of a user in a client/server environment, you are committing to ten times the purchase price over the next five years (Langel, 1995). The acceptance of and satisfaction with a new system can be derailed by an unreliable infrastructure or a poorly supported desktop environment, yet these components are often inadequately addressed because justification for their development is not incorporated into the project business case.

3) User departments often drive technology decisions because the central information systems (I/S) organization has become either unresponsive or ineffective. As the organization's need to provide comprehensive data access to growing numbers of information workers drives the move to implement institution-wide client/server systems, the struggle between the need for centralized standards and operation versus the users' desire to be in control of their own systems becomes increasingly acute.

People and Processes

People use processes and technology to get work done. The organizational impact of a reengineering-based technology initiative is sometimes thought of in terms of job restructuring or layoffs. It goes much further. The new process often challenges the existing culture and authority structure. For example, if purchase orders currently require many approval levels, a new process that encourages individual budget responsibility may challenge basic assumptions held by executives or staff involved in the existing process.

Another organizational impact results from the level of integration of technology into the business process. In the traditional technology environment of legacy systems, relatively few people use the system directly, and the function provided is very specific. The system is designed to do a particular task—for example, general ledger—and the users who have access are essentially information gatekeepers with specialized roles and a unique knowledge of the system. When management wants information from the system, the information gatekeeper interprets the request and queries the system. One advantage of client/server is that it enables the creation of a system with a broad range of duties that support the whole business process. Instead of merely tracking expenditures, the system is responsible for every aspect of budget, requisitions, purchases, payments, approvals, exceptions, and reporting. It is no longer a tool that is checked prior to requesting a purchase order; it is the one place for all departmental finance information. Each staff member has access to the system and relies on it to do work. Gone is the information gatekeeper who interprets system output and restates it in human terms. Gone also is the paper or spreadsheet process used to check on the system. When managers need information, they enter the query themselves. This represents a fundamental change in the work experience and in the definition of roles for many employees. It also raises questions about the relevance of traditional job descriptions and performance measures.

Returning to the advising example, the new system automates routine transactions (e.g., seeking basic information about schedules, policy, degree requirements) freeing the faculty advisor to focus on the value-added advising functions including mentoring, selecting programs of study, and addressing policy exceptions. The faculty member may now be expected to devote more time to advising, and the impact of advising may be measured to determine its contribution to institutional objectives. This may conflict with the faculty member's own expectations of his or her job and relationship to the institution. While all these changes are good for the student and the institution, they may be viewed negatively by faculty or staff and be expressed as resistance to the project. It is difficult to anticipate the source of the resistance; it is best prevented by open communications and avoidance of hidden agendas.

A MODEL FOR PREDICTING CLIENT/SERVER PROJECT SUCCESS

There are many potential problems when implementing a client/server project. How can you predict whether or not you will be successful? The Chantilly study (IBM Consulting Group, 1994) developed a management model that could be used to plan successful client/server projects. The study also highlights the benefits and pitfalls. By retrospectively analyzing 24 enterprises that had completed the implementation of a production application with different degrees of success, the Chantilly study found that risk in client/server projects is essentially a misalignment of the technical complexity of a project with the organization's readiness to implement it. Both factors can be measured and assessed prior to implementation. This identifies the potential pitfalls of the project. Using a number of benchmarks, among them the Malcolm Baldrige National Quality Awards criteria, ISO 9000, and an alignment model developed by the IBM Consulting Group, a multidimensional rating system was developed to evaluate organizational readiness.

The technical complexity of client/server applications reviewed in the study was determined by examining the four main components of the solution design and how they were deployed across a network (Figure 12.2). The more distributed the components, the higher the technical complexity.

Six indicators were used to determine the degree of the project's success. The results of this analysis showed that projects within the low risk zone, where technical complexity is aligned with organizational readiness, are much more likely to succeed than those that fall outside (Figure 12.3). There is risk in initiating projects that exceed the organizational readiness level. There is also risk in those with complexity below the organization's readiness level. The risk, in this case, is that end-users receive less value either because the functionality is too simple or because the underlying process was not reengineered (Figure 12.3).

FIGURE 12.2

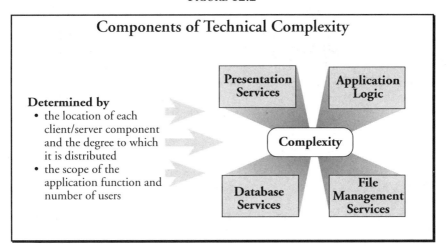

FIGURE 12.3

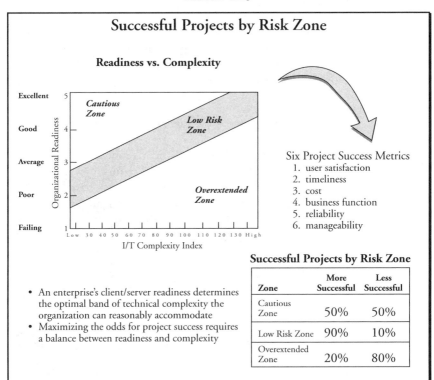

Based on the results of the Chantilly study, the IBM Consulting Group developed an assessment tool to predict client/server implementation success. They applied the concept of quality maturity stages developed for use in IBM internal software development to organizational readiness (Kaplan, Clark, & Tang, 1994). The four stages of organizational readiness are: awareness, coping, management, and integration (Figure 12.4).

FIGURE 12.4

Organizational Readiness Indicators by Stage

MATURITY STAGE	QUALITATIVE INDICATORS
Integration	Optimizing processes; learning organization; closed loop management; robust measurements; enterprise wide teamwork; adaptive culture; end user/customer driven; hardened infrastructure; I/T enables change; I/T business value in evidence
Management	Process managed; robust measurements; feedback loop closing; cross-functional teaming; end user-I/T partnership strong; user buy-in high; process efforts facilitated by I/T; alignment of goals high; proactive management; beginning of end user/customer driven culture
Coping	Defined processes; functional team driven; measurements in place; high level of end user involvement; user I/T partnership in evidence; management involved to facilitate needed changes; infrastructure can sustain change; investment prioritization scheme to assure alignment; solid project management controls; good fit with reengineering efforts; cultural inhibitors corrected when encountered
Awareness	Anecdotal process; limited repeatability; limited user buy-in; some alignment with business goals; beginning user-I/T partnership; emerging development approach; management awareness of need to change; small work team approaches emerging; infrastructure investment in evidence; limited standards; poor change tolerance

APPLYING THE RISK ASSESSMENT MODEL TO HIGHER EDUCATION

In 1995, IBM Higher Education developed an assessment based on the Chantilly study model to help higher education institutions undertaking campus-wide client/server projects anticipate potential pitfalls and address these early in the implementation planning stage. We developed a 14 point questionnaire to capture the perspectives of the key stakeholders which would allow us to rate the institution's organizational readiness with respect to the client/server project (Figure 12.5).

FIGURE 12.5

Organizational Readiness Topics	
CAPABILITY TOPIC	**ORGANIZATIONAL READINESS ATTRIBUTES**
User Satisfaction	The level of satisfaction expressed by the end users of the project
Data Analysis	The institution's use of data for decision-making and operations management
Organizational Culture	The alignment between the institution's culture and the project approach
Business Value	The linkage between the project and the institution's business goals
Training and Education	The degree of investment in training and education
Success Criteria	Whether success criteria have been defined for the project
Project Governance	Roles and ground rules established for the project
Implementation Process	The extent to which the implementation approach is appropriate for the client/server project
Project Management	The extent to which project management disciplines are in place for this project
Infrastructure	The deployment of the I/T infrastructure needed to support the project
Systems Management	The extent to which system management disciplines are in place for the project
Executive Sponsorship	The leadership characteristics of the project sponsor
Management Unity	The degree of support by departmental managers impacted by the project scope
Strategic Planning	The linkage between the institution's business and I/T strategies

METHODOLOGY

The underlying methodology was adapted to higher education. To reflect the shared governance structure of the institution, a multiconstituency analysis was performed. Key stakeholder groups in the project were interviewed and analyzed separately. Stakeholder groups typically included administrative department heads, faculty, students, information technology providers, and when applicable, the outside implementation team (consultant or vendor). Studies focused on implementation of student, human resource, and finance applications supplied by industry software vendors. Implementation processes which, among other things, look at the degree of process reengineering underlying the project, substituted for questions on internal development. Technical complexity was determined from information provided by the vendor with the aid of IBM's Client/Server Business Advisor tool. In addition to the organizational readiness data points, one-on-one interviews were conducted to ensure that each topic area was explored in depth.

Five higher education institutions were studied. Of these, two are large public research institutions, two are private research universities, and one is a land grant, four-year instructional university. Two have major teaching hospitals and medical centers. Findings from each assessment were used to develop a set of specific recommendations for each university to address pitfalls and, if necessary, move the project into the low risk zone (Figure 12.3). However, when taken as a group, certain themes began to emerge which have broad applicability in the higher education environment.

FINDINGS IN HIGHER EDUCATION: WHERE DO THE PITFALLS LIE?

Institutional Culture

Institutional culture in higher education is an amalgam of several cultures blending entrepreneurial components with a shared governance model. As one frustrated university executive described it, higher education consists of "... institutional change agents, entrepreneurs, and heads in the sand." He then asked, "How do we appeal to each of the cultures within our institution to drive this project forward?" The culture of the institution both supports and rejects the essential tenets of the client/server approach. In support of the culture, client/server provides users with an unprecedented degree of involvement and control in application development as well as deployment. In addition, it greatly enhances direct access to data. Client/server has the potential to reduce or eliminate trivial and rote tasks, allowing individuals to focus on their core missions. This appeals to what one human resources director described as "the genius of the university, the independent spirit which makes us great." But there is a price to pay. A successful client/server system requires standards for processes, infrastructure, data, and definitions. It also requires the willingness to rethink where work is best done and to place the good of the institution as a whole above individual wants or needs. To deliver on client/servers' promise, data, processes, and people must be shared across departmental boundaries. This may seem at odds with the institutional culture of independence and autonomy.

FOCUS ON CUSTOMER SERVICE

Client/server demands a new emphasis on and definition of customer service. The organizational readiness assessments that IBM Higher Education conducted with five universities confirms this need in higher education.

Figure 12.6 shows the aggregate rating for each readiness topic. Topics with data points that fall within Stages 3 and 4 (Management and Integration) are generally considered strengths; those that fall within Stages 1 and 2 (Awareness and Coping) are considered potential pitfalls which, if not addressed, can adversely affect the success of client/server implementation.

Interview comments also guided our analysis. For this discussion, we selected the topics that surfaced repeatedly as pitfalls either in the analysis of aggregate data or the interviews.

MISMATCH OF EXPECTATIONS

Beware of perception gaps between different stakeholder groups. For example, in our study of five universities, providers had unrealistically high expectations for data, infrastructure, and systems management. This may be because the provider view of service often focuses on operations rather than user support. The information systems mission may not mirror the users' stated or assumed requirement for more comprehensive support. Providers often fail to seek direct information from the users they serve.

In another example, the average score of the five institutions indicates that executive sponsorship is a particularly strong asset. Both academic and administrative executives tend to adopt reengineering principles, looking not only for efficiency but for qualitative leaps in service to students, faculty, and staff. The executives communicate the importance of the project to key stakeholders, and, to a lesser degree, to the campus community at large. Executives also tend to have a clear understanding of the project's institutional value. If problems occur, it is likely to be at the departmental level where there are varying degrees of buy-in or a lack of it. In one extreme case, the user departments found the stated business case for the project so unbelievable that no one was willing to pilot the system.

FIGURE 12.6

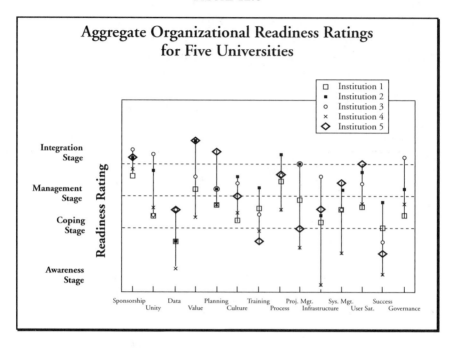

DATA AS AN INSTITUTIONAL ASSET

In all the readiness assessments we conducted, users and executives pointed to data analysis as the number one issue in the current environment. While in agreement that insufficient or inaccessible data is the problem and that the client/server system will fix it, very few respondents understood the trade-off they would be making. Compensatory mechanisms that had allowed them to get by without data pose as much of a potential problem to successful client/server implementation as the data issues themselves.

The topic area included questions on data access, timeliness, and accuracy. It also probed how data is currently used to improve business operations and management decision-making and to monitor service improvements. Respondents identified easy access to timely data as the number one issue. As one executive pointed out, "... because access (extracting data from the mainframe system) is so difficult, people don't validate gut level decisions." A second important issue was accuracy and reliability of data which, in one example, resulted in students graduating before enrolling.

Most respondents believed that their departments would use data effectively if it were accurate and if they were given easy-to-use query and reporting tools. They believed, therefore, that the client/server system would provide the necessary tools. Their concerns revolved around adequate training and on-line help for the applications.

In two of the universities, however, respondents voiced concerns that identified some key underlying issues. One I/T manager described the underlying issue as a cultural one: "...in the current culture, information is hoarded; we lack the training and skills to use data, but more fundamentally, we don't like to work with people outside our own department. Information doesn't leave the fiefdom." One administrative department head stated that absence of proactive thinking and failure to measure performance have limited their use of data in decision-making. In interviews the issue of departmentalism surfaced again and again, but most respondents did not think it would inhibit the success of the client/server project. In our experience, the pitfall is this: In order to cope with administrative systems that do not provide the data they need, departments have built extensive shadow systems that deliver high levels of function for their particular needs. The value of the new system and its integrated database comes at the cost of department-specific functions, with the result that the replacement system often cannot match the expectations of the users.

The second pitfall is that most institutions lack a history of viewing data as an institutional asset and using it to measure performance in a cross-departmental context. Without specific training and skills and a certain level of experience in data analysis techniques, many users are unlikely to use the system effectively to drive quality improvements. The impact on the implementation comes in the form of user resistance and dissatisfaction assigning to the system the role of scapegoat.

In response to these issues, one of the project implementation teams chose to use a low-risk data analysis pilot. This allowed them to demonstrate the value of data analysis to the institution, establish skills in data capture, analysis, and metrics, and implement a mechanism for skills transfer and organizational learning. They selected a subprocess, preregistration advising, which is tied to the goal of increasing student retention. Their goal is to define the desired metrics and capture data from the automated degree audit system which they will install in the first phase of the project.

DEFINING SUCCESS

I have not seen any defined or detailed success criteria. 'Save us money' and 'make purchasing easier' is what I hear. I will probably never celebrate because success is a moving target. It will be successful if completed on time and within budget. That is the only thing stated.
(Interview comments from Organizational Readiness Assessments)

Since the essential purpose of a client/server system is to deliver value by enabling the deployment of reengineered processes, linking project success criteria to goals is not only fundamental but inescapable. How else will you know when you have succeeded? This is a major departure from traditional project success measures such as "on time" and "under budget." The Chantilly study reports that "... organizations which specifically state the value they expect to derive from a client/server implementation have a better chance of actually getting and measuring it." In fact, the data gathered by the Chantilly study showed that even late projects that ran over budget were considered successful by the organization because business value was delivered and users participated. However, those projects not based on reengineered processes or projects which were too limited in scope were not viewed as successful, even when they met time and budget objectives. The study also demonstrated that successful projects are likely to be those in which the business unit has a high degree of control and participation.

Our study participants expected to derive important value from their client/server projects and were able to describe it in general terms (improved information access to students, better quality of student services, increased student retention). No university in our assessment had yet defined a concise set of three to five success criteria for the project or knew how they were going to measure performance and capture the data. Instead, they expressed an intuitive belief in the correctness of their approach.

The pitfall here is that in the absence of formally communicated project success criteria, informal, individual, or departmental criteria will fill the void. Without a shared vision of the project, key stakeholders may end up dissatisfied because their unofficial objectives were not met. In some cases, these informal criteria may be at odds with the official project. The dissension this may cause within the implementation team or amongst initial users may slow down or even halt the project.

Not-for-profit institutions typically have no history of evaluating project success. Lack of accountability is often cited as a weakness in higher education, giving rise to cynicism on the part of many about the utility of success criteria in their environment. However, do not underestimate the unifying effect of defining a common set of project objectives and continually communicating the progress made toward their attainment to all project stakeholders. The process builds buy-in and fosters collaboration among the different constituencies. In fact, we have suggested that one way to measure the success of the definition process is when all groups affected by the scope of the project can articulate a common message about the project's three to five objectives.

One university adopted the following approach to address this issue. The project team built a straw-man set of performance indicators based on the project's business case, the institution's key goals, and the departments' prioritized objectives. They then received endorsement from the executive sponsors. They quantified each performance measure by using baselines and targets to create a scorecard to track and report project progress. The scorecard consisted of 1) predictive measurements: Are we on track to achieve the desired results on a sustained basis? 2) results measurements: Did we achieve the expected results? and 3) stress test measurements: Did we test the capabilities of our organization to implement a client/server application? They plan to update and communicate the scorecard results quarterly to all key stakeholders.

TRAINING AND EDUCATION: THE SHOEMAKER'S CHILDREN

Training is critical for the successful adoption of client/server technology within an organization. It is of particular concern in client/server projects because of the size and diversity of the user population, some of whom may have never used a PC. Now that the information gatekeepers in their organization have been removed, these novice users are expected to integrate the new system into the fabric of their daily work. Many are anxious and ill-prepared. This anxiety may manifest itself in various forms of resistance to the system. The most effective way to remove resistance is to assure the users of adequate training.

What needs must be addressed in the training? First, basic training on the PC, especially for those with minimal exposure to personal workstations. Next in importance is application usage, that is, how the work processes will change and how the application can be used to the best advantage. The training format should address these areas holistically and focus on helping people integrate the technology into their business process.

While the assessment results from our five universities indicate that all three groups (users, executives, and providers) had concerns about their institutions' ability to adequately prepare its constituents for client/server, the users were consistently the least confident that the projects being implemented at their institutions were adequately funded to provide enough training or the right training. They were most concerned that individual departments would have to shoulder the burden of training. Users know from prior experience that this area is often neglected in system implementation (some examples cited were new telephone systems and campus e-mail). The issue of funding surfaced repeatedly in interviews. There is a good reason: With an average total training cost of $2,400 to $2,800 per user (The Gartner Group, 1994), training is seldom adequately funded. It is appropriate for both central administration and the departments to bear a portion of the cost, assuming that the training is in support of well-articulated project objectives.

Most respondents felt that training was not evaluated in their institution. When it was, the metrics were typically limited to classroom satisfaction surveys. The true contribution of training to a successful client/server implementation is determined by measurements at three levels:

1) The degree of comprehension at the conclusion of the course

2) The degree to which knowledge has been incorporated into job behavior

3) Whether the new behavior has produced the desired outcomes

Return to our early example of advising. Assume we train the advisor along with the student to use the new system to select the semester course load. At the conclusion of training, we measure satisfaction/understanding with a short questionnaire. For level two we measure the percent of advising sessions in which the advisor and student used the new system together. For the third level, we measure the drop/add ratio for these students (compared to baseline and target).

INFRASTRUCTURE: HIGHWAY OR BYWAY

There's a backbone to every building but no LAN within the walls. . . . Departmental LANs are not consistent with the central network. . . . Students have given up trying to get into the network. . . . We fear that we will have standards that require a costly upgrade. . . . Mice have eaten the wires. (Interview comments from Readiness Assessments)

Many institutions have invested time and resources in network improvement projects, yet reliable, responsive, ubiquitous client/server infrastructures remain elusive. The definition of infrastructure is often limited to the backbone network, occasionally extending to the departmental local area networks (LANs), but rarely considering the client or server as part of the campus infrastructure. In order to adequately prepare for client/server implementation, the infrastructure must include all the components necessary to run the new application including the appropriate skilled professionals. With this broader view, infrastructure was a pitfall for four of the five institutions we assessed—including an institution that had just completed a $30 million network upgrade.

The most commonly raised issues are uneven access and nonstandard technology. Because of the decentralized nature of the institution, departments are often allowed to establish their own client, LAN, and network standards—or to not establish any. Some departments (e.g., graduate and/or professional schools) invest heavily in technology and support it well, while others (e.g., undergraduate departments) do not. The result is a have/have-not culture that impedes any project that requires a common infrastructure.

Infrastructure reliability is also an issue. Expectations of the network are beginning to resemble the reliability levels expected of utilities. Reliability depends, in part, on the selection of hardware and software, but far more on proactive management (See also, Systems Management in the next section).

Even when a robust infrastructure exists within a department, the skills necessary to implement and support the new system are frequently lacking. In most institutions, mainframe skills have developed over many years in a structured, centralized environment. Client/server skills are less available, are developed in a less structured way, and are rarely centralized. Thus the institution has difficulty drawing on what little client/server skills are available. One I/T executive summarized, "Our resources are low in quantity, low in C/S experience, and we have no plans to train them."

To provide a suitable infrastructure for client/server, institutions should plan to:

▶ Consolidate responsibility into a single campus-wide organization that has responsibility for the backbone network and departmental LANs (up to and including the network adapter card).

▶ Increase infrastructure reliability and performance to a level consistent with other utilities (e.g., telephone, electric).

▶ Establish institution-wide standards for client/server infrastructure that allow for diversity. Let departments determine their destiny at the workstation as long as it conforms to minimum standards. Limit options to what the central I/S organization can comfortably support but realize that failure to offer and support diversity in workstations may be a showstopper in some university settings. "Technical support (i.e., help desk, training, service, preventive maintenance, software distribution) in this mixed environment will cost more, but users will have a better attitude toward I/T and be more willing to compromise in other areas when the time comes" (Langel, 1995).

▶ Use a funding strategy that will lessen the disparity between the haves and have-nots. It may be appropriate for the institution to make the initial capital investment and then have the departments pay their share of ongoing network costs.

SYSTEMS MANAGEMENT: DON'T DISTRIBUTE WHAT YOU CAN'T MANAGE

In the institutions analyzed, information system providers typically rated themselves higher than did the users who received the service. Factors contributing to poor systems management performance include:

▶ Lack of a help desk that can resolve a problem on the first call. Typically, the user must determine what is broken, call the right help number and, in many cases, end up on a call-back queue. Even if users correctly follow all these steps, they may not get someone who can provide the resolution, or they may simply get transferred to someone else. The level of frustration is such that two of the institutions analyzed call it "the no help desk."

▶ Tension between centralized support which is often unresponsive and decentralized support which is often uneven.

▶ Low management priority and inadequate resources for the development of systems management. As one university administrator said, "Our data center does not have the resources to even look at systems management."

▶ Insufficient funding also contributes to poor systems management performance. However, institutions must consider the hidden cost of an unofficial help desk—where peers help peers. In institutions with medical schools, for example, it was not unusual to find medical doctors serving in this capacity.

As Langel (1995) has pointed out, client/server implementations magnify the need for effective systems management because C/S depends on the coordination and synchronization of clients and servers. Areas to be explored include numbers of PCs, decentralization of problems, physical security of devices, disaster recovery, viruses, software distribution, network bandwidth, administration, and asset management. Lack of comprehensive systems management will quickly compromise user support because of system unreliability or instability.

FIGURE 12.8

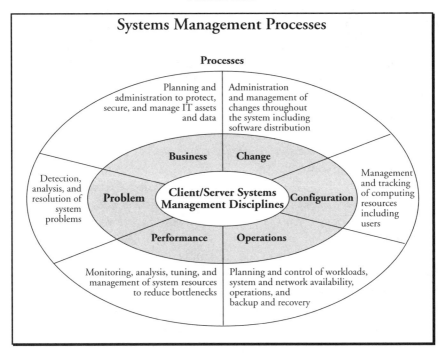

When addressing systems management, take a holistic approach. Figure 12.8 shows the six systems management processes that need to be addressed in institution-wide client/server implementations. When establishing each process area, consider the cultural issues such as ownership and the balancing of centralized and decentralized support. For example, control back-up and software distribution centrally, but deliver first-line support through a person in the department. Be sure to adequately fund the support structure. The average real cost is $350 per user per year (Langel, 1995). Again, there are both capital and ongoing support needs. We recommend the same approach as with infrastructure: The institution funds the initial capital investment, then ongoing costs of system management are distributed among the users.

PROJECT MANAGEMENT: WOULD THE REAL PROJECT MANAGER PLEASE STAND UP?

By definition, institution-wide client/server implementations are projects that cross departmental boundaries. A key challenge is the selection of a project manager with that rare mix of business and technology expertise who can ensure proper representation of the disparate groups that must come together to implement the system. Since client/server depends on user involvement, it would be preferable to select a project manager from among users. Even though you are more likely to find a person with that specific skill-mix among the providers, choosing a provider may give the appearance that it is an I/S project and could lead to resistance or lower participation from the users. Overall, most institutions have not undertaken large projects in recent history; they lack skilled project management candidates. One executive noted, "We haven't done anything significant, therefore we have limited project management skills. We send people to a two-day class and expect them to come out project managers. The team lacks a project manager who can pull the business functions and technology teams together."

Another obstacle is that colleges and universities are uncomfortable with formal project management. The project manager has to keep his/her team focused on task and goal. This enforced discipline is foreign in a culture that resists any kind of control. Yet projects of this scope cannot be accomplished without it.

The project manager is also charged with building a team, empowering its members, and holding them accountable for the results. One I/S leader said, "Teams need to create, develop something, not just review or provide input." If building the team and communication within is troublesome, consider the effort required to implement an effective communication plan with the user community. Because success in client/server projects is principally defined as satisfied users, communication between the project team and users sets the tone of the entire project. Poor communication can defeat a project before it even starts. Failure to manage user expectations effectively will make it very difficult to satisfy them.

Project management suggestions:

▶ If you don't have sufficient project management skill, you must buy it. Don't settle for less than is needed.

▶ Provide opportunities for individual departments to take leadership in project tasks where consensus needs to be built.

▶ Define and execute a pilot or phase that will demonstrate early project success.

▶ Put in measures and incentives to encourage teamwork.

▶ Consider an external project management review board.

▶ Communicate. Communicate. Communicate.

IMPLEMENTATION IMPERATIVES: FOREWARNED IS FOREARMED

Client/server is not for the faint of heart; however, we are not trying to dissuade you from proceeding. The benefits of a successful client/server implementation can have a dramatic impact. When implementing an institutionwide client/server system in higher education, the critical success factors require you to:

▶ Ensure that business value is well-understood and agreed to by all stakeholders.

▶ Be willing to radically change the way you function.

▶ Plan and budget twice the training time and expense as your best estimate.

▶ Establish a robust and well-managed client/server infrastructure.

▶ Commission a project management team that effectively communicates with the user community.

The bottom line: Know your strengths, and address your weaknesses before the project uncovers them!

REFERENCES/SUGGESTED READINGS

The Gartner Group. (1994). *A guide for estimating client/server costs.* Client/Server Strategic Analysis Report, R-810-105.

Hammer, M., & Stanton, S. A. (1995). *The reengineering revolution.* New York, NY: HarperCollins.

IBM Consulting Group. (1994). *The IBM Consulting Group report on client/server.* White Plains, NY: IBM.

Kaplan, C., Clark R., & Tang, V. (1994). *Secrets of software quality: Forty innovations from IBM.* New York, NY: McGraw-Hill.

Langel, R. (1995). *Client/server: The 10% you need to know.* Costa Mesa, CA: IBM.

13

Designing Classrooms for the 21st Century

Kathryn L. Conway

Information technologies are increasingly digital, personal, and available on demand. The pace of technological change is no longer measured in years, but in months. Technology developers speak of time on the basis of "Web years" or three months chronologically. We are forever in a transitional mode, trying to assimilate new technological capabilities into our economic, cultural, and social systems as rapidly as they arise.

In this rapidly escalating environment of technological change, it would be useless to write a book that recommended equipment models and specifications. No matter what equipment you put into a classroom or building, it will not be state-of-the-art technology within two to three years of its purchase. What I will try to provide, instead, is practical advice for the process of designing a classroom. The goal is to summarize the fundamental issues in designing a learning environment and to suggest the framework for addressing these issues, thereby helping you create classroom facilities that are flexible and functional for years to come.

To design a classroom is to define its purpose. The clearer and more specific your definition of the purpose, the more functional your classroom will be. Whether you call them "electronic classrooms," "classrooms of the future," or "smart classrooms," any learning environment that incorporates technology requires careful analysis and planning to insure that it meets its functional requirements.

There is no ideal design or set of hardware for a high-tech classroom. This is because the fundamental driving force and unifying theme for designing classrooms is the activity that will take place there, not the technology we install in it. Obviously we want to select hardware and networking configurations that enable and support these activities, but the design of the electronic classroom does not start with the selection of the hardware.

For the last few years, people have sought to define electronic classrooms. Too often these were classrooms designed to accommodate state-of-the-art equipment but not state-of-the-art learning. The justification for the budgetary outlay required to renovate and equip these facilities usually involved the following:

▶ To provide leading edge technology for the foreseeable future

▶ To transform teaching

▶ To encourage innovation and infuse information technology into the curriculum

▶ To enable the institution to compete more aggressively to attract top students

▶ To reduce the cost of instructing and graduating more competitive, technology-literate students

Can a classroom full of hardware really do all these things? Experience suggests that it cannot. "The introduction of information technology has led to changes in the way the nearly universal standard classroom is used. However, simply replacing the classroom with an equally universal update, including computers, networking, and electronic presentation equipment, is unlikely to be possible" (Stuebing, 1994b).

Short (1994) describes the usual outcome of searching for the magic list of equipment in hopes that it will transform education by its sheer physical presence. "Perhaps the most common of the false trails is the quest to identify and acquire the hardware and software that will catapult the academy into the 21st century. The usual exercise is to secure funding and embark on a rigorous round of comparison shopping to squeeze as many model numbers and software titles out of the funding as possible. It is an exercise repeated at random intervals at virtually every campus in the country. Twelve to 18 months after the capital expenditure, what do we find? Countless clusters of PCs and Macs underutilized or used primarily for word processing. The real promise of instructional technology—the delivery of interactive course materials, self-paced mastery of basic skills, access to the rich array of networked databases and much else—remains elusive" (Short, 1994). So, hardware in itself cannot spark a learning revolution on your campus. But a well-planned and thoughtfully implemented learning environment could be a fundamental component of your institution's strategic plan. Let's examine the factors that transform a roomful of equipment into a functional learning environment.

CREATING A LEARNING ENVIRONMENT

A classroom is an intentional learning environment. All the participants come with a common objective. For centuries, the most common way for an instructor to teach students has been by giving lectures in classrooms. The educational strategy depended upon the ability of the teacher to transmit the appropriate knowledge directly to the student. It also depended upon the student's ability to listen, comprehend, and remember the knowledge provided by the instructor.

The difference in the classroom scenario described above and the classrooms that will be built tomorrow is in the students' learning activities. New perspectives on the learning process, teamed with new technologies, have created new opportunities, strategies, and options for the way students learn in the classroom. In fact, a classroom may not be necessary to put some of these strategies into practice. Educators look toward the computer lab to allow for:

▶ Student collaboration

▶ Project-based work

▶ Use of other tools, equipment (e.g., robotics and other control equipment), books, or paper

▶ Visual connection between the computer lab and other related study areas (Stuebing, 1994b)

Teachers may give students group or individual projects as well as research that they must complete outside of class. Increasingly, analogous activities are taking place inside the classroom. Today's classroom is becoming much more than a meeting place. Tomorrow's classrooms will become more complex learning environments, because tomorrow's classrooms will be part of an integrated human and technological system that enables students to learn in a more dynamic and participatory way.

Learner-Centered Education

The traditional, lecture-based model of teaching is predicated on the transfer of ideas and information from the teacher to the student. It is a transmissive process in which the student receives the ideas or products of others' knowledge, along with selected facts, and reassembles these mentally to create knowledge for him or herself. Carol Twigg dramatically points out the difference between the roles of teacher and student in this model and the emergent learner-centered model.

> Right now, teachers stand in front of a group and convey information that new technologies will soon enable kids to get and interact with themselves. Kids simply learn best when they teach themselves and each other, and this may necessitate a different role for teachers. ... To do this, teachers have to stop teaching and get out of the way of student work; they have to stop thinking they're conveying information and, instead, focus on strategies to help students learn (Twigg, 1995).

Constructive and Participatory Learning

Increasingly the lecture-based learning model is being replaced by a more active and creative process, one in which teachers plan learning strategies, design activities, and guide students through the process of creating knowledge for themselves. The learners are often asked to collaborate or work in teams to accomplish these activities. They may discuss or critique each other's work in addition to receiving feedback from their instructor.

In contrast to earlier learning models that used computers for drill and response, the current trend is toward using computers, networking, and multimedia technology to create multidimensional "microworlds" through which the learners explore and learn while interacting in the social context of specific "communities of practice." Lewis Perelman explains the basis for changing technology's role in the learning process: "The success of these programs stems from applying the lesson of extensive cognitive science findings: Knowledge and skill are acquired most effectively when learning takes place in the 'context' where it is to be applied to solving problems that have real value and meaning" (Perelman, 1995).

Multiple Activities, Multiple Focal Points

Even when the emphasis is on an active, constructive approach to learning, there may be lectures and discussion. The difference is that the lecture component takes a smaller proportion of time in the overall mix of learning activities. Because there are multiple kinds of activities, there are usually multiple focal points. The studio classrooms at Rensselaer Polytechnic Institute (described later in this chapter) are a good example of this. Of course, multiple activities make multiple demands for flexibility in classroom design. Research on these settings indicates that with this change, there is also a need:

▶ For an additional floor area within the room

▶ To consider the physical setting as an important component to enhance collaboration and project-based work

▶ To offer teachers support to reorganize the typical classroom organization (Stuebing, 1994a)

Learning Styles

Another change in our perception of learning involves learning styles. Howard Gardner gave us the concept of multiple types of intelligences or learning styles. He identified seven different types of intelligences, or styles—verbal, mathematical/abstract, musical, visual, kinesthetic, interpersonal, and intrapersonal (Gardner, 1985). Carol Twigg also notes a revealing finding in the Myers-Briggs typology of learners. "The largest group of college students consists of concrete-active learners, who learn best from concrete experiences that engage their senses, that begin with practice and end with theory . . . while the majority of college faculty prefer the IN (abstract reflective) pattern, creating an increasing disparity between teacher and learner" (Twigg, 1994). This information supports not only the use of more active learning strategies, but the use of multiple media as well. Providing information and learning challenges that use multiple approaches, examples, and media gives students the flexibility to choose the learning mode that works best for them.

Student Mobile Computing

Student mobile computing is a term used to denote the personal ownership of portable computers and their use in different environments such as home, school, the workplace, and in places and times in between these destinations. Student mobile computing creates a number of challenges to facility designers. The nomadic use of technology means that areas not previously considered part of the instructional environment, such as cafeterias, lounges, hallways, and even some exterior locations, require network and electrical connections. Providing that same level of connectivity to each student in the classroom creates dilemmas: Bringing network connections and power to each student seat without creating a maze of wires along the floors and walls of existing facilities is difficult. Wireless networks hold promise, but currently cannot provide the necessary bandwidth for transmitting digital media and other high bandwidth applications.

Distributed On-line Learning

In the future, will we even need classrooms or the campus itself? In many cases the answer is that we will not need classrooms or campuses in order for students and teachers to communicate and interact. There are compelling reasons for today's adult students to seek learning opportunities that do not require them to go to a campus or classroom. The near ubiquity of computers and Internet connectivity creates a very different world of options for these students, as well as for many educational institutions. The use of the World Wide Web as a resource and a platform for creating virtual learning environments is one example. The options are multiplying yearly. A fundamental question for classroom designers is: What can be done best in the (face-to-face) classroom environment, and what can be done best in the (virtual, or asynchronous) on-line environment?

Focus on Learning

Designing a classroom that facilitates learner-centered instructional strategies is different from designing a classroom for teaching. It is not what the teacher does but what he or she gets students to do that results in learning (Glick, 1990). We might say that the major difference between yesterday's classrooms and tomorrow's classrooms comes down to this: Yesterday's classrooms were defined by what the teacher did; tomorrow's classrooms will be defined by what the learner does. John Seely Brown (1993) suggests the challenge of designing technological systems for these learner-centered environments: "We find it quite difficult to address these questions—not because it is impossible to build technology to support learning, but because that is a different problem from building technology for teaching." Clearly, this approach to learning environments presents complex demands to technology designers.

DESIGN ISSUES

When designing classrooms that must enable and support a variety of learning activities, it is helpful to visualize what the students and instructors will be doing within the classroom space. Describe the activities that will take place. Answer questions such as:

▶ What will the students be doing physically?

▶ What tools and materials will the students need to use?

▶ How will students be interacting with each other?

▶ Will students be working individually, in pairs, or in small groups?

▶ How will they interact with the instructor?

▶ What kind of information will they need to access?

▶ Do the students have any special or unusual characteristics that should be taken into account?

▶ Do the students really have to be in the same place at the same time to do what you want them to do?

▶ Could you consider moving this activity out of the classroom, perhaps to be done individually, or collaboratively through on-line discussions?

Answering questions such as these will help you to define the range of activities and to describe the types of spaces that will accommodate them. *Campus Classroom Connections* (Stuebing, 1994b), a case study guide of higher education facilities, provides the following list of potential elements in your educational strategy for facility design:

FIGURE 13.1

Elements to Consider when Strategizing a Facility Design		
TYPE OF EDUCATIONAL DELIVERY	TEACHING METHODS	OTHER
Lecture	Collaboration	Number of students
Lab or other hands-on experiences	Teamwork	Size of spaces
Long distance	Individual	Nature of spaces
Electronic network	Lecture	Services
Database	Inquiry	
Video	Project-based	
Audio		
Mixed mode		

Hardware and Software

The selection and implementation of software and hardware is where instructional strategies are translated into learning activities. Learning activities must be defined in terms of the tools and resources necessary for successful participation. Decisions must be made about minimal hardware requirements such as operating system, memory, hard drive capacity, processor speed, media capabilities, necessary peripherals, display size and resolution, and CD-ROM drive speed. Appropriate drivers must be provided for all the peripherals and special equipment which may need to be connected to students' machines.

Many students want to bring their computers into the classroom and connect them to the campus network. As we design new facilities and classrooms, we must be cognizant of the need to provide nearly ubiquitous network connectivity for students and their computers while on campus.

There are five basic hardware components in most learning environments:

1) Network infrastructure (your building, classroom, or departmental intranet)

2) Computer(s)

3) Multimedia devices

4) Display or projection system

5) Control system

The software used in these facilities is often customized as well and plays a significant role in the instructional function of the classroom. In fact, in any technology-rich learning environment, the software is often the active ingredient in the mix. It is the software or courseware which allows the students to actualize their learning or create knowledge through their learning activities. This element of the learning environment is often less obvious than the hardware itself, but it can be more challenging and just as expensive (in terms of human resources) as the hardware.

Physical Characteristics of the Facility

Students and teachers must be able to see, hear, and participate in what is going on. They must have reasonably comfortable seats, sufficient space in which to work, and tools with which to communicate. There must be temperature controls and sufficient ventilation to keep the equipment working and the students comfortable. Above all, the physical characteristics of the room should facilitate and not distract from any of the learning activities required of students. A desk or chair may be very low on the technology chain, but an uncomfortable seat can prevent a student from concentrating on higher order activities. The lack of a whiteboard marker can prevent a teacher from reinforcing an important point visually. A stuffy, hot room can make everyone miserable and inattentive. First, eliminate all possible environmental distractions by making sure that each of the physical elements is optimized for the types of activities that will occur in the facility.

The nature of the learning activities affects many physical dimensions of the room, including spatial requirements, lighting levels, acoustical treatment, material selection, access conditions, and degree of overall spatial flexibility (Stuebing, Martin, Wolfshondl, & Cousineau, 1992). In considering these requirements you should take into account the following physical characteristics of the facility.

Capacity. When calculating the seating capacity, be sure to provide enough for building code requirements for entrance and egress, for easy movement within the room, and for flexible seating arrangements.

Seating workspace for each student. Depending on the type of activity, students may need room for books and supplementary materials, paired collaborative activities, resources and reference materials, team or small group discussion, experiments, digitization of multimedia materials, etc.

Furniture selection and configuration. The layout of the desks determines the teaching methods available. No matter what layout is selected, it is important to recognize that each student requires a certain amount of desk space for the tools used and a certain amount of floor space, leg space, and elbow room to perform required functions and enter and leave the classroom safely (Stengel, 1996).

Placement. When choosing furniture, you have several options for the placement of computer equipment: on top of the work surface, recessed within the work surface or desktop, or placed completely below a transparent desktop.

Ergonomics. Careful choice of a student chair is an important decision, because it determines many of the ergonomic characteristics of the work space. Important attributes for the classroom workstation chair are flexibility in height adjustment, back tilt to adjust eye-to-monitor distance, durability and stability, and a seat and back design that is sufficiently broad to suit most body types (Stengel, 1996).

Data, video, and communications wiring. The network wiring infrastructure is the lifeline for any technology-intensive learning environment. It would be difficult to overstate the importance of your network design to the functionality of your learning environment. The critical decisions you must make about the network concern conduit size/capacity, topology (physical design), physical medium (fiber, copper, wireless, etc.), and speed or bandwidth.

Electrical wiring (power supply and distribution). Your facilities should have sufficient circuits and power to operate all the equipment and systems they contain. The outlets should be located convenient to various equipment which must be operated. In some cases surge protectors or backup power supplies may be necessary.

Acoustical treatment. In larger rooms audio amplification may be necessary. In others, acoustical treatment such as acoustic panels, carpeting, upholstered seats, or electronic echo-canceling systems may be required to reduce the reverberation or audio feedback within a room or audio system.

Lighting control (window treatment, dimmers, etc.). Conducting multiple activities in a room requires the ability to adjust the light at any given time to provide more or less light on a given area, to provide light in either a direct or diffuse manner, and to control glare from a variety of surfaces such as the monitor, the desktop, whiteboards, etc.

HVAC (heating, ventilation, and air conditioning). Microcomputers and related equipment generate quite a bit of heat in addition to that of the people using them. Rooms housing a concentration of equipment place a heavier demand on building HVAC systems than do regular meeting rooms.

Security measures and systems. These can include options such as room motion detectors and alarms, surveillance cameras, equipment locks, installing equipment in locked cabinets or racks, keypad or magnetic card controlled electronic door locks, etc.

Control system for equipment and room lights. Integrated control systems can simplify the operation of a classroom and reduce the confusion faculty members feel when confronted with the multiple options and controls for a room full of equipment. These systems are available in wired and wireless versions. Most systems are modular and software-configurable so that equipment can be added, removed, or upgraded at any time. Interfaces for equipment control systems can be manipulated by remote control devices, touch-screen panels, or physical knobs and controls. Some systems also support multiple control configurations so that different users can each have a software-configurable, customized control interface tailored to their particular needs or preferences.

CLASSROOM MODELS

There are several methods for allocating different types of classroom functionality on a campus. Some use technology-based learning suites in which several classrooms are located adjacent to each other, each having a different configuration and/or capacity, and suited for a different teaching or learning mode (Stuebing, 1994a; Manuel & Quest, 1988). In a case like this, students move from room to room to participate in different learning activities for the same course. A typical example of this is meeting in an auditorium for a large lecture session, breaking up into smaller classroom groupings for discussions, and working individually in a laboratory to complete a lab requirement. At the other extreme, there are classrooms which accommodate a wide variety of equipment so that many different types of courses can be taught in them. And there are specialized classrooms that are scheduled on an ad hoc or as needed basis for a class session. The particular strategy used by a campus often has more to do with the historical policies for owning and scheduling classrooms than it does with academic planning.

Although there is no one magic classroom design that meets all the instructional needs on a campus, there are several generic configurations. The teacher-centered models generally use technology to enhance the lecture-based course. Often these types of facilities will not have computers for the students. There will usually be one or two (depending on the number of operating systems supported) computers available and connected to the network and a projection system. The instructor typically uses a computer for presentations, simulations, demonstrations, etc. Of course, a student or visiting speaker might also use the computer. In some cases students may have their own computer stations in the classroom, but the classroom is still used to support a lecture. In this instance, the computers tend to be used for polling the students about the course, taking notes, etc. When a classroom is used in this way, it is still a teacher-centered application since the teacher is the one who has access to the technology and determines access to information. Learner-centered facilities have computers and network connections for the students and generally focus on team or collaborative exercises in the classroom or extensive use of courseware.

There are many terms being used to denote a physical learning environment that integrates information technology as a significant part of the instructional strategy. Terms such as "electronic classroom," "classroom of the future," "high tech classroom," and even "virtual classroom" have no standard definition.

In this document we are using several terms such as "master" or "multi-media" classroom, "computer classroom," and "teleclassroom" which will consistently refer to a particular set of technological capabilities. We will also describe examples of a basic computer classroom which has been customized for a particular campus's pedagogical strategy (i.e., the University of Maryland's "Teaching Theaters" and Rensselaer's "Studio Classroom").

Computer Lab

Some people use the terms "computer classroom" and "computer lab" interchangeably. We will use these as two different terms indicating different learning approaches.

The term computer lab indicates a facility that is generally used in the context of an individualized instructional strategy rather than a group one. That is, the students go into the lab at varying times and at any given moment different students in the lab will be doing different things. Some students may use the lab in lieu of purchasing their own computer; they may use the lab for applications such as word processing. Some students may have assigned exercises from a course or may be doing optional work. Arrangement of the machines is not as critical in a computer lab, because there is no need for a common focal point (a projected image) if no group instruction is being conducted.

Computer Classroom

By contrast, in a computer classroom a common focal point or projection surface is usually provided. The focal point may shift as activities change. When the students are listening to a lecture, watching a demonstration or discussing a topic among the group, everyone is usually facing the common focal point (e.g., a projection screen at the front of the room or, perhaps, the teacher). When the students are working individually or collaboratively at their computers, they will be focused on the computer and any adjacent equipment.

A very practical arrangement for a computer classroom is to have the students facing outward, away from the front of the room so that the teacher can easily move around behind the students and observe or stop to give a student some help. This works well when the activity involves using software or courseware in some learning activity, as opposed to trying to learn to use the software itself.

The typical configuration for a training facility, on the other hand, is to have all the students facing forward, toward the teacher when they are facing their machines. This way the students can easily shift focus between their monitor and the projected image or the teacher at the front of the room.

This is a typical scenario for training students to use software. Because it is more difficult for the teacher to move around to each student's station in this kind of set up, there will often be an assistant or additional person to move among the students, looking over their shoulders and offering assistance when needed.

The computer classroom includes all the multimedia presentation capabilities and connectivity of the master classroom while also providing workstations for individual students or student teams. The addition of machines for the students increases the cost, requires the internal networking of the classroom machines, and necessitates selection of a room and furniture configuration appropriate for the learning activities and their focal points within the room. Depending on the nature of the learning activities, peripheral equipment such as printers, scanners, scientific, or other equipment may need to be in the classroom.

Master/Multimedia Classrooms

Master classrooms integrate a wide range of computer, media, projection, communications, and control capabilities, including connections to the campus network for data reception and transmission. The master classroom is different from a computer classroom or laboratory in that it does not have individual computers for each student, but has a single computer that can be used by either a teacher or student(s) for presentations, demonstrations, simulations, on-line access, multimedia, etc.

The teacher has real-time access to text and multimedia databases, courseware, software tools of all sorts, simulations, supercomputers, on-line services, electronic mail—any resource accessible over campus and regional data networks—as well as Internet resources and the World Wide Web. The classroom can also receive live instructional events—workshops, satellite teleconferences, foreign language newscasts, teleconferencing of visiting lecturers—as well as the more traditional film and video materials via video feeds from either on- or off-campus.

Equipment costs for a master classroom are relatively predictable and inelastic. The primary variables (as the room size and seating capacity changes) are projector characteristics and screen size. The equipment (including control interface) costs about one-fifth the cost of the typical small computer lab/classroom. Therefore, master classrooms are a relatively cost-effective means of integrating computing and communications power into a teacher-centered learning environment. A master or multimedia classroom can also be used as a transition strategy between teacher-centered and learner-centered environments if the initial planning provides sufficient spatial and networking flexibility to accommodate computer workstations for the students (or wiring to accommodate their mobile computers) at a later time. The initial investment in equipment for the master classroom is not wasted since the same components would be necessary in a computer classroom or studio classroom.

Laptop-Enabled Classroom

The laptop-enabled classroom is essentially a traditional classroom or a master classroom which is wired (or outfitted for wireless network transmission) so that students may bring their own portable computers into the classroom and connect to the classroom and/or campus network. There must also be sufficient power and outlets for students to plug their laptops into the building electrical supply rather than rely on internal battery power for their machines.

The laptop-enabled classroom can function as either a teacher-centered or learner-centered environment, depending on what the students actually do with their laptops in the classroom. Because these rooms tend to be used for traditional lecture style courses when students do not have their own laptops, the configuration is typically the same as for a lecture classroom.

Retrofitting traditional classrooms for laptop connectivity is not a trivial matter, since there is usually no conduit in the necessary places to run network and power connections to each of the student ports. This can result in a messy improvisation of cabling along the floors and walls of rooms. Wireless systems are available and require a special card in each student's machine to enable them to receive and transmit data. At this time wireless systems do not have sufficient robustness to support multimedia and other high bandwidth applications.

Studio Classroom

Technologically, the studio classroom is a form of computer classroom. The primary difference is in the nature of the peripheral equipment and the way it is used with the computer and specialized software. A studio classroom is essentially a computer classroom that has input devices or other specialized peripherals or software which allows students to generate or work with authentic data within the discipline they are studying. The studio classroom is a good example of a pedagogical approach that combines collaborative effort with participatory and situated learning.

Rensselaer Polytechnic Institute pioneered the use of studio classrooms to reengineer the way they taught their physics courses (Wilson, 1997). Previously, Rensselaer faculty taught large sections (700+ students) of physics in the lecture/laboratory/recitation format. For their studio classrooms, they designed computer classrooms to accommodate about 60 students working in pairs at 30 computers. Various types of input devices were connected to the computers to enable the students to do their laboratory exercises in the classroom using the computer and the Comprehensive Unified Physics Learning Environment (CUPLE) software. The CUPLE software provided students with interactive learning activities custom-designed for their curriculum and classroom (Wilson, 1997).

Teaching Theater

The teaching theater is another variation of the computer classroom. The term teaching theater is one used by the University of Maryland at College Park for two customized facilities on their campus. As with any computer classroom, there are computer stations on which the students work either individually or in pairs. The distinction between Maryland's teaching theaters and other computer classrooms is principally in the software; the facilities combine a variety of synchronous and asynchronous communications capabilities. Some courses use the teaching theaters for lecture enhancement while others use the classrooms for more participatory learning activities. Each of their teaching theaters accommodates 40 students at 20 computer stations. The classrooms feature a variety of multimedia capabilities as well as notetaking and collaborative communications software. Since student notes are stored on a server connected to the campus network, students can access their notes from any computer that has network access. Some of the collaborative applications provide access from outside the classroom, allowing the network to support both face-to-face and asynchronous learning activities for the students. Similarly, one of the classrooms is equipped with video conferencing capabilities so that students in the teaching theater can meet with students or teachers at other locations.

Teleclassroom

Teleclassrooms come with many different appellations and a variety of media configurations. Basically, we are using the term teleclassroom to denote classrooms which are equipped with some form of live video and audio communications capability so that individuals or groups at different physical locations can meet together in virtual proximity provided by the video and audio links. The video links may be one-way or two-way. In a one-way link, the video of individual(s) at the originating site is transmitted to individuals at all the other sites (the receiving or distant sites). Audio links typically go among all the sites, because audio can be originated and switched less expensively than video. Two-way systems provide for origination of video and audio from all sites.

Teleclassrooms vary widely in the type and configuration of equipment as well as the means of video and audio transmission. Video transmission requires very high bandwidth compared to the bandwidth required for typical data communications. For that reason, digitally compressed video may be used to send the video and audio over a smaller bandwidth medium, thereby reducing the cost.

Courses in teleclassrooms usually occur in real time; i. e., everyone is participating at the same time even though they are not physically at the same location. A variety of auxiliary technologies can be used in conjunction with teleclassrooms. Analog media such as video, slides, graphic images, etc. can be used as well as digital media such as computer graphics and a variety of outputs from a personal computer. The primary use of teleclassrooms is to provide virtual proximity for individuals who cannot come to a common location to meet together. The virtual proximity of the teleclassroom contrasts with the social proximity provided by the virtual classroom.

Virtual Classroom

The virtual classroom is not a physical classroom at all. It is a form of asynchronous communication (i.e., not in real time) enabled by the use of computers interconnected over a network. It is a classroom made out of software and network connections rather than out of bricks and mortar. Computers connected to the Internet or other common servers can be used to communicate asynchronously with others at any time of the day or night. This provides a flexible and convenient way for students who cannot (or don't want to) go to a campus or other classroom at a specified time to participate in courses. Using groupware such as Lotus Notes, the World Wide Web, or electronic lists and bulletin boards, students are able to interact with each other and the instructor. Just as e-mail lets people communicate or work with each other without having to be on-line at the same time, groupware or collaborative communications software can be used by groups of students and teachers to communicate at their own convenience.

Unlike the virtual proximity provided by teleclassrooms, virtual classrooms enable social proximity. Students can interact from many different physical locations and at different times. Because the available time is not limited to a typical class period, there is much more opportunity for each student to participate. The window of opportunity is now 24 hours a day, seven days a week, instead of three hours a week. The opportunity for interaction provided by asynchronous communications can be used for class discussions, group project coordination, role playing, student critiques of each other's work, instructor feedback, on-line debates, homework submission, or collaborative writing. The possibilities are virtually unlimited.

PLANNING, BUDGETING, AND SUPPORT CONSIDERATIONS

Planning

Do not assume that your architect, physical plant personnel, facility planner, or even your technical support staff know how to design a classroom to meet your needs without your input. They will all understand a given aspect of the facility you need, but in most cases, no one individual has the breadth of experience to integrate all the requirements for a successful classroom. Each person tends to see the project from the perspective that he or she has. In other words, while your technical staff may solve the technical problems quite elegantly, they may not address the pedagogical issues. To get a facility that really does what you need it to, you must integrate solutions to both the pedagogical and the technological challenges. In these circumstances, the instructional strategies must drive the technological choices. Due to the complexity of the task, facility planners increasingly suggest that a multidisciplinary team be involved in the planning process. The team may include educators, administrators, facility managers, architects, and technology providers (Stuebing, 1994a).

Unfortunately too many educators leave the instructional decisions until the end of the building process—often until after the building is finished. This is the most expensive way to design your classrooms. No matter how recently a facility was completed, it will always be more expensive to retrofit the technology than it would have been to design and implement it from the beginning. Effective planning is critical to containing costs and optimizing the functionality of your technology-intensive learning environments.

Budgeting

Project your up-front and longer-term costs for facilities. Facility cost is traditionally evaluated on the basis of first cost, operation and maintenance cost (O&M), and the cost of changes or adaptations of the design. Since generations of technology change so quickly, adaptation becomes a large factor in the cost equation. Computer hardware and software may need to be replaced every two to three years (Oberlin, 1996). A replacement schedule for equipment should be considered in your annual equipment and maintenance budget. Equipment maintenance and facility alteration costs are frequently underestimated or ignored. Costs for additional staff to maintain networks and other technical equipment are often overlooked when planning the technology-rich facility (Stuebing, 1994a).

The capital cost of equipping learning facilities is usually obvious because it is itemized and budgeted separately from other building costs.

Don't ignore the less obvious technology-related expenses that contribute to overall facility cost. These include:

▶ Networking

▶ Site services such as excavation and placement of conduit for networking

▶ Additional demand on ventilation and air conditioning systems (from computers and related hardware)

▶ Zoning of heating and air conditioning systems

▶ More specialized lighting requirements

▶ Larger, more reliable electrical services that may take a greater percentage of the total cost of the building

▶ Security systems

▶ Built-in casework or furnishings that accommodate particular learning activities (Stuebing, 1994a)

Support

You should have a migration strategy for helping your faculty obtain the knowledge, skills, and resources necessary for using technology in new ways in the classroom. A migration strategy should take into account the types of materials, media, technology, and activities faculty are currently using in their classrooms as well as the facilities and support personnel that will be needed for transferring information and materials into digital media.

Bear in mind that technology-intensive classrooms usually create a need for more and different types of support facilities. "The use of information technology in teaching and learning requires increased teacher support and professional development. At the same time, new materials are required such as software, videos, and other multimedia and database materials. Expertise and maintenance requirements also suggest the potential needs for educational support centers" (Stuebing, 1994b). These resources and services must be available to teachers for them to rethink and redesign their approach to teaching.

There are significant resource and organizational challenges in supporting technology-intensive learning environments. The cost of training, professional development, and support services for faculty and staff is generally the greatest expense in using information technology in higher education.

Rethinking your pedagogical and technological strategies may necessitate reengineering your support services and organizational structure as well.

Miller (1992) suggests that, "... institutions should think about how to organize their ... development and media resources to allow for more flexible combinations of media as required by individual programs." This often requires consolidating or restructuring support services which previously operated independently of each other. In many institutions, the media center or learning resources staff, computing support staff, and the telecommunications support staff have been incorporated into a single information technology support structure.

Restructuring your support services is not easy. Media support personnel, microcomputer user services personnel, and mainframe support staff generally have worked in different organizational cultures which interpret their role in relation to instruction in significantly different ways. It is important to find inclusive models for integrating divergent support staff. Otherwise turf wars and games of technological one-upmanship can interfere with the real work at hand.

CONCLUSION

Any learning environment is a complex system mixing both human and technological elements. Remember, the foundation of any learning experience is what happens in the learner, not what happens with the technology. Technology is a tool, an enabler, a way of facilitating a variety of interactions between the learner, other learners, teachers, and information. It is a tool for creating and communicating knowledge. The driving force in any classroom—whether virtual or concrete—is the human activity and interaction that constitute the learning experience. If we design our classrooms and learning environments around those experiences, we will be using technology appropriately to create state-of-the-art learning.

REFERENCES/SUGGESTED READINGS

Brown, J. S., & Dugruid, P. (1993, March). Stolen knowledge. *Educational Technology,* 10-15.

Gardner, H. (1985). *Frames of mind.* New York, NY: Basic Books.

Glick, M. (1990). Integrating computing into higher education: An administrator's view. *EDUCOM Review, 25* (2), 35-38.

Manuel, S., & Quest, J. D. (1988, July). Computer class: Curriculum and environment interact. *AS&U,* 22-23.

Miller, G. (1992). Long-term trends in distance education. *DEOSNEWS, 2* (23). http://www.ede.psu.edu/ACSDE/DEOS.html.

Oberlin, J. L. (1996). The financial mythology of information technology: Developing a new game plan. *CAUSE/EFFECT, 19* (2), 10-17.

Perelman, L. (1995). The future of technology in education. *Multimedia Today, 3* (4), 10-21.

Short, D. (1994). *Enhancing instructional effectiveness: A strategic approach.* White Plains, NY: IBM.

Stengel, P. (1996, May 15). *Computers in the classroom—Space planning and furniture design issues.* URL: http://www.clark.net/pub/peter/cidesi1.htm#top.

Stuebing, S. (1994a). *Campus classroom connections.* Newark, NJ: New Jersey Institute of Technology.

Stuebing, S. (1994b). *Redefining the place to learn.* Newark, NJ: New Jersey Institute of Technology.

Stuebing, S., Martin, E., Wolfshorndl, A., & Cousineau, L. (1992). *School design notebook: Case study analysis of exemplary schools.* Newark, NJ: New Jersey Institute of Technology.

Twigg, C. A. (1994). The changing definition of learning. *EDUCOM Review, 29* (4), 23-25.

Twigg, C. A. (1995). The future of technology in education. *Multimedia Today, 3* (4), 10-21.

Staff. (1993, Fall). No more pencils, no more books, no more teachers' dirty looks. *ChAPTER One: The AIChE Magazine for Students, 7,* 50-53.

Wilson, J. M. (1997). Reengineering the undergraduate curriculum. In D. G. Oblinger & S. C. Rush (Eds.), *The learning revolution: The challenge of information technology in the academy.* Bolton, MA: Anker.

14

Prepare Today for the Digital Library of Tomorrow

Richard P. Hulser

Throughout their history, libraries have played many important roles in archiving, information retrieval, and knowledge dissemination. There are many reasons for wanting to use technology in libraries: to improve the quality of services they offer, to provide new types of service, and to overcome some of the problems with which libraries are faced. Problems confronting libraries include the following:

▶ The information explosion

▶ Handling the new forms that knowledge can take, such as multimedia and hypermedia

▶ Ensuring the security of information

▶ Provision of access control

▶ Facilitating efficient and effective sharing of information

▶ Maintaining copyright protection

▶ Providing help and assistance for library users (Barker, 1994)

If knowledge is power, then leveraging the volume and nature of information is critical to higher education. With the library's critical information role, the first step is to be sure the library is integrated into any strategic plans. In addition, faculty, students, and administrators will need new capabilities to manage information as institutions migrate toward a digital environment. The emergence of vast, distributed repositories of educational materials will necessitate new capabilities for storing, searching, retrieving, and managing digital information.

INFORMATION TECHNOLOGY STRATEGIC PLANNING

Before attempting to implement a digital library, it is important to have an information technology plan. As discussed in other chapters of this book, such a plan enables the appropriate implementation of information technology for current and future needs in alignment with the mission and goals of an institution. Those responsible for information management at an institution, such as librarians and information managers, must ask themselves a number of questions:

▶ What are the current information services and resource requirements of the people at my institution?

▶ How do the current services and resources provided by my organization, including the use of technology, address those needs?

▶ What information services are needed to support the mission?

▶ What are the minimum information services that can be provided based on the particular context (money, people, space, etc.)?

▶ What are the priorities of the services provided?

Alignment with Mission

At one institution, for example, it was determined that supporting students in distance education programs required the ability to deliver information stored as physical reserves in the library to the students in electronic form with the same ease afforded students on campus. An assessment had to be made as to whether this service was central to the mission of the institution and of the library services organization. Once it was determined to be essential, an analysis of current operations and procedures was done to understand how best to carry out this service.

A process was devised to minimize the long-term impact on faculty and library staff when making such materials available. A scanning area was created near the library reserve desk where library staff worked with faculty to digitize reference materials. Although the initial implementation took many weeks, refinements were made to the process that reduced turnaround time to just a few hours. The results were highly successful due to careful assessment, planning, and alignment with the institution's priorities.

Trends in Information Technology

Information technology trends should be considered in tandem with short-term needs assessments. Planning for applications of technology should include an understanding of how much information can be transferred in a short amount of time, as well as how much storage capacity is needed for the variety of information to be stored digitally. For instance, it is possible to transmit close to 1.2 gb (gigabits) of information over a network with 1997 capabilities. This is roughly equivalent to 85 books or 39,000 pages of text per second. This speed of transmission also can support scientific visualization. Compare this to the capabilities available in 1989 when transmission speeds enabled a mere two pages per second to be sent across a network. If today's technology plan was based on the transmission speeds of 1989, that technology plan would be sadly inadequate.

High network transmission speeds are imperative in moving large amounts of digitally stored information, especially high resolution color images and video. Consider, for example, how much information can be stored in one terabyte (1 tb) or one million megabytes (1,000,000 mb):

- 300,000,000 pages of text

- 20,000,000 pages of scanned documents

- 1,000,000 pages of scanned color images

- 100,000 medical X-rays

- 1,800 hours of CD-quality audio

- 500 hours of good quality video

- 250 movies

To transfer 1 tb of text would require approximately 128 minutes, or over two hours using the fastest transmission speed (1.2 gb/second) available in test laboratories today (1997). Even with today's technology, the transfer of information across a network can still take time. In addition, consider the operating reliability of a network; such transmissions need to occur accurately. Most of us have experienced the frustration of losing an Internet or World Wide Web connection which interrupted a download process and required starting the process again. Without reliable networks, undue effort and network traffic will be consumed with repeated transfers of information.

The rapid advances in transmission technologies, along with increases in reliability of networks, will significantly reduce the time and increase the effectiveness of such transmissions. This is important, for example, when providing interactive information access in support of distance learning.

Physical Resource Issues

Books are not going away. Contrary to popular belief, print and other analog information will persist. Everything is not on-line, nor will it be soon. It is naive to assume that buildings will no longer be necessary or that everything will be stored and available on-line. Neither of these assumptions is valid. One way to test such assumptions is to make a list of the materials often used locally by a particular academic department, as well as information materials requested on loan or as photocopies from other institutions. A determination of how many of them are available (or are soon to be available) in digital form should then be made. It may be that a large percentage of the materials are yet to be made available in electronic form. Thus, storage of and access to materials in print and other nondigital forms will be needed in combination with the implementation of digitally stored information.

Legacy Systems

Application systems which are already in use, such as integrated library systems, are often referred to as legacy systems. These should be assessed on their capability to meet new functional needs (e.g., management and delivery of digital multimedia), as well as their capability to be upgraded to meet such needs.

Consider a university where the collection of books and other materials are currently managed by an integrated, automated library system. This system has been in place for several years, with regular maintenance upgrades applied to the installed system, along with some enhancements as new products have become available from the system vendor. This university is now assessing incorporation of a digital library of high resolution images from archival materials and one of electronic reserves with their current library system. While use of the 856 fields of the MARC record enables them to achieve access to these electronic materials through the library system, this connection does not enable the system to take full advantage of advanced search and rights management technologies. Such capability will require significant investment in programming by either the university or the library system vendor. As a result, the university is analyzing alternative systems to explore the technological and financial feasibility and timeliness of moving to a new library system with these advanced capabilities. Another option is to work with the current vendor toward enhancing their existing system.

Centralization Versus Decentralization

Assessment of the appropriateness of centralized and decentralized technology and support is needed. The move toward decentralized computing services (using client/server technology, for instance) has many benefits. However, it may be more efficient and effective to have some management and support of technology centralized at an institution. Costs, in long-term support and maintenance, should be considered in addition to the short-term expenses of hardware, software, and installation.

Outsourcing

Outsourcing of management, support, and even services has been done in a variety of ways in higher education. Libraries have often outsourced the retrospective conversion of card catalogs into electronic form, as well as outsourced article delivery services through contracts with commercial and nonprofit information providers. This is relatively common in today's information management environment. In the emerging digital library world, there are more possibilities for paying for access instead of paying for ownership and obtaining information from a source external to the institution.

Human Resource Issues

Changing role of information professionals. Higher expectations by library and information systems users of what is acceptable information access and service are part of the reason for the changes in the role of information professionals. The information professional's role could be that of information provider, mediator, facilitator, or maintainer of a repository, or some combination of these roles.

Training. Information professionals have always been service providers, but the advent of many new technologies for information access and retrieval requires new skills and knowledge. It is not unusual to have a staff with varied knowledge of and experience with technology. In addition, new technical skills are required of staff already employed by an institution, as well as of potential new hires into the organization. Thus, more frequent training—both formal and informal—is needed in order to keep up with technological advances.

How much time or budget should be allocated for training? A rule of thumb used by many organizations is that each employee or staff member should have at least 40 hours of education and training each year. Such training could be formal, such as a one-week class, or based on informal, self-paced instruction. Attendance at professional or technical conferences and seminars also can be considered part of training and professional development.

Based on the extent, methods, and places of education and training needed, a budget can be devised to support it. An alternative way to allocate education and training funds is to analyze training programs at peer institutions or at organizations implementing similar technology projects, even if outside the academic arena.

For institutions assessing incorporation of a digital library with their current integrated library system, the assessment of current staff programming, maintenance, and other technology skills should be matched against short-term and long-term needs. Does the current staff have skills in client/server technology? If not, will training position them to be capable of handling such technology or would a gradual turnover of staff be more appropriate?

Addressing people issues in the changing world brought about by technology is not enough. The leadership of the institution must have vision, while giving consistent support to initiatives to accomplish that vision, particularly in relation to adoption of information technology into the mainstream of institutional operations. Therefore, continuing education in the use and management of information technology for these leaders, as well as their staffs, should occur on a regular basis.

Organizational Issues

Organizational structures and cooperation are among the people issues of strategic planning. Beware of the empire builders and maintainers, as they may block moves to incorporate information technology with current or future requirements. It is also helpful to assess current organizational structures and management techniques to determine whether a hierarchical or a team structure is most effective in addressing identified needs.

There is a variety of organizational structures and changes being tried by academic institutions as they grapple with technology implementation. Several colleges and universities have consolidated computer services, the library, telecommunications, and other information-related services under a chief information officer or chief technology officer. However, in most cases the management hierarchy has been maintained rather than transformed. The failure or success of this type of organization has not yet been determined.

Creation of formal and informal teams to tackle issues and provide services on a temporary or permanent basis also should be considered.

Interdepartmental cooperation across the institution is imperative to achieving success, as is cooperation within a department.

Policies and Procedural Issues

Strategic planning must also address policies and procedures. There is increasing emphasis on information access instead of ownership as well as on paying for access rather than paying for ownership. Careful assessment should be made of what materials need to be provided locally and which ones can be obtained from other sources, as needed. This enables an organization to do some things differently instead of doing more with less.

Budget planning should include requirements for probable upgrades or outright replacement of technology-related systems. The design should be flexible enough to enable implementation of previously unknown or unaffordable systems. In budget planning, there will be the need for greater staffing and/or services.

EVOLUTION TOWARD THE DIGITAL LIBRARY

Part of the strategic planning process is determining the "to be" state. Most would paint a future vision of a digital library. The emergence of digital libraries does not exclude the need for access to books or for teachers and librarians to be information access facilitators or knowledge navigators. Teachers and librarians are integral in most cases to learning (Thorin, 1995). However, there are some trends that ensure that more institutions will move towards digital libraries.

New Types of Information

For centuries, information was mostly paper-based. Today, in addition to traditional textual information, data accessible through the network includes nontextual information (photographs, drawings, illustrations, works of art, etc.), streams of numeric data (satellite information, cosmological data, etc.), digitized sound and moving visual images (music, movies, animation, etc.), multidimensional representations of forms or data (e.g., holograms), and the capacity to integrate these data into new representation forms from many different sources, augmenting the passive presentation of knowledge by adding interactive knowledge bases.

Space

Current space use for collections of materials will not scale into the 21st century. Institutions cannot afford to provide new buildings for storage of information in print form (which is expanding exponentially).

Expense

Traditional libraries are becoming increasingly expensive to operate and maintain while funding is not keeping up with costs. Hawkins estimates that if current trends continue, by the year 2026 the acquisitions budgets of libraries will have only 20% of the buying power they had 45 years earlier (Hawkins, 1994). Digital technologies may help with expense issues. For example, the costs for digital storage of information are declining at a rate of approximately 40% per year; estimates for storing information digitally average 20 cents per megabyte. The contrast with physical storage is dramatic. To put a book on the library shelf costs approximately $40; storing the same content optically is closer to $2.

Access

The evolution, availability, and affordability of various enabling information technologies is creating a major paradigm shift in the use of information. Users have come to accept that as long as they can access the information they want when they want it, they do not have to collect it. This shifts emphasis from acquisition or ownership to access. Global networks make access to digital information much more rapid and flexible than is possible with traditional libraries.

Improving access to information or dealing with data from multiple locations are also reasons for digital libraries. Many geographically dispersed institutions are providing instruction under cooperative arrangements, and many students are often dispersed beyond the convenience of the main campus. They have a need for access to research materials in a timely fashion that emulates the convenience of being physically on the campus. Digital libraries can include instructional applications and therefore enhance distributed learning environments.

Searching

With a seemingly infinite amount of information available, how can anyone find what they really need? Powerful search capabilities are needed so users can comb through vast amounts of data to find specific information they need quickly and easily. These search capabilities are needed for textual information. Even more challenging is the development of searching and indexing capabilities for multimedia information. Consider searching for a specific 35mm slide, or series of slides, among many thousands in a collection. Manually, the task is almost impossible. Often those slides have not been indexed or cataloged in any detail, thus it may require many hours to search for such slides. Technologies now exist that enable searching for digital images by color percentages, texture, shape, and position. Combining these capabilities with a natural language search on textual descriptions that may exist for a set of slides is indeed a powerful and efficient capability provided by a digital library.

Management of Large Amounts of Data

Colleges and universities typically manage very large amounts of data. Consider, for example, that one side of one page of a book, scanned as an image, requires approximately 50 kb of storage. If it is assumed that an average book volume is approximately 500 pages, then 1 million books would require 50 tb (terabytes) of storage. One terabyte is approximately 1 million gigabytes or 1 billion megabytes or the equivalent of a three mile high stack of diskettes.

Similarly, a typical one-hour, stereo-quality audio compact disc (CD) requires approximately 635 mb of storage. Multiplying that by the number of CDs in a particular collection results in a significant amount of storage. Thus, a collection of just 1,000 CDs would require 635 gb (gigabytes) of storage. Some other storage requirements for a single, color image, and video are

Image	8x10, color, desktop quality	22 mb
	8x10, color, near-photo quality	2,880 mb
Video	1 hour, VCR-quality	720 mb
	1 hr, uncompressed broadcast	108,000 mb

Preservation of Unique Collections

Another reason to have digital libraries is to preserve the intellectual content of unique materials such as illuminated manuscripts. Access to such information in digital form not only enables a wider audience to access the information, but also preserves the originals by reducing the need to handle them, thereby limiting their exposure to potential damage.

Protection

With information readily available over networks, there is increasing concern that individuals and institutions will lose control of their intellectual assets. If anyone can copy digital information from the network, how do you determine ownership and authenticity? Developments in rights management allow the owners of information to make their words, sounds, and images available in digital formats while protecting them from unauthorized copying and excessive distribution.

For example, there is often reason to protect the content owner's information, or be able to obtain revenue from the intellectual content through direct sales or royalty payments. Scholarly research, which has been rigorously tested, then published in electronic form, is one example where protection of content is required. Although subsequent additions or even challenges to such research may occur, there must be a way to ensure the integrity and authenticity of the original information, particularly as more of this information becomes available in electronic form.

Similarly, intellectual content developed through research may provide income through book sales. If this information is provided in electronic form, digital library rights management technology enables this revenue attainment to be possible.

Definition

There is no universal agreement on the definition of a digital library. Imaging systems, full text databases, and World Wide Web servers filled with home pages of information are all digital libraries, of sorts. Digital libraries can be thought of as architectures for creating, storing, managing, and retrieving information in a variety of formats. Digital libraries allow institutions to store and manage their multimedia information including books, movies, music, documents, pictures, letters, etc., in an electronic environment. The network allows this information to be accessible any place at any time.

IBM has created an integrated infrastructure for the digital library which is defined by five functional areas: creation and capture, storage and management, search and access, distribution, and rights management.

Creation and capture. Information can either be created in digital form, such as through the use of a word processor, a graphics program, or other methods. It can also be transformed from analog form by scanning into digital form, such as when a page of printed text is scanned and optical character recognition applied to that scanned information.

Storage and management. Once information is in digital form, it must be stored and managed for future retrieval. Such storage can be on optical or magnetic disk or tape. It can be accessible directly on-line or held in separate storage, for physical mounting into a storage system. Knowing where the information is located, as well as how to get to it, is part of the function of the storage and management component.

Search and access. When information is needed, search and access becomes important. Searches of text databases using keywords or Boolean logic have been used for a number of years. New advances in natural language query; searches of images based on characteristics such as color, texture, or shape; and other advances comprise the search and access component. Access is the other component which can be accomplished using a variety of interfaces and methods.

Distribution and rights management. The information found in a digital library may need to be sent to others over a variety of networks and in a variety of ways and forms. There is also the possibility that payment for the distributed information will be required. Rights management encompasses payment as well as authentication of documents.

INFORMATION LITERACY

Large amounts of information are available through networked sources. However, what is "good" information? Will you know it when you see it? Addressing these two questions determines the level of information literacy. Good information is defined as that which is accurate, real, and dependable. Dealing with the deluge of information requires the ability to discern useful information from information that is not needed. Though it is important to surf the net and gain skills in using technology-based resources, it is also important to maintain the fundamental skills associated with assessing and using printed materials. These skills can often be applied in the electronic or digital arena.

An example of the need for information literacy can be seen by examining print and on-line technical journals. Such journals available in print typically have a team of editors and reviewers to assess content for accuracy before it is published, ensuring a certain level of quality. Providing such information in electronic form does not preclude the need to ensure that the information meets criteria applied to its printed counterpart. Accuracy of data, properly cited references, and authentication of primary research are a few of the criteria used to assess submissions to technical journals. These provide a base for publication credibility to the reader or researcher by making certain conclusions about the information presented. Failing that, the reader must become the judge and may need to do all the investigation normally done by reviewers. If not done, the reader could accept erroneous information.

SUMMARY

Digital library and other technologies can be applied broadly across higher education institutions. Such technologies are being applied now, with an accelerating pace of change anticipated. Development and proper implementation of a technology plan tied to the mission and goals of the institution will enable that institution to incorporate emerging technologies effectively and efficiently.

REFERENCES

Barker, P. (1994, August). Electronic libraries—visions of the future. *The Electronic Library, 12* (4), 221-229.

Hawkins, B. (1994). Creating the library of the future: Incrementalism won't get us there! *The Serials Librarian, 24* (3/4), 17-47.

Thorin, S. E. (1995). The national digital library. *European Research Libraries Cooperation: The LIBER Quarterly, 5,* 145-181.

15

Managing Innovation: Project Implementation in Higher Education

D. Lawrence Bivins

There is nothing more difficult to plan, more doubtful of success, if not more dangerous to manage than the creation of a new system. For the inventor has the enmity of all who profit by the preservation of the old system and merely lukewarm defenders in those who would gain from the new one.

(Machiavelli, *The Prince,* 1513)

Effective project management is a key component of any strategic technology initiative (Short, 1994). In surveys of information technology projects in higher education, a firm understanding of project goals by all affected personnel and systematic procedures for resolving unforeseen technical barriers are two commonly mentioned critical success factors (Boettcher, 1993). This chapter explores various approaches to managing complex projects and the issues that campus executives, midlevel managers, and project personnel must address when planning and implementing such initiatives given the unique physical and organizational constraints that exist at today's colleges and universities.

One need not look long to find examples of successful project implementation. The pyramids of Egypt, the ancient cathedrals of Europe, the homes we live in, the office buildings we work in, along with the highways, railroads, and bridges that connect them are all products of ageless principles for harnessing human, natural, and capital resources in pursuit of an agreed upon objective. History is also littered with examples of failed projects. In 66 A.D., Petronious Arbiter lamented the confusion, inefficiency, and demoralization that occurred as a result of frequent reorganizations of the Roman army (Devins, 1968). Several centuries prior and half a world away, Sun-Tzu, the ancient Chinese military strategist, cited the mastery of what amounts to five basic management principles—organization, command, control, procurement, and resource allocation—as the difference between victorious generals and those who are defeated (Griffin, 1963). So it comes as no surprise that the earliest contemporary application of project management principles took place in the military. In the early 1950s, the U.S. Air Force used a matrix management structure in its Atlas Project, a complex "crash" program that successfully developed the West's first Inter-Continental Ballistic Missile (ICBM). Prior to this, Defense Department initiatives were undertaken within established hierarchical management organizations, with functional managers given responsibility for specific components of the project and top-level management retaining overall responsibility. Though this approach was usually successful, it was rarely executed without constant organizational tension (Easton & Day, 1981b).

Project management can be defined as a set of methods, principles, tools, and techniques for the effective management of objective-oriented work, in the context of an organization's unique environment. It is based upon assigning the success or failure of a given project to one or occasionally more persons of responsibility. Project management evolved in response to the managerial problems that arise in today's increasingly complex systems. The equally complex tasks associated with resolving the inevitable problems occurring in such systems also require a project management approach. Senior executives periodically rediscover the virtues of project management when, sensing a major job on the verge of disaster, they seek a single individual "who can take charge of this whole infernal mess and keep me informed as to what's going on" (Stuckenbruck, 1981a).

THE NEED FOR PROJECT MANAGEMENT

Project management principles are applicable to organizations and projects, large and small, that involve complexity. Though the approach is closely associated with construction and product development ventures, project management is today used in all sectors of our economy and society, including government and nonprofit institutions (Easton & Day, 1981a). It is particularly useful in instances where coordination is required between a client and a contractor. Given the historic opportunities and challenges facing colleges and universities at the dawn of the 21st century, it is inevitable that higher education will look to integrated, multidisciplinary management models that offer more effective budgetary and scheduling control and more efficient allocation of finite resources.

In establishing the need for project management, several universal premises must first be recognized. Foremost is the fact that every organization—public or private—produces a product or provides a service—or does both. Organizations strive to perform in such a way as to provide goods and services to consumers at the right time, at minimum cost, and to the satisfaction of the consumer. In industry, failure to do this results in lost profits, layoffs, and bankruptcies. In higher education, it can mean reduced enrollments, overrun budgets, frustrated students and parents, loss of the most gifted faculty, fewer alumni contributions and corporate gifts, and public cries for replacement of an institution's top leadership. Occasionally, these problems arise from external stimuli (i.e., adverse economic or political conditions), but more often they are rooted within the organization. The tendency is for management to respond to increased complexity by expanding or reorganizing existing hierarchical management structures. If for no better reason than that of simplicity, managers are comfortable with a one-boss reporting system. Hierarchies also lend themselves to convenient subdivisions; e.g., into groups and departments representing specific specialties and functions. Higher education is uniquely attracted to this paradigm because academic disciplines have traditionally been divided and subdivided (Easton & Day, 1981a).

Though the so-called line or functional structure can, in some cases, enhance efficiency and productivity, it contains the following problems:

▶ The ability of specialized organizational groups to coordinate effectively in their service to consumers (e.g., current or prospective students, faculty, staff, alumni donors, etc.) is critical to the overall success of the institution. Functional managers frequently suffer from tunnel vision: They either do not know or do not subscribe to the institution's larger objectives. What a dean perceives as good for the division can take precedence over what's best for a campus-wide initiative or for the university.

▶ Competition between line divisions can result in inefficiency and failure to communicate vital information.

▶ Inadequately defined or overlapping responsibilities can create chaos in crucial external coordinating functions.

❱ Overlapping lines can inhibit effective and rapid response to changing project requirements.

❱ Growth in size and complexity of institutions themselves can distract top campus leaders with concerns over the day-to-day problems of individual projects.

Projects can fail due to one or more of these reasons, leading presidents and chancellors to try to determine—amid the finger pointing of their deans, division directors, and department chairs—what went wrong (Easton & Day, 1981a).

Benefits of Project Management

By far, the single greatest advantage to accrue from the project management philosophy is the organized, concentrated, planning and control function embodied in the project manager's constant and consistent leadership. Such an approach centralizes responsibility for the following key issues:

Budgeting and cost control. Budgeting is a function of the planning process and serves as a control mechanism upon which performance can effectively be measured, compared, explained, and corrected. In the event numerous organizational entities have a degree of cost impact on the initiative, cost control efforts can converge at the project manager's office.

Scheduling. No cost control program can be effective unless it is complemented with a definitive schedule showing distinct, measurable, and identifiable milestones. Scheduling should also highlight interrelationships between the execution of one group's tasks and those of other groups. The schedule should be easily understood and agreed upon by all participants and should be flexible enough to allow adjustments for changes in project conditions.

Resource allocation. Along with time and money, materials, equipment, and manpower constitute crucial project resources. Close coordination of these resources is a central task of the project manager, who is also responsible for an orderly and objective allocation of fixed resources—primarily personnel—as competing divisions jockey for a greater share.

Technical quality. As part of an overall quality control plan, project management draws together technical expertise and second-line supervisory personnel to conduct a design review of predesignated segments of work. Established, sound methodologies for monitoring and documenting quality will alleviate future problems before they occur.

Customer satisfaction and public relations. As a representative of top management, the project manager performs a central function in maintaining good customer and public relations. At the day-to-day working level, no one interacts more frequently with the client than the project manager. This role is especially sensitive when the initiative in some way touches on environmental, marketing, or public safety issues (Easton & Day, 1981a).

FIGURE 15.1

Top 10 Reasons Projects Fail

Losing sight of or lack of clear objectives

Lack of approval and commitment in the project initiation phase

No clear conflict resolution procedure

Inappropriate members on the project team who can be neither trained nor transferred

Poor estimating skills

Lack of relevant experience or technical skills on the project team or in the human resource pool

Change in the thrust or direction of the project as personnel change

Lack of "political" support

Poor change management procedures

Poorly defined specifications due to communication problems

(IBM Skill Dynamics, 1993)

There are clear limits to project management. A project management structure may require top management to give up some of its prerogatives and line management to be partially or wholly subordinated to the project management team. The introduction of a matrix organization, in particular, will likely run into stiff resistance from more conservative managers of the old school. In determining the need for a project management approach, campus leaders should ask the following questions:

▶ Is this a large initiative?

▶ Is this a technically complex initiative?

▶ Will the proposed initiative dramatically disrupt the current institutional structure?

▶ Will more than one participating division be dealing directly with clients or consumers?

▶ Does the initiative create a true system that comprises many separate components or subsystems which require operation integration?

▶ Does the initiative create a subset of some larger system under which it must be closely integrated, and does the overall system have a project orientation?

▶ Do top campus executives believe strongly that a single point of information and responsibility for the initiative is needed?

▶ Is the institution committed to a firm completion date?

▶ Are strong fiscal and budgetary controls required?

▶ Are tight scheduling and budgetary constraints envisioned?

▶ Will rapid responses to changing conditions be necessary?

▶ Is there a high likelihood that changing conditions will seriously affect the initiative's completion?

▶ Does the initiative cross many disciplinary and organizational boundaries?

▶ Are other complex projects being conducted concurrently?

▶ Is there a high likelihood for conflict among line managers involved in the initiative?

▶ Will the initiative require major procurements outside the institution?

▶ Will the initiative require subcontracting outside the institution?

▶ Will it be necessary to have some or all features of the initiative reviewed or approved by government regulatory agencies and/or accreditation bodies?

If the answer to most of these questions is yes, or even if there are only a few affirmative answers but they apply to key phases or components of the initiative, a project management approach should be seriously considered (Easton & Day, 1981a).

Alternatives to Project Management

There are four alternative organizing structures capable of providing some of the benefits of project management. These alternatives are recommended in cases where top-level campus executives either can not or will not relinquish authority, or in projects that are deemed insufficiently complex to necessitate a project management structure.

▶ Designation of a "lead" division with responsibility to coordinate or direct the activities of affected divisions. This approach may work for small initiatives at smaller institutions, though for large, complex projects, conflicts-of-interest within the "lead" organization may create more problems than this approach will solve.

▶ Direction and control of the initiative by top campus executives. This approach is workable to the extent executives can invest the time and energy needed to resolve the project's inevitable day-to-day problems. If this is not the case, both the project and the institution will be adversely impacted under this approach.

▶ Clear definition of responsibility and authority of each division involved in the initiative. This alternative is appropriate in cases where everyone involved is on-board and willing to cooperate fully, though it is not recommended for complex projects where there is a high likelihood for misinterpretation or misunderstanding of instructions. This approach works far better in theory than in practice.

▶ Assign a project coordinator the responsibility of keeping campus executives informed. Since the individual would not be vested with decision-making authority for the project direction, an accountability vacuum may arise (Easton & Day, 1981a).

Laying the Groundwork

For project management to be successfully implemented, several crucial actions must be undertaken by top campus executives, participating functional managers, and by the project manager(s). The most important first step rests with top administrators. They must assume responsibility for

▶ Completely selling the project management concept to the institution

▶ Choosing the project management structure to be used

▶ Issuing a project charter that clearly demarcates the responsibilities and authority of the project manager(s) vis-à-vis functional management

▶ Selecting and offering visible, ongoing support to the project manager(s)

▶ Assigning the appropriate functional managers to the project organization

▶ Providing adequate financial and human resources, equipment, and technical support to the project organization (Stuckenbruck, 1981a)

Functional managers involved in a project management organization must ensure that their unit's personnel are supportive and understanding of the initiative, the project management concept, and their responsibilities to the project team. At this point, the project manager's duties have only begun. Among them is the initial task of issuing a Project Implementation Plan—the first step in actually getting the project going (Stuckenbruck, 1981a).

FIGURE 15.2

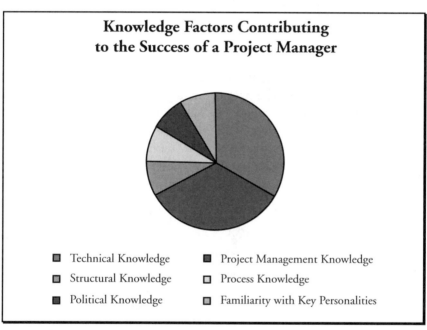

**Knowledge Factors Contributing
to the Success of a Project Manager**

- ◼ Technical Knowledge
- ◼ Structural Knowledge
- ◼ Political Knowledge
- ◼ Project Management Knowledge
- ◻ Process Knowledge
- ◼ Familiarity with Key Personalities

(IBM Skill Dynamics, 1993)

The implementation plan—necessary under any project management model—serves to inform functional managers and project personnel as to the following central questions about the initiative:

▶ What is to be accomplished?

▶ What are our specific goals and objectives?

▶ What are our constraints regarding budgets and scheduling?

▶ Which organizational units will be involved in the initiative?

▶ What are the project's milestones?

▶ What are the key points where project components (e.g.,. hardware, software, facilities, training, etc.) converge?

▶ What planning responsibilities for the project are required of the functional units, and how early must they be completed?

Much of this information will have been addressed during the proposal stage of the initiative, though the implementation plan should be a detailed, official document that formally turns the project on, educates management as to the actual scope the undertaking, and informs the project team about what they are expected to accomplish (Stuckenbruck, 1981a).

Organizing for project management—determining the structure and depth of the organization needed to successfully complete the initiative—begins with an analysis of the project characteristics. How big is it? How complex is it? How many components (i.e., subprojects) are involved? How visible (read: important) is the project to top campus executives? Much can be revealed in the history of the institution and in the experiences of other, like-minded institutions that have undertaken similar projects. Has this college or university ever embarked upon anything like this? If a previous attempt failed, what was learned?

To the extent that the initiative involves one large project, a "pure project" organization is recommended. This approach can best be described metaphorically as the creation of a small company inside the institution, a more or less freestanding unit charged with the successful completion of the project. Though a pure project orientation will create the most disruption to the existing functional management framework—occasionally a desirable goal for campus executives, especially newly appointed ones brought in from outside the institution to "shake things up"—this approach is frequently needed for high-end projects with sensitive requirements in the areas of cost control and scheduling. The model also puts the greatest amount of authority in the hands of the project manager, who in effect becomes an absolute ruler of his/her own "empire," a risk that necessitates careful consideration of interpersonal skills and leadership style when selection of a project manager is made (Salapatas, 1981; Easton & Day, 1981b).

A matrix organization—defined as an organization in which there is dual or multiple managerial accountability and responsibility—offers the advantage of scale economies in the management of numerous, relatively small projects (i.e., more efficient use of equipment, facilities, and—most importantly—human resources). It also creates the least amount of institutional disruption as it merely adds another reporting dimension: Chains of command will exist along functional and project lines (Stuckenbruck, 1981b; Easton & Day, 1981b). A third chain of command—for example, based on geography—may be easily added under this model, an important consideration when projects span across multicampus institutions. One clear advantage of the matrix approach is that it provides an excellent training ground for prospective project managers and develops an institutionalized, permanent unit that can cultivate flexible, proven, transferable, and multidisciplinary skill sets for the human resource pool (Stuckenbruck, 1981b). The major disadvantage of the matrix lies in its complexity. The multiple-boss structure is rife with possibilities for conflict, confusion, and excessive consultation, risks that can only be controlled with careful planning and sensitivity in the selection of functional and project management personnel (Stuckenbruck, 1981b).

FIGURE 15.3

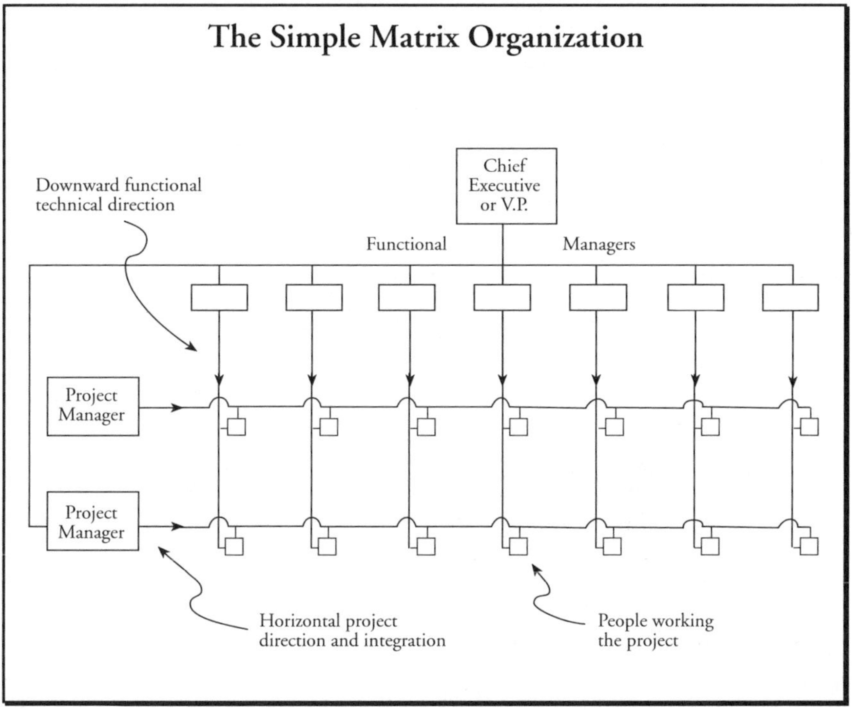

The Simple Matrix Organization

Another project management organizational model involves a "simple liaison" role for a project coordinator, who serves as a conduit for moving messages across forbidden lines of divisional demarcation. A weak matrix model is one where the authority and responsibility of the project manager—usually a part-time position—is clearly subordinated to that of functional managers. A strong matrix—the reciprocal—is also an option (Salapatas, 1981; Stuckenbruck, 1981b).

Planning for Change

Planning is the most basic function of management. It is defined as the process of stating project objectives and then determining the most effective activities or accomplishments needed for reaching them. It should logically take place prior to other management functions like organizing, staffing, directing, and controlling. Since all management functions intermesh, planning involves more than simply setting the stage. It is an ongoing process requiring constant updating and revision. Projects are rarely completed exactly in the manner originally planned (Michael & Stuckenbruck, 1981).

Change—the only constant in life—should be anticipated and understood by the entire project management organization. In other words, the original project plan serves as a baseline against which progress can be measured over the lifetime of the project. It is vital for the project team to be able to distinguish between changes that occur in the project plan and those made to the project's objectives. Both are possible, and each must be addressed through a distinct process. Changing project objectives will mandate changes in the project plan (e.g., recalculations of time, budget, and resource estimates). The inverse—though it is commonplace—is an unwelcome and, ideally, wholly avoidable scenario.

Changes to the project plan should be anticipated from four factors:

- *Client-driven.* Look for possible changes regarding the needs, resources, and expectations of consumers of the institution's instructional and administrative services and programs.

- *Regulatory.* Changing statutory and regulatory requirements from government and the demands of accreditation bodies can necessitate project plan changes.

- *External.* Macroeconomic and demographic fluctuations are examples of how outside pressures can impact a plan's key assumptions.

- *Internal.* A turnover in the office of a top campus executive is an example of one event inside the institution that will likely force a reassessment of the project plan.

Adoption of a project management model and the design of the project plan should take into account the likelihood of such changes, factoring in an adequate level of flexibility.

CASE STUDY: THE WAKE FOREST UNIVERSITY PLAN FOR THE CLASS OF 2000

Given that most of the literature available on project management assumes either a decidedly theoretical perspective or focuses on construction-oriented projects, it is useful to look to real-time, working examples of project implementation in higher education, projects that do not necessarily produce tangible, concrete products (i.e., buildings or labs). One such effort is taking place at Wake Forest University (WFU) in Winston-Salem, North Carolina, where a multidisciplinary, campus-wide project known as the Plan for the Class of 2000 is taking place.

In 1993, faculty, students, and administrators at WFU began planning for an initiative that would position the institution in the top tier of the nation's private liberal arts universities. The resulting Plan for the Class of 2000 was built with the objective of providing more personal opportunities for faculty and students to collaborate in the learning process. In achieving this goal, WFU has rededicated itself to its historic liberal arts emphasis, the development of stronger writing and critical thinking skills, an appreciation of global perspectives, smaller class sizes, and computer competency (Hearn, 1997).

The plan has engaged faculty, students, and administration in a set of projects involving academic, residential, and technical components. The most visible aspect of the plan is the placement of notebook computers into the hands of each incoming freshman. Upgrades were also made in the campus networking infrastructure, making WFU a truly learner-centered environment.

Partnership agreement. To manage such a sweeping and complex initiative, a project implementation plan was designed for the technology component. Two project managers were selected, one from the institution and the other from the WFU's corporate partner in the venture, IBM. A partnership agreement was drafted that documented in detail each of the project's goals, clearly delineating the responsibilities of both WFU and IBM, and formalizing the business partner relationship.

FIGURE 15.4

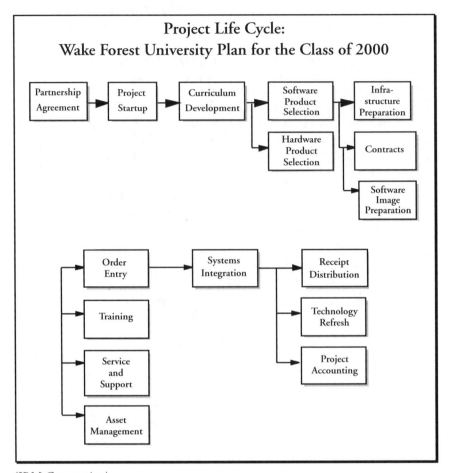

Project Life Cycle:
Wake Forest University Plan for the Class of 2000

(IBM Corporation)

Project startup. The project startup phase began with the organization of project workgroups, the definition of roles and responsibilities of project personnel, and the establishment of a project office. This phase also included the creation of a project plan and the development of project planning, tracking, and controlling methodologies.

Curriculum development. Curriculum development involved a consideration of WFU's vision for what role technology would play in teaching and learning. This phase included determinations about collaborative learning, e-mail access, multimedia-based presentations, and advanced applications like digital libraries.

Software selection. The process of software selection began by looking at the curriculum design changes and other pedagogical considerations. An operating system, application software, and utilities were selected; a determination was made as to the documentation that would be needed (both standard and customized); media requirements were determined; system assurance was performed; and end-user support requirements were set. Based upon these tasks, finalization of software configuration occurred.

Hardware selection. Consideration of software requirements and curriculum/pedagogical issues were key to beginning the hardware selection phase. This process began with preparation of configuration requirements for not simply laptops, but also for desktop computers (for staff/faculty), servers, printers, and networking gear. Availability and pricing were determined, and warranty, service, and support issues were addressed. Finally, hardware configuration was completed and a delivery channel was selected.

Infrastructure preparation. Infrastructure preparation involved a long list of subprojects and tasks. A determination of networking requirements was made based upon an analysis of the existing infrastructure and projections of future network use. A network topology was designed based upon the requirements of classrooms, residence halls, computer labs, and commons areas as well as the needs of administrative and academic units. Server requirements were determined using similar criteria. Determination of printing requirements took place once a strategy for printer sharing and a charge policy were developed. A review of workstation printer requirements and a plan for addressing special (i.e., high quality or high volume) printing needs were needed. Remote network connectivity was also considered at this point, and a system for tracking network problems was designed.

Contracts. A phase was included in the plan for the handling of contracts. This included review and submission to in-house legal counsel for software licensing agreements, leasing and financing agreements, insurance contracts, hardware maintenance agreements, consulting contracts, and an agreement with an Internet access provider.

Software image preparation. The software image preparation phase involved construction of a software master image, building registration scripts and programs, determination of user IDs and password standards, and the design of a system for software distribution and upgrading. This step also included a testing program for measuring user acceptance, systems integration, and problem identification and management. Finally, hardcopy and on-line documentation were developed to support system operations, software applications, and the help desk.

Order entry. Order entry centered around forecasting equipment requirements and laying out timeframes in which equipment would be needed. Orders were placed, and delivery dates and special instructions for receiving were set.

Training. The training phase was an extensive undertaking that began with a skills assessment questionnaire and survey. Based upon those findings, a training program was designed that included instruction in laptop computer operation and care, end-user fundamentals for e-mail and office suite applications, and World Wide Web home page design. A brochure was developed about the training offerings. Finally, a system was designed for using feedback from course evaluations and the help desk to monitor and update training offerings, as needed.

Service and support. The first step in the service and support stage was to formulate a strategy for handling telephone and walk-in support requests (i.e., local and remote clients). Hardware maintenance concerns required the training and certification of technicians and the creation of a spare parts inventory. Procedures for administering a loaner pool were adopted, and a system for tracking problems and analyzing trends was implemented.

Asset management. Asset management tasks included registration of assets along with user information for tracking purposes. A system for handling insurance and warranty claim submissions, service requests, and asset replacement was designed. Procedures for managing the loaner pool were also needed. Asset recovery procedures for instances of student transfer and employee separation were put into place.

Systems integration. Systems integration began with an inventory of products received. From there, component installation, system burn-in testing, software image loading, and system customization were completed. Shrink-wrap packaging included the insertion of necessary documentation, getting started information, instruction on accessing the network, insurance materials, and user IDs and passwords. Once this was completed, each package was registered and shipped either to a campus location or to the student's home address via Federal Express.

Receipt and distribution. Receipt and distribution of equipment required the identification of an appropriate storage facility. Was the site secure enough? Was it insured? A distribution process was then developed. Instruction on basic care and use as well as training information was provided. Confirmation of receipt by the user was obtained in writing.

Technology refresh. The technology refresh phase included development of procedures for handling and tracking asset returns and construction of a system for dealing with missing or broken parts. Planning was also done for disbursement of used equipment. What can be refurbished? What must be returned to the leasing company? Plans were also made regarding a system for distributing new materials.

Accounting. Project accounting started with identification of a central control point for product receipt paperwork. Invoices were then paid, and books reconciled. Contract requirements are being administered.

Process evaluation. The final phase is process evaluation. It began with a review of process effectiveness based upon focus groups, surveys, training class evaluations, and help desk problem reports. It will end with a new process and/or a refinement of the existing process for the next project cycle.

CONCLUSION

The successful experiences at Wake Forest University and elsewhere have come about not by luck, but as a result of sound project management principles: careful planning, effective implementation strategies, coordination and communication, and strong top-level leadership. From community colleges to the largest research universities, public or private, the management of innovation requires that the right questions be asked, the appropriate individuals become involved, the proper skills be identified, and the appropriate expectations be established. A project management approach is strongly recommended as a way of insuring that the resources invested into meeting the challenges of the Information Age are maximized.

REFERENCES/SUGGESTED READINGS

Boettcher, J. V. (1993*). 101 success stories of information technology in higher education.* New York, NY: McGraw-Hill.

Devins, J. H., Jr. (1968*). The Vaagso raid: The commando attack that changed World War II.* Philadelphia, PA: Chilton Book Company.

Easton, J. L., & Day, R. L. (1981a). The need for project management. In L. C. Stuckenbruck (Ed.), *The implementation of project management: The professional's handbook.* Reading, MA: Addison-Wesley.

Easton, J. L., & Day, R. L. (1981b). Planning for project management. In L. C. Stuckenbruck (Ed.), *The implementation of project management: The professional's handbook.* Reading, MA: Addison-Wesley.

Griffin, S. B. (1963). (Translator) *Sun-Tzu: The art of war.* Oxford, UK: Oxford.

Hearn, T. K., Jr., (1997). Tradition and change in quest of excellence. In D. G. Oblinger & S. C. Rush (Eds.), *The learning revolution: The challenge of information technology in the academy*. Bolton, MA: Anker.

IBM Skill Dynamics. (1993). *Fundamentals of project management: Course handbook*. Purchase, NY: IBM.

Machiavelli, N. (1935). *The prince*. Oxford, UK: Oxford University Press.

Michael, S. B., & Stuckenbruck, L. C. (1981). Project planning. In L. C. Stuckenbruck (Ed.), *The implementation of project management: The professional's handbook*. Reading, MA: Addison-Wesley.

Salapatas, J. N. (1981). Organizing for project management. In L. C. Stuckenbruck (Ed.), *The implementation of project management: The professional's handbook*. Reading, MA: Addison-Wesley.

Short, D. D. (1994, November). *Enhancing instructional effectiveness: A strategic approach*. IBM White Paper.

Stuckenbruck, L. C. (1981a). Implementation of the project: Getting off on the right foot. In L. C. Stuckenbruck (Ed.), *The implementation of project management: The professional's handbook*. Reading, MA: Addison-Wesley.

Stuckenbruck, L. C. (1981b). The matrix organization. In L. C. Stuckenbruck (Ed.), *The implementation of project management: The professional's handbook*. Reading, MA: Addison-Wesley.

PART 5

MEASURING SUCCESS

16

KNOWING HOW IT IS ALL WORKING: THE ROLE OF PERFORMANCE MEASUREMENTS

James W. Cortada

The citizens of California had gone through a turbulent period of economic change, downturn, downsizing, shrinking budgets, and then a return to prosperity. Along the way, the University of California system felt the same pain as budgets shrank and government research and development (R&D) funding became more scarce. Both the nation and the citizens of California looked to the nine campus system to maintain quality of service, research, and teaching. Quickly all nine campuses came together and decided to begin by improving administrative operations. Step one was to implement a series of new performance measures that would help each institution understand how it was performing. Two years later, teams made up of representatives from multiple campuses had formed to look at such diverse issues as how to measure performance of environmentally hazardous waste management to the more traditional financial indicators. Teams created measures, implemented them, and now they are beginning to become a way of life. Many of their lessons are reflected throughout this book. In short, administrators all over California once again set a trend for the nation, this time in measures of performance.

The University of Wisconsin-Madison, under the encouragement of its chancellor, Donna Shalala, sought to improve its operations across-the-board in administration. At the same time, she promoted the use of quality management practices in both the School of Engineering and in the Business School as pilots for the faculty. On the administrative side, she sought to implement performance-based assessments linked to processes. The university first implemented quality management practices and process management, then added measures to indicate how well processes were working, ranging from registration to law enforcement activities.

When faced with the enormous pressures of change, particularly change of a type new to higher education, it is inevitable that we would be concerned about the risks of failure, while eager to understand when we are succeeding. As other industries discovered during the 1980s and early 1990s, the more they changed the more they needed to understand the consequences of change. That need to know led to fundamental changes in the way organizations measured their own performance. The result is that today we have measurement techniques that can help higher education understand how they are progressing with their transformations while gaining insight that will make it possible to continue the process of change safely, cost-effectively, and to the satisfaction of all the constituencies that depend on them. It is to the issue of measurements that this last chapter is devoted.

Ask experienced executives why they should measure something and you invariably hear answers such as:

▶ People like to measure ("I lost four pounds over the past month, so I guess I will recover from the holidays!").

▶ They help us form intelligent assumptions about the future (e.g., the oil gauge in the car says we are low; probably need to take it in for an oil change and check for a leak).

▶ You cannot really know if quality and performance are improving without measuring results (e.g., costs are going down, the number of errors are declining, the unit is doing more per hour).

▶ Measurements help keep people focused on what has to be done well and what must be improved (e.g., meeting three to four objectives).

▶ They reduce the amount of randomness in cultural change improvements in an institution.

▶ Measurements make it possible to celebrate real results.

▶ They allow one to balance a variety of activities for the greater good of the entire organization (e.g., process improvements and results achieved).

▶ Measurements make it possible to experiment or run pilot programs to learn how to improve and change (e.g., by forcing one to answer the question, "What would make this a successful project?").

▶ One can be held accountable in a more precise, fair manner by using measurements (e.g., staying within budget, achieving a specific graduation rate).

▶ Measurements get people into the mindset of asking for very precise answers to open-ended questions (e.g., How good is our faculty? How good is the education my child is receiving?).

In the final analysis, measurements help people understand what is happening better. They help people to communicate that insight to each other, to legislators, to parents, and to students. Measurements help us gain insight into what really needs to change and how well we are doing. In survey after survey conducted by various higher education organizations, it has become clear that whether you transform the institution, or simply desire to maintain the status quo, you must articulate very precisely what you are doing and why. Measurements can help because they lead to precise discussion.

Precise discussion, for our purposes, is the use of numerical data and simple tools which grew out of statistical process control techniques designed to measure change. The use of numeric data is useful because many with whom a university or college must work come from businesses or industries that have become very comfortable with the language of modern measurements.

Perhaps the most important lesson that managers in higher education have learned—and that IBM's own change management experts have found in over a dozen industries—is that senior executives are the ones who really initiate the process of using measurements to understand their organizations. It is their leadership that creates the facilitative environment where employees use numeric data to understand better how things work and what the results are of improvements and change. Like the dashboard on a car or a pilot's instrument panel in an airplane, an effective set of measurements helps you understand where you are going and how to protect yourself from avoidable problems.

To date, most of the innovative work done on measurements in higher education has focused on administrative functions because they most closely parallel what occurs in business. However, faculty experimenting with performance measures are finding them useful, as well. Although most of the comments in this chapter are targeted towards administrators, the same lessons apply to faculty and the academic enterprise. Some examples illustrate the point.

Professor Ronald E. Turner, who teaches economics at Eastern Maine Technical College, applies quality management practices in his classroom. He now argues that student grades do not tell the full story about the quality of instruction. Student feedback, when analyzed statistically, helps provide insight into what to fix or seek to improve.

In business schools across the United States there is an increasing use of benchmarking to determine the quality and attractiveness of programs. Besides measuring starting salaries and hiring rates of their graduates, business schools are also measuring skills and classroom performance. Outcomes assessments are becoming increasingly popular with these faculty, as they compare their own institutions with others. External evaluation systems are being implemented in Pacific Rim nations to do just that.

Muhlenberg College in Allentown, Pennsylvania has implemented a series of quality management programs to improve a wide range of campus activities, from administrative services to teaching and quality of faculty. A great deal of focus has been on the supremacy of teaching where professors use a faculty center for teaching in which they learn about the scholarship of teaching but also about the measurement of the results of their work. The outcome has been better teaching and better discipline throughout the process.

Higher education surveys tend to report that improvements in the management of teaching methods usually means the application of quality management practices. Process management and outcome-based measures of performance are increasingly appearing on campuses, usually as experiments, not necessarily applied across the entire curriculum—yet. Common areas of focus involve teaching methods (about 50% of both community and senior colleges) and student achievements (nearly 20%). This contrasts with the 65%-68% for administrative functions. When faculty are involved, they tend to approach measures by addressing problems with processes. For example, faculty at El Camino Community College decided to reduce the complexity of their grade check system by addressing the problem with process. After measuring its current state and understanding how it worked, they were able to reengineer it and measure positive results. Faculty at American River College in Sacramento, California, track how many students work in teams since that is a skill these students will need to have in the workplace.

Faculty are increasingly teaching courses that involve the application of measurement techniques such as those described below. Our own research indicates that most of this training occurs in schools of management (77%), followed by those teaching statistics (51%), engineering (49%), continuing education programs (29%), and education (14%).

Faculty are measuring many things:

▶ Percent of major writing assignments as a result of new writing emphasis programs

▶ Amount of classroom time per semester per student

▶ Results from campus-wide, faculty-endorsed instructional goals

▶ Percent of departments adopting senior exit examinations

▶ Faculty evaluations

▶ Portion of a university's budget devoted to instruction

▶ Student satisfaction with specific classes and with their overall education

▶ Use of group or team grades

In short, faculty—often characterized as the last holdouts against any important change in higher education—are applying the lessons of modern measurement systems to their own work as well.

INSTITUTIONAL ARCHITECTURES FOR MEASUREMENTS

Counting noses or looking at budget spreadsheets will not suffice. Today, those organizations that have demonstrated great skill in using measurements effectively all display similar behavior. First, they aspire to link measurements to a well-articulated set of objectives for their organizations, objectives that make sense to all members of the institution and that are measurable. Second, they create measurement architectures and frames of reference that can serve as a way to coordinate and link measurements across the organization. Third, they involve people at all levels of the organization in the creation and use of measures. The very best have turned measurements over to their staffs to use to improve operations, not simply to reward or punish based on the numbers. Fourth, measurement systems have been broadened to take into consideration such categories of information as financials, attitudes of constituent groups, performance of key processes, and the capabilities of the organization to learn and improve. Moreover, they have come to realize that all of these collections of measurements must be viewed in total, not individually, because one set of activities can have an influence on others. The old Japanese saying is true here, "When a butterfly flaps its wings, it creates a tornado in another part of the world." The holistic view holds: If you stub your toe, the rest of your body is painfully aware of what just happened, especially your brain, which could be well over six feet away from the problem.

It all begins with an architecture. Simply defined, an architecture is a conceptual framework for understanding a set of related concepts or issues. They do not need to be complex or arcane. Figure 16.1 is a simple yet real example of a high level architecture. The nine campuses of the University of California system have used this model for many years to help guide administrators as they developed measurements of their own performance. It allowed them to ask more questions of themselves about what needs to be measured and why. Each column led to discussions about what was needed. Each campus and every segment of administration could ask what measures they needed in order to align with the model.

FIGURE 16.1

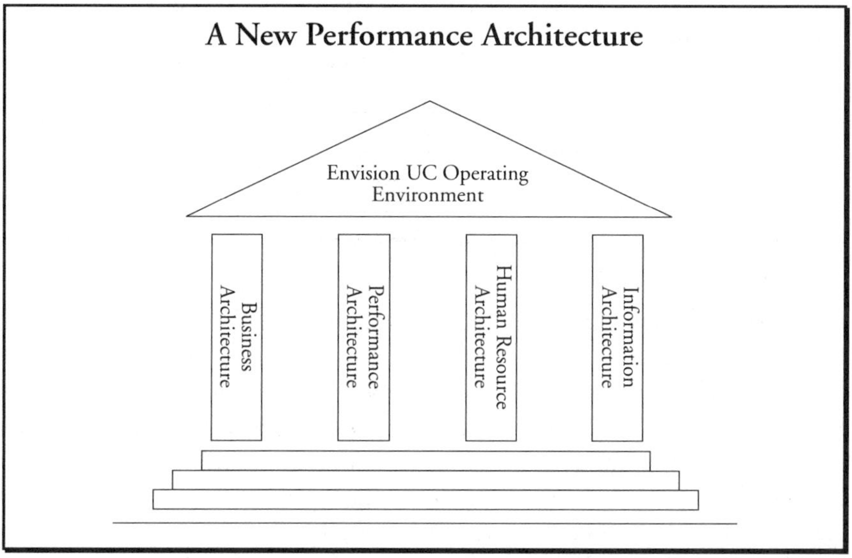

A New Performance Architecture

Envision UC Operating Environment

Business Architecture

Performance Architecture

Human Resource Architecture

Information Architecture

A second example of a model is depicted in Figure 16.2 which is widely used by corporations and is now spreading across higher education. What is particularly attractive about this model is that it acknowledges the linkage and relationship among various classes of measures. For example, values of the organization are cherished; it recognizes that the vision and mission of the enterprise must be congruent with its values. Goals must support vision and mission as must strategies. Processes, where the daily work is done, should be the playout of the strategies, and so forth. With such a model one can build a set of measures that inform a department or an individual to what extent they are 1) carrying out the overall objectives of the enterprise, and 2) how well they are performing and improving.

FIGURE 16.2

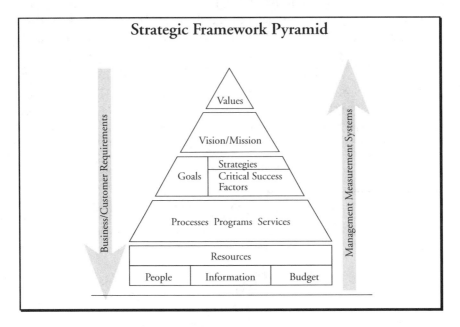

Invariably, such high level frameworks quickly lead individuals to ask about the categories of modern measurements that can be deployed. Is there an ideal measure to inform us exactly about what we need to know? Since every department and institution is unique, there are no hard and fast answers. However, what we have learned is that there are categories of subjects which are important to consider measuring. Moreover, we are learning how they affect each other. Figure 16.3 summarizes these categories of measures and how they influence each other. For example, using waste we can trace the ripple effect. Suppose a letter has a typographical error. It must be retyped, so the cost of the second sheet of paper and the salary of the individual correcting it can be considered a waste since these expenses could have been avoided if the job had been done right the first time. That waste makes the amount of time it takes to get the letter done longer (cycle time is expanded), resulting in lower productivity, possibly less flexibility in spending a few minutes helping a student standing there waiting (flexibility) while lowering everyone's satisfaction. Other ways of deciding what categories of measures are needed can include risk, efficiency, effectiveness, and growth. Irrespective of the model, the value lies in the categories chosen. For example, a decision-maker must decide whether or not he or she needs to understand flexibility (e.g., very critical to many of the topics discussed in this book), or customer satisfaction (e.g., the extent to which we are graduating students who obtain meaningful employment).

FIGURE 16.3

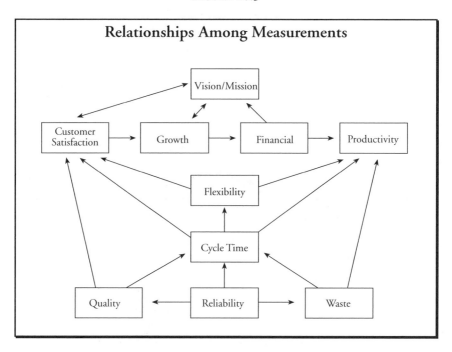

Those best at using measurements also understand the level of detail required to achieve the desired transformation. Figure 16.4 has been used by many management teams across a wide variety of industries to help address that point. The key is understanding how to link various levels of detail so that the ideals suggested in Figures 16.1 and 16.2 are attainable. It emphasizes the need for more process and task-specific measures of performance the lower in the organization or activity one goes. It also demonstrates that measures can be "rolled up" into higher orders of measures.

FIGURE 16.4

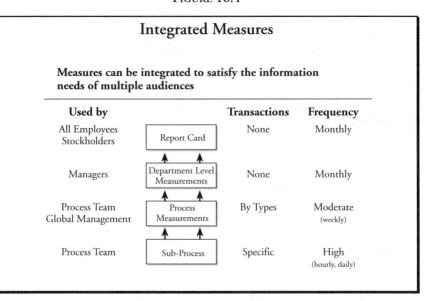

Integrated Measures

Measures can be integrated to satisfy the information needs of multiple audiences

Used by		Transactions	Frequency
All Employees Stockholders	Report Card	None	Monthly
Managers	Department Level Measurements	None	Monthly
Process Team Global Management	Process Measurements	By Types	Moderate (weekly)
Process Team	Sub-Process	Specific	High (hourly, daily)

FIGURE 16.5

Types of Measures by Level

Report Card

Indicates performance vs. targets
Customer satisfaction
Employee morale indices

Department Level Measurement

Indicates numbers, percentages
End-user satisfaction with IS

Process Measurements

Trends by month
Error types by month
Employee survey statistics
Overtime in programming

Subprocesses

Numbers
Transactions
Hours to respond to end
Unanswered phone calls today

FIGURE 16.6

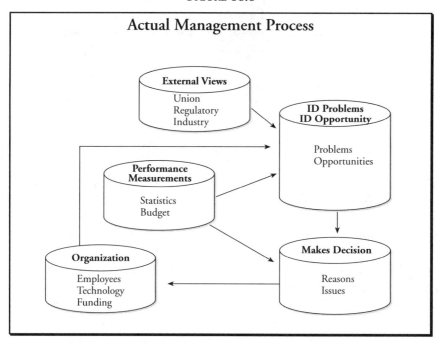

FIGURE 16.6

Actual Management Process

What kind of data are gathered at each level? Figure 16.5 is a catalog of the types. Both are best applied when they measure the performance of processes and the overall results of a department. Both can be mixed, indeed must be, in order to arrive at a clear understanding of how such a diverse and complex organization (i.e., a college or university) is doing.

Universities, corporations, and local and national governments have learned that management teams live in an environment within which certain basic activities take place: Most of these activities are measurable. Figure 16.6 illustrates what people do: The external environment creates problems and opportunities which causes them to make decisions and compel the organization to take actions. Along the way, they measure some activities (e.g., costs). As managers have come to realize what they really do, they have found their performance improves if they can set their activities into a more measurement-centric mode. What is critical to understand is that at every point where activity occurs, effective managers have created formal bodies of data and measures to inform them of what is going on and to measure the consequences of all actions.

In this model of management behavior, many of the issues raised in this book drive through the institution starting at the top (External Views) of either figure, create the problems and opportunities, and finally work their way through the organization for activity. Think of the organization much like an office supply cabinet. One goes to it for resources needed to carry out the work of the institution: buildings, computers, people, budgets, and campus culture. Measurements serve as a gateway from what we intend for an organization to do to actual performance. Over time, measurements appear that help address what is going on in each of the half dozen buckets presented in these figures (Cortada, 1995).

USING BALANCED SCORECARDS

One of the most effective tools that allows management to apply the intent and theories described above is the use of the balanced scorecard approach to performance measures. The purpose of the balanced scorecard is to carry out an old admonition, "Count what is countable; measure what is measurable; and what is not measurable, make measurable" (Galileo Galilei). Leaving aside discussion of what is wrong with most traditional measurement systems for discussion elsewhere—they focus too much on financial issues and not enough on performance or comparative data—concentrate on the trend of modern systems becoming more holistic (Lynch & Cross, 1991).

The modern balanced scorecard is the brainchild of Robert Kaplan and David Norton, developed in the late 1980s and refined during the 1990s (Kaplan & Norton, 1996). In this schema, vision and goals superseded audits and controls as more important because vision leads to goals, while measures indicate how well goals are achieved. In this scenario goals are road maps for behavior and action, while measures draw everyone's focus on carrying out the intent of the institution's vision. The idea of a scorecard is simply to have concise sets of measures that meet the needs of those who worry about strategy and those who focus on operational decision-making.

Kaplan and Norton liken their scorecard to a pilot's set of cockpit indicators; all are necessary for a safe and successful flight. If you leave out one (e.g., altitude, speed, or bearing) you are left with a possible accident. Similarly, running an organization with only one instrument (e.g., budget) would be fatal. Is such an approach possible in higher education? Figure 16.7 illustrates one in use at the University of California.

All scorecards have four categories of measures and targets which are presented simultaneously, just as all dials in the cockpit are visible to a pilot at the same time. For the same reasons as for the pilot, a manager must have a variety of data at the same time in order to decide what to do next.

FIGURE 16.7

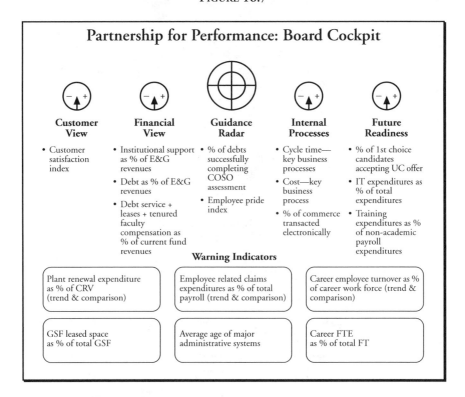

Partnership for Performance: Board Cockpit

Customer View
- Customer satisfaction index

Financial View
- Institutional support as % of E&G revenues
- Debt as % of E&G revenues
- Debt service + leases + tenured faculty compensation as % of current fund revenues

Guidance Radar
- % of debts successfully completing COSO assessment
- Employee pride index

Internal Processes
- Cycle time— key business processes
- Cost—key business process
- % of commerce transacted electronically

Future Readiness
- % of 1st choice candidates accepting UC offer
- IT expenditures as % of total expenditures
- Training expenditures as % of non-academic payroll expenditures

Warning Indicators

Plant renewal expenditure as % of CRV (trend & comparison)	Employee related claims expenditures as % of total payroll (trend & comparison)	Career employee turnover as % of career work force (trend & comparison)
GSF leased space as % of total GSF	Average age of major administrative systems	Career FTE as % of total FT

Customer Perspective

Leaving aside the commercial connotation of the word "customer," substitute the concept of constituencies who *de facto* act like customers of an institution's services, making Kaplan's and Norton's idea of customer perspective an easy carryover to higher education. This perspective is the notion of having performance indicators which take the view of your constituents (e.g., students and legislators), and document the degree to which (from their point of view) an institution or department is satisfying their needs and wants. These measures should cover both customers of the institution (e.g., students, faculty, staff, and their families) and stakeholders who influence the institution or pass judgment on its performance (e.g., legislators, regents, trustees, grant agencies). Our experience demonstrates clearly that the first step is to identify who your customers are, what they need and want, and why. That exercise then can lead to specific measures that answer those questions continuously.

Internal Business Process Perspective

These are the measures that tell people how specific processes are performing. Many of the quality management practices in process management fall in this area. For example, measuring how well an institution maintains its buildings, registers students, controls traffic, and graduates ABDs are all process-centric considerations. These are the measures that tell management how timely and accurately payroll is processed, the speed with which employee inquiries into benefits are met, and the degree to which one is complying with federal environmental regulations. Here is where one houses measures on productivity, cycle time, waste, use of resources, and many information technology performance indicators.

Financial Perspective

This is the collection of measures which is probably most familiar as well as most mature in all institutions. They include such obvious measures as those dealing with budgets, revenue growth, operating income, and forecasts of possible future expenditures.

Innovation and Learning Perspective

This fourth dimension of the balanced scorecard helps to answer such questions as "How well are we improving and creating value?" "How innovative are we?" These are more than intellectually interesting issues. This category does for the institution what the human brain does when it tells itself that in the future one should avoid stubbing one's toe! Our experience indicates that this is the one area that requires the greatest amount of work by institutions of higher learning because it addresses the heart of its performance in organizational transformation. This is the category where one puts measures that indicate the ability of the institution to create and sustain the environment necessary to achieve its goals and vision. For example, measures might include employee skills and training, the appropriate use of all kinds of technology (not just computers), and encouragement of innovation and continuous improvement.

When fully operational, there are measures in the four categories as well as numerically defined goals for each. One compares performance against goals. Goals are created once we understand what current performance is and have reached a decision as to what it must be. Over time, measurements in each category come and go, driven by such issues as changing vision and goals, or learning which indicators are better or less effective in indicating how one is doing. Pilots do the same thing. When they take off with a full tank of gas, they spend less time looking at the gas meter than they do the altimeter to see how high they are climbing. An hour into the flight, they have a different objective; they are less concerned with how high they are flying than on how much fuel remains.

Benefits of the Scorecard

This tool has now been used by so many organizations that we can confidently catalog four classes of benefits for its use.

1) Translating the vision leads to consensus building around an institution's vision and strategy.

2) Communicating and linking makes it possible to communicate strategy at all levels of the institution while linking these to both departmental and individual performance objectives.

3) Business planning enables one to integrate financial (e.g., budget) and operational (e.g., business) plans.

4) Feedback and learning permits the institution to monitor short-term results from many points of view while evaluating strategy in light of recent and long-term performance.

With so many organizations now using this tool, are there some best practices emerging for making the balanced scorecard work well? Both Kaplan and Norton and several thousand IBM consultants appear to be merging into a consensus answer on the question. Already mentioned is the most obvious: One must build consensus around a clear vision, mission, and goals that can be articulated, bought-into, and implemented. Once past that substantial task, there are several other actions to be taken to insure a successful implementation of scorecards (Kaplan & Norton, 1996).

Define the scope. Define the scope of the "service delivery unit" for which the tool is to be used. The best people to involve in this activity are normally managers and employees who have direct responsibility for the process and departmental results being measured.

Involve senior management. Make sure senior management of either the department or institution is involved. Their involvement requires that they learn what the balanced scorecard is about, arrive at a set of expectations about its benefit, and understand how it will link a department's activities to the vision-driven approach to the overall management of the institution.

Involve these same senior managers in the development of the vision and goals which will serve as the overall context of the measurement system. This is an ongoing process that must be revisited from time-to-time, usually annually. Many institutions attempt to include key constituents, which makes this step a lengthy and complicated process. For all practical purposes, this becomes an ongoing process rather than a single annual event, often blending into the overall communications activities of the organization.

Collect input and feedback. Closely related to this process is the need to collect input and feedback from all key stakeholders and constituents. The purpose for their participation is to insure that their expectations are included (customer perspective) and are understood rather than assumed by higher education decision-makers.

Always involve departmental or unit managers in converting institution-level goals into terms that make sense within their own operations and involve them in selecting which measures they feel will best track progress toward these goals.

Develop different measures. Do not forget to recognize that you need different types of measures at various levels in the organization (the point made with Figure 16.5). For example, the board of regents may only need to see four to six indicators while, in the registrar's office, employees may require eight to ten, all of which are very different than what the regents see. The experience of many organizations is that they have too many measures in the beginning, and eventually pare down to a small but mighty set of measures that give them true insight into their operations. They arrive at this smaller list by trial and error over time.

Assign responsibilities. Make sure there is a clear understanding of who owns the process for developing, collecting data for, and improving the scorecard. This is a very important point, especially in institutions of higher education where data and responsibilities are highly decentralized. Measurement is a process; it needs to be managed as such.

Communicate. It is extraordinarily important for management to communicate clearly what the role of the scorecard will be and to reinforce that message constantly through communications and actions. To improve confidence and trust, scorecards should be widely available to employees, other constituents, and stakeholders in an open and honest manner. Refer to them often, make decisions based on the data they present, and allow employees to improve the scorecards as circumstances warrant. Ultimately, weave the scorecard into the fabric of the institution's way of doing things.

Modify the scorecard to reflect current realities. No effective scorecard is static. As the institution revises its vision, goals, and measures as part of its overall strategy for delivering value to society through its various transformations, scorecards must be modified to reflect current needs and realities. It is crucial to the relevance of a scorecard that it always represent an accurate view of the institution's areas of focus and where it intends to evolve. Some organizations use techniques such as benchmarking and national assessment models, such as the Baldrige framework or National Association of College and University Business Officers (NACUBO data) to improve the measurements process itself.

Role of Benchmarking in Institutional Transformation

No measurement or assessment tool has been so widely embraced as benchmarking. As one expert facetiously put it, "Benchmarking has legitimized plagiarism!" Put another way, it has provided a way to obviate the need to reinvent the wheel. Every industry and thousands of industry associations have embraced the concept, including higher education.

What is benchmarking? It is the act of continually comparing the performance of one process against that of another, usually of comparable or greater performance and frequently on a continuous basis. The primary goal of benchmarking is to find out who has the best practice regarding a process, approach, or issue so that one can use that insight to improve one's own operations. For example, the University of Wisconsin might want to compare its telephone-based student registration process to the reservation system used by hotels at Disney World. Or one of the research laboratories at M.I.T. might want to compare how effectively it disposes of hazardous materials with some of the U.S. National Laboratories. The Sorbonne in Paris might want to know how its graduates are doing in their careers in computer science compared with those of Cal. Tech. The hunt is always for better ways to do things. Better is defined by the vision and goals of an institution.

Benchmarking comes in many forms. Companies benchmark their competitiveness against rivals. Sports teams do this all the time. Functional benchmarking is the process of comparing operations or processes of one organization to those of others. A great deal of NACUBO's activities center around this kind of benchmarking. Strategic benchmarking is one of the newest variations which deals with comparisons of business strategies. What are alternative ways of running an organization, and what is best? Should I continue to teach all my classes on campus or aggressively deploy distance learning? What is better for my constituents, campus residence halls or off-campus housing? Why?

Benchmarking is also a set of formal steps and techniques. Essentially what happens is that two or more organizations agree to share information in some structured format to compare performance on an agreed upon set of issues. For example, universities may come together to measure how much budget they expend for commonly performed activities (e.g., writing a purchase order, registering a student). In this scenario, a group of similarly-sized institutions would agree to share data on these topics and periodically discuss their implications. IBM continuously benchmarks a variety of information technology issues ranging from best practices in operating data centers and networks to identifying what is of value to end users. In this case, IBM typically will identify several dozen organizations in multiple industries and work with them to collect and analyze a variety of data. The results will suggest who has figured out how to do things better and why.

Benchmarking is one of the most versatile tools available; it can be applied to just about any topic. The most convenient benchmarking projects are those that rely extensively on numeric data as opposed to information acquired through surveys, roundtables, and other forms of conversation and textual analysis. It is an ideal tool for those who measure performance because once armed with data on one's own performance, individuals can then compare their data to others.

If your university has decided that its students must have outstanding starting salaries (a goal many MBA programs have), you could easily measure the starting salaries for graduates. You find wages continually rising over time but do not know if they are rising fast enough to attract students to your campus. By benchmarking with similar institutions, you might discover that Harvard MBAs actually outperform your graduates on starting salaries. You might also find out that half the institutions you benchmarked with have lower starting salaries than your graduates. Now you have perspective. You now better understand what questions to ask Harvard concerning its program. Alternatively, you could go to employers and ask why it is that they are willing to pay more for a Harvard MBA than for yours even though both groups of students might have used the same textbooks, the same case studies, and even had professors who had done their graduate work at the same institutions.

Organizations that effectively use measurements to chart their course always include benchmarking as yet another form of assessment. Sitting side-by-side with departmental and process measurements, they will either benchmark periodically (e.g., once every several years on an issue) or make it part of their annual audit duties.

There are many benchmarking-related activities and frameworks which are useful in higher education. Most familiar to officials in higher education is the work of NACUBO, CAUSE, and the research by such consulting firms as the IBM Consulting Group and industry and professional associations, such as the American Society for Quality Control (ASQC). But other frameworks exist to help structure the issues on which to focus. There are two widely used sets of frameworks in North America: the Malcolm Baldrige National Quality Award and ISO 9000. The Baldrige criteria clusters into seven chapters with issues ranging from management leadership, to process management and data use, to customer-focused results. The other, even more widely deployed approach is the documentation in ISO 9000. ISO 9000 is also the most widely used set of quality-centric documentation procedures in the world. In fact, it is the *de facto* standard to achieve (e.g., ISO certification) if as a company one is to operate in East Asian or West European economies. ISO 9000 is a collection of procedures for insuring documentation of quality practices which includes measures of performance. Many campuses are familiar with ISO 9000, particularly engineering schools and science laboratories. Increasingly, higher education management is becoming interested in ISO 9000 standards. East Asian universities not only teach ISO 9000 standards, they implement them.

Attempts to turn some frameworks into higher education format are well underway. For example, the US Department of Education began the process of translating the Baldrige Award criteria into higher education language in the early 1990s. This project concentrated on administrative functions because those were so similar to business and industry. Some universities, however, have simply stuck to the original Baldrige criteria rather than the education version in the belief that the original business-centric ones met their needs more closely on the administrative side. Benchmarking and other audit frameworks for teaching and scholarship are beginning to emerge but not with the same speed as tools for administration.

Mistakes to Avoid in Benchmarking

Benchmarking is such a quickly understood and endorsed process that most decision-makers do not require a great deal of time to figure out why they want to do it and how. It is not complicated. What they are really interested in doing is finding best practices. Solutions to the problems people run into are not normally found in benchmarking, but in best practices data. There are several easily avoided errors that often grow out of both measurements and benchmarking.

Copying a best practice "as is." This is the sin of literally reproducing in your institution a practice the way someone else does it. The problem with this approach is that the reason it became such an effective practice elsewhere was that an organization tailored it to their specific needs which are not necessarily yours. Since no two organizations perform a process exactly the same way, just porting over someone else's way of doing things could result in poorer performance than before.

Not validating a best practice. You hear that another institution is reputed to have a best practice, you see it, like it, and try to emulate it back on your campus. Before doing that, however, validate that it is, in fact, a best practice before trying to learn from it. How do you validate it? Either look at benchmarking data or benchmark it against your process or department, then measure its value against your objectives.

Adopting a practice that is outdated. Best practices do not remain best practices forever. Just because NACUBO data indicated that a particular process performed best at a campus in 1991 does not mean that in 1998 it is still performing best. Furthermore, as institutions change, some practices will deteriorate or disappear while others, now more relevant, get the attention they need.

The relevance of a practice is not established. Put another way, some people will not determine what the business value of implementing a particular practice is before adopting it. Normally we see this error committed with processes that are not linked to what the institution is attempting to accomplish. Since the effort of implementing a practice of dubious value takes the same amount of resources as one of considerable value, one might as well expend effort on the higher value practice.

Adopting a best practice because it is fashionable. This is a real problem, but one which few wish to acknowledge. Professors in business schools ask "Is TQM a fashion?" Business executives are often puzzled by what they see as the "in" thing to do on campuses and the concern over political correctness. Reengineering of corporations became very fashionable in the early 1990s, and downsizing has proven a bestseller. Fashion in practices does exist and can be very harmful because the dangers are masked behind the rubric of "best practices," "world class," or "best of breed." To avoid this pitfall ask a very basic question: "How will a refurbished process or practice help my organization achieve its objectives?" If you do not arrive at a good answer and proceed ahead anyway (because instinct or political circumstances compel you) you may be succumbing to fashion.

In the final analysis, measurements, benchmarking data, and the hunt for best practices comes down to decision-makers understanding what is best for their institution. This is a good point on which to focus as your institution undergoes accelerating change. Managers who have successfully led their organizations through great periods of change cherish information that is insight-based, which means that management is looking less at how one mechanically does a task within a process, and more at the effects of the process on institutional culture, customer perceptions, productivity, and the ability of the organization to carry out its institution-wide objectives.

HOW TO GET STARTED AND HOW TO SUSTAIN THE MEASUREMENTS PROCESS

Where major revisions of existing and proposed measurement processes have occurred, a common pattern has emerged. Many of the elements of that pattern have already been introduced in this chapter, but a quick review of them suggests what should happen.

▶ A senior executive or manager must decide that existing measures need to be refurbished. That person must also be prepared to change roles, alter how people are rewarded for their work and measured on performance, all as a consequence of changing measures.

▶ At the detail level, those who do the work which is being measured should form a team to explore what measures they want in order to bend their daily work to the goals and objectives of the institution. That exercise also requires that they define what data are needed to develop a measure, where it is to come from, who will gather it, and how this information will be presented (e.g., weekly report, etc.).

▶ The results of each proposed measure need to be thought out and discussed. Simultaneously, the old measures which are no longer needed should be reviewed.

▶ The team must attempt to build the measures (e.g., gather the data, calculate the numbers, design the measurements report) to see if what they want can be done. Once possible, then they and management must decide whether to start using it or not.

Figure 16.8 summarizes the work done by the three groups of individuals involved in the creation of new measures. Expect that this work might take anywhere from a few weeks to several months. Teams in higher education normally are formed within departments, although we are now seeing some cross-functional teams composed of people who participate in a specific process regardless of department. For example, a conventional approach might be to have librarians working on library-related measures. A process-focused approach might, using a purchase order process as an illustration, include representatives from multiple campuses in a system, people who requisition supplies, and others who run the purchase process.

The move to cross-functional teams is particularly attractive when implementing a balanced scorecard where a variety of perspectives are important. Figure 16.9 illustrates the enormous variety of measures that different perspectives can generate. In the case of purchase orders, the secretary

FIGURE 16.8

Roles of Management and the Measurement Development Team		
SENIOR MANAGEMENT	SENIOR MANAGEMENT TEAM MEMBERS	TEAM MEMBERS
Articulate strategic goals	Determine how managers will review the team's performance and measurement system	Design and develop a measurement process
Ensure that the team understands its role in translating goals into measures	Decide which measures need to be changed and how	Articulate unit/department goals in support of strategic goals
Provide appropriate training to team	Define a framework for gathering, analyzing, and communicating measurement information	Develop • Measures • Data definitions • Frameworks for diplay of results of the measurement process
Require the team to decide which measures will provide the unit/department with the best information		Audit input data

in the history department might want a measure of how fast orders are delivered; the finance organization might want to know how many national contracts cover purchases and what the average discount list is; the budget office might want to know what is being bought and the effect on individual departmental budgets; vendors would want to understand how many items are being ordered so that they can calculate a profitable yet attractive bid to the institution; other parts of the organization might want to know the quality of the items being purchased since that has an effect on such other issues as waste and productivity.

Once an initial set of measures is up and running, their relevance must be maintained. Simply put, measures should always be treated as a process. Our experience strongly demonstrates that organizations in transition need to manage this process in two ways:

FIGURE 16.9

Performance Indicator and Measure		
	Performance Indicator (example)	Performance Measure (example)
Customer View	customer satisfaction	responsiveness to complaints length of service delivery time quality of service provided
Financial View	invoice quality procurement	% error-free invoices lost revenue due to late invoices
Internal Business View	efficiency	# transactions/employee # employees served by a function (e.g., HR benefits)
Innovation and Learning View	employee morale	perception of training adequacy effectiveness of decision-making

1) Process owners should have as part of their responsibility the maintenance of a relevant set of measures.

2) Department heads and general management have responsibility for managing the departmental and higher order sets of measures as well.

Once the measurement process owner is assigned, that individual can put together a team responsible for creating and nurturing the process. That same team would also use benchmarking, as appropriate, to do its job. The best teams and managers review measures on a predetermined schedule. Process owners might do that weekly, department heads monthly, and chancellors on a monthly and quarterly basis. Reviews are not just of the numbers but also include a discussion of what the data reveal. Annual audits, while very popular, suffer from the problem of being a year late. When an organization is changing rapidly, an audit-like mentality (appreciating how the data are gathered and calculated) must exist on a daily basis and in the minds of the measurement collectors, not in the minds of others coming in to inspect. However, a formal annual review of information not normally gathered is an excellent way of testing the data and one's assumptions. The most widely used of these annual processes are surveys of constituents and customers as well as a review of how overall performance has changed since a previous Baldrige-like review. When surveying constituents who use the measurements, the key issues are normally about the usefulness of information, format of the data, and to what extent it causes the institution to perform better.

As a measurements process owner, one normally should inspect the act of collecting measures by asking questions that are routinely applied to all process management. These include asking about

▶ Cycle time needed to produce the measures

▶ Costs of producing measures

▶ Waste and defect rates in measurements reports

▶ Resources required for the job and their productivity

▶ Effectiveness of the measurements process

▶ Quality of the process

▶ Linkage of the process to institution-wide objectives

If a process owner falls down in performance, it is usually in communicating findings. Often, not enough time is spent determining who needs to see the data, in what format, and with what frequency. If the measures indicate weak performance, that in turn strains communications. Chancellors, for example, normally do not want the public to see hard data indicating problems on campus, yet process owners and their constituents need to know what problems exist and why. Thus the issue of communications creates its own tensions, making it a delicate one for organizations in change. But people need to understand how things are operating, must comprehend what the data mean, know when there are changes in schedule, content, format, and so forth. Otherwise, why have measures?

SOME FINAL THOUGHTS

All institutions have a massive collection of measures of performance. The challenge in a period of transformation is to decide which measures to continue looking at as relevant and realistic while disposing of those that are no longer useful. As institutions change so will the measures. Behind those changes will be how people are rewarded or penalized. The theme woven throughout the chapters of this book is that change is comprehensive and holistic: Once started, you cannot be selective. Change begets its own change. Some individuals will benefit personally from change; to others it will be detrimental. Some departments and organizations will thrive; others will shrink. What we have observed in many industries, including higher education, is that change can be harnessed in very positive ways. Those best at it recognize that the one basic tool that helps them contain random undesired consequences and gives them the best insight on what to do next and why is a robust set of measurements. These must be practical, capable of being changed, and supported by senior management. It is as simple as that. The opportunity to shine in a growing world of personal and departmental accountability and to do extraordinary things for constituents asking for fresh approaches in higher education are facilitated in a practical way through the use of measures.

REFERENCES/SUGGESTED READINGS

Cortada, J. W. (1997). *Best practices in information technology.* Upper Saddle River, NJ: Prentice-Hall.

Cortada, J. W. (1995). *TQM for information systems management: Quality practices for continuous improvement.* New York, NY: McGraw-Hill.

Kaplan, R. S., & Norton, D. P. (1996). *Translating strategy into action: The balanced scorecard.* Cambridge, MA: Harvard Business School Press.

Lynch, R. L., & Cross, K. F. (1991). *Measure up!: Yardsticks for continuous improvement.* Oxford, UK: Blackwell.

Thor, C. G. (1994). *The measures of success: Creating a high performing organization.* New York, NY: Oliver Wight.

INDEX

Academic institution transformation
  forces causing transformation, 4
  importance of vision, 6-8
  and information technology, 26-28,
  31-34
  opportunities for change, 5-6
  people side of, 20-21
  reengineered course, 12-15
  role of benchmarking, 263-266
  successful transformation, 8-12
Academic processes, 11
  transformation, 12
Administrative processes, 11-12
Adopters, 134-145
  chasm between, 135-137
  cumulative distribution over time, 144
Adoptions
  distribution over time, 134
  life cycle, 135
  mainstream, 142
  and support strategy, 145-148
Alavi, M., 121, 129
Alexander the Great, 132
American Heritage Dictionary, 166
American River College, 251
American Society for Quality Control
  (ASQC), 264
Andriole, S. J., 120, 129
Aristotle, 132
Asset management, 244
Asynchronous classroom, 203
Asynchronous courses, 124-126
Asynchronous Transfer Mode (ATM),
  171, 173
Awareness stage, of organizational
  readiness, 184, 188
Babson College, 82-83
Baker, W. J., 107

Balanced scorecard approach, 258-263
  benefits of the scorecard, 261-263
Barker, P., 218, 229
Beede, M. A., 68
Bellamy, D. L., 178
Benchmarking, 11, 263-266, 269
  mistakes to avoid, 265-266
Benson, R., 52
Berge, Z., 95, 107
Bivins, D. L., 230
Bligh, D. A., 119, 129
Boettcher, J. V., 230, 245
Boston College, 83
Botkin, J., 2, 23
Bottom-up innovators, 157, 161
  success of, 155-156
  and technology, 151-153
Brigham Young University, 81
Brown, D. G., 109
Brown, J. S., 203, 216
Bryson, J. M., 67
Budgeting, 233
Bureau of Labor Statistics, 69
Burnett, D. J., 68
Bush, V., 131, 149
Business processes, 16-20
  keys to transforming, 21-22
  and organizational boundaries, 17
  reengineering, 12
Cal. Tech, 263
California, University of, 81-82, 253,
  258
Campus Classroom Connections
  (Stuebing), 204
Campus computer networks, 167-169
  benefits of, 168-169
  expectations for, 167-168
Campus Computing (Green), 137, 142

Campus network infrastructure, 166-177
　defining infrastructure, 166-169
　determining value, 175-177
　integration of voice, video, and data,
　　171
　power of the plan, 174-175
　strategic planning, 170-171
　upgrading networks, 173-174
　wiring, 171-173
Carnegie Institution, 131
Cartwright, G. P., 95, 107
Champy, J., 4, 7, 12, 23, 83, 86
Chantilly study, 182-184
　defining success, 190
　and IBM Higher Education, 185
Chasm, between adopter groups,
　　135-137
Chief information officers (CIOs), 137,
　　144, 223
Chief technology officer, 223
Clark, R., 184, 197
Classroom design, 198-216
　classroom models, 208-214
　creating a learning environment,
　　200-203
　design issues, 203-204
　hardware and software, 205-207
　planning, budgeting, and support
　　considerations, 214-216
Classroom of the future, 208
Clayton State College, 94, 100, 107
Client-driven changes, to project plan,
　　240
Client/server projects, 178-197, 222
　applying models to higher education,
　　185
　balancing people, process, and
　　technology, 180-181
　data as an institutional asset, 188-189
　defining success, 190-191
　driving business value, 179-180
　elements of success, 180
　findings in higher education, 186-187
　focus on customer service, 187
　implementation imperatives, 197

methodology, 186
　mismatch of expectations, 187-188
　predicting success, 182-184
　project management, 195
　systems management, 194-195
　training and education, 191-192
COGNET, 169
Collaborative learning, 118-129
　and asynchronous courses, 124-126
　definition of, 118-119
　enabling computer collaboration,
　　122-123
　enhancing video distance education,
　　126-127
　fostering collaboration among
　　students, 123-124
　and higher education, 121-122
　success of, 119
　and technology, 120-121
Collabra Share, 122
Collins, M., 95, 107
Communication, and mobile
　computing, 93
Communications management, and
　strategic planning, 51
Comprehensive Unified Physics
　Learning Environment (CUPLE), 212
Computer classroom, 209-210
Computer facilitated collaboration,
　three elements of, 122-123
Computer laboratory, 200, 209
Congressional Record, 10
Constructive learning, 201
Contracts, and project management,
　　243
Conway, K. L., 198
Coping stage, of organizational
　readiness, 184, 188
Copyright Office Registration,
　Recordation, and Deposit System
　(Cords), 10
Cortada, J. W., 248, 258, 271
Cost control, 233
Cousineau, L., 206, 217
Cross, K. F., 258, 271

Cross-functional teams, 78
Curriculum development, 242
Customer perspective, 259
Customer satisfaction, 233-234
Data
    access, 188
    management of large amounts, 226
    reliability, 189
Davis, S., 2, 23
Day, R. L., 231, 232, 233, 234, 235,
    236, 238, 239, 245
Delaware, University of, 80-81
Developmental advising model, 74
Devins, J. H., Jr., 231, 245
DeVry, J. R., 149
Digital libraries, 218-228, 242
    evolution toward, 224-228
    information literacy, 228
    information technology strategic
    planning, 219-224
    integrated infrastructure for, 227-228
Dill, D., 4, 23
Direct information access, 78
Distance education, 28-29
    versus distributed instruction, 29-31
Distributed instruction, 29-31
Dolence, M. G., 69, 86
Drexel University, 120
Dugruid, P., 216
Duke University, 125
Early adopters, 134, 135, 136, 146
    nurturing, 147
Early majority, 134, 135
Eastern Maine Technical College, 251
Easton, J. L., 231, 232, 233, 234, 235,
    236, 238, 239, 245
Educational models, changing, 92-93
Ehrmann, S. C., 95, 107
El Camino Community College, 251
Electronic classroom, 199, 208
Electronic conferencing, and campus
    networks, 169
Electronic Forum Discussions, 123
Eng, L., 69, 86
Epper, R., 86

Equipment
    disbursement of used, 245
    order entry, 244
    receipt and distribution, 244
Executive support, and planning, 50
Expectations management, and strategic
    planning, 51
External changes, to a project plan, 240
Facility design, 204
    planning, budgeting, and support,
    214-216
Faculty collaboration, and campus
    networks, 169
Farrington, G., 11, 23
Ferri, C., 82, 86
Financial perspective, 260
Financial planning and management,
    for students, 77-78
First Class, 122, 126
Floyd College, 107
Fourteen fundamental concepts, of
    computers, 113-117
Functional silos, 4
Funding, and strategic planning, 51
Funding models, for student mobile
    computing, 99-100
Fuqua School of Business, 125
Galilei, G., 258
Gardner, H., 202, 216
The Gartner Group, 180, 192, 197
Geoghegan, W. H., 131, 140, 149
Gilbert, S. W., 93, 107
Glick, M., 203, 216
Gloster, A. S., 107
Graves, W. H., 26, 34
Green, K. C., 93, 95, 107, 133, 137,
    138, 140, 142, 144, 145, 149, 150
Greene, J. A., 149
Gregorian, V., 3, 23
Griffin, S. B., 231, 245
Groupwise, 122
Hafner, K. A., 2
Hall, J. W., 91, 107
Hammer, M., 4, 7, 12, 23, 58, 67, 83,
    86, 179, 197

Harasim, L., 120, 129

Hardware components, in learning
  environments, 205

Hardware selection, 243

Harvard University, 264

Hawkins, B. L., 3, 23, 225, 229

Hearn, T. K., Jr., 246

Heller, K., 69, 86

Henderson, J. C., 43, 52

Henry, T., 86

Heterick, R. C., Jr., 34, 88, 100, 107

Higher education
  applying risk assessment model to,
    185
  challenge assumptions, 14-15
  challenges to, 3-5
  and collaborative learning, 121-122
  considering the future of, 69-70
  increasing the relevance, 96
  institutional culture, 186-187
  process view of, 15-20
  and project implementation, 230-245
  and strategic information technology
    planning, 36-52, 219-224

High tech classroom, 208

Hiltz, S. R., 120, 129

Hollowell, D. E., 80, 81, 86

Holt, J. C., 154, 163

Hooker, M., 15, 23

Human resource issues, and digital
  libraries, 222-223

IBM, 54, 63, 227, 250, 261
  and benchmarking, 264
  Chantilly study, 182-184, 190
  Client/Server Business Advisor tool,
    186
  integrated infrastructure for digital
    libraries, 227-228
  partnership with Wake Forest
    University, 241-242

IBM Consulting Group, 43, 179, 182,
  197, 264

IBM Global Network (IGN), 110

IBM Higher Education
  and the Chantilly study, 185

organizational readiness assessments,
  187, 190, 192

IBM Skill Dynamics, 246

Identity processes, 15-16

Illinois, University of, 92

Implementation planning template,
  53-67
  compelling business case, 56
  critical success factors, 55-56
  design and process requirements,
    56-63
  development of, 54
  expanded view of planning, 55

Information integration, 78

Information systems (I/S), 181

Information technology (I/T), 10,
  151-162
  and authenticity, 159-161
  defending the value system, 154
  defining quality, 157-159
  demonstrating feasibility, 154
  functional examples, 153
  implementation planning, 53-67
  investments, 26-34
  maintaining quality, 154
  and organizational readiness
    indicators, 184
  planning, 36-52
  strategic planning, 219-224
  strategy for investments, 26-34

Information technology planning,
  36-52
  critical success factors, 50-52
  current planning, 39-43
  strategic alignment, 43-50

Infrastructure, 78, 166-177
  and client/server projects, 192-194
  defining, 166-169
  for the digital library, 227-228
  and mobile computing, 98-99
  preparation, 243

Innovation, adoption of, 134-135

Innovators, 134, 135, 136
  nurturing, 147

IN pattern, of learning, 202

Instructional design, 147-148
Instructional support, and individual
    departments, 148
Instructional technology, 131-149
    adoption and support strategies,
    145-148
    growth in use, 138
    history of the revolution, 132-137
    making a successful innovation,
    139-143
    signs of change, 137-139
    the support crisis, 143-145
Integration state, of organizational
    readiness, 184, 188
Internal business process perspective, 260
Internal changes, to a project plan, 240
The Internet
    access providers, 243
    access to, 78
    and access to experts, 169
    and collaboration, 122
    and faculty/student contact, 33
    growth of, 84
    and higher education, 31-32
    and on-line learning, 203
    and student mobile computing, 90
    and student recruitment, 75
ISO 9000, 182, 265
Jefferson, T., 10
Kaplan, C., 184, 197
Kaplan, R. S., 258, 259, 261, 271
Kramer, G. L., 74, 86
Kulik, C. L. C., 119, 129
Kulik, J. A., 119, 129
Laggards, 134, 135
Langel, R., 180, 194, 195, 197
Laptop computers, 111-113
    and access information, 112
    and level playing field, 112-113
    and nomadic learners, 112
    personal and individual education,
    111-112
    technological transformation, 112
Laptop-enabled classroom, 211
Late majority, 134, 135

Leadership, and change, 50
Learning environment, 200-203
    constructive and participatory
    learning, 201
    distributed on-line learning, 203
    focus on learning, 203
    hardware components in, 205
    learning-centered education, 201
    learning styles, 202
    multiple activities and focal points,
    201-202
    student mobile computing, 202-203
Learning perspective, 260
Learning styles, 202
    Myers-Briggs, 202
    IN pattern, 202
Lewis, M., 83, 86
Libraries
    and campus networks, 169
    digital, 219-228
    human resource issues, 222-223
    problems confronting, 218-219
Library of Congress
    THOMAS, 10
    U.S. Copyright Office, 10
Local area networks (LANs), 168, 172
    departmental, 192-193
Lonabocker, L., 83, 86
Lotus 1-2-3, 59
Lotus AmiPro, 59
Lotus LearningSpace, 127
Lotus Notes, 110, 113, 120, 122, 126,
    213
Lotus Notes Mail, 110
Lynch, R. L., 258, 271
Lytle, R. H., 120, 129
Machiavelli, N., 230, 246
Mainstream, 136, 137, 142, 144
    definition of, 135
    focus on adoptable uses of
    technology, 147
    focus on teaching and learning,
    146-147
    involving, 146
    need for peer-based support, 146

Malcolm Baldrige National Quality
    Award, 182, 263, 265, 269
Management, role of, 268
Management stage, of organizational
    readiness, 184, 188
Manuel, S., 208, 216
MARC, 221
Martin, E., 206, 217
Maruyama, M. K., 34
Maryland, University of, 209
Maryland, University of at College
    Park, 212
Massachusetts Institute of Technology
    (MIT), 131, 263
Massy, W. F., 4, 8, 12, 14, 23
Master/multimedia classrooms,
    210-211
Matrix organization, 238-239
    simple, 239
Mayadas, A. F., 120
McCall, D. C., 178
Measurement development team,
    role of, 268
Michael, S. B., 240, 246
Microsoft Excel, 59
Microsoft Office 97, 110, 114
Microsoft Project, 59
Microsoft Windows 95, 110, 114
Microsoft Word, 59
Millard, S., 149
Miller, G., 216, 217
Miller, M. A., 129
Mingle, J. R., 88, 91, 92, 93, 96, 100,
    108
Minnesota, University of, 126
Minnesota, University of at Crookston,
    92, 93, 97, 99, 100, 103, 104, 122
Molnar, A., 96, 107
Moore, G. A., 135, 150
Moran, C. R., 36
Mosher, D. N., 108
Muhlenberg College, 251
Multimedia, and campus networks,
    169
Myers-Briggs, style of learning, 202

National Association of College and
    University Business Officers
    (NACUBO), 263, 264, 266
Netscape, 110
Networking, and collaboration, 122
Networks, specialized, 169
Nichols, R., 166
Noblitt, J. S., 95, 96, 107, 151, 156,
    163
Norris, D. M., 69, 86
Norton, D. P., 258, 259, 261, 271
O'Banion, T., 74, 86
Oberlin, J. L., 157, 163, 214, 217
Oblinger, D. G., 2, 34, 88, 91, 92, 93,
    96, 100, 108
Oldach, S., 43, 52
On-line learning, 203
Operational processes, 15-16
Organizational infrastructure and
    processes, 43-46
Organizational readiness
    assessments, 187, 190
    indicators by stage, 184
    ratings, 188
Outsourcing, 148, 222
Parker, M., 52
Participatory learning, 201
Perelman, L., 201, 217
Performance architecture, 253
Performance indicators, 269
Performance measurements, 248-271
    actual management process, 257
    benchmarking in institutional
        transformation, 263-266
    getting started and sustaining,
        267-270
    institutional architectures for
        measurements, 252-258
    integrated measures, 256
    relationships among measurements,
        255
    types of measure by level, 256
    using balanced scorecards, 258-263
Performance measures, 269
Peterson, E. D., 81, 86

Petronious, 231
The Pew Higher Education
    Roundtable, 27
Philip of Macedon, 132
Piaget, J., 119, 130
Pinheiro, E. J., 92, 108, 118
Priority processes, 15-16
Processes, 10-12
    and client/server projects, 181-182
    example of, 18-20
    and higher education, 15-20
    internal business perspective, 260
    systems management, 195
    transforming business processes,
    21-22
Project implementation, 230-245
    need for project management,
    231-241
Project management, 99, 231-241
    alternatives to, 235-236
    benefits of, 233-235
    case study, 241-245
    and client/server projects, 196-197
    laying groundwork, 236-240
    planning for change, 240-241
    reasons for failure, 234
Project manager
    and simple matrix organization, 239
    success factors, 237
Projects, success by risk zone, 183
Project startup, 242
Public relations, 233-234
Quest, J. D., 208, 216
Regulation and compliance processes,
    15-16
Regulatory changes, to a project plan,
    240
Rensselaer Polytechnic Institute (RPI),
    202, 209, 211
Resmer, M., 88, 91, 92, 93, 96, 100,
    108
Resource allocation, 233
Risk zone, 183
Rogers, E. M., 134, 135, 139, 147, 150
Rossman, P., 86

Salapatas, J. N., 238, 240, 246
Scheduling, 233
Shalala, D., 249
Short, D., 199, 200, 217, 230, 246
Sine, P., 149
Skinner, R. A., 89, 94, 108
Smith, D. G., 119, 130
Software
    for collaboration, 122-123
    image preparation, 243
    selection, 243
Sonoma State University, 98, 100, 101,
    103
The Sorbonne, 263
Sorkin, V. D., 10, 23
Stanford University, 132
Stanton, S. A., 58, 67, 179, 197
Stengel, P., 206, 217
Strategic alignment, 43-50
    framework, 44
    planning approach, 46-50
Strategic framework pyramid, 254
Strategic planning, 219-224
    alignment with mission, 219-220
    centralization vs. decentralization,
    222
    human resource issues, 222-223
    legacy systems, 221-222
    organizational issues, 223-224
    outsourcing, 222
    physical resource issues, 221
    policies and procedural issues, 224
    trends in information technology
    (I/T), 220-221
Stuckenbruck, L. C., 231, 237, 238,
    239, 240, 246
Student admissions, 75-76
Student advising, 73, 74, 78
Student mobile computing, 88-107
    assessment of, 102-104
    characteristics of, 90-91
    definition of, 90-91
    educational impact, 95-97
    implementation, 98-102
    and learning environment, 202-203

models, 97-98
need for, 89-90
questions to ask, 104-106
Student process, 76-77
Student records, and campus networks, 169
Student recruitment, 75
Student services, 68-85
exemplars, 80-83
and mobile computing, 93-95
role of technology, 83-85
traditional model, 70-71
21st century vision, 71-80
Studio classroom, 211-212
Stuebing, S., 199, 200, 204, 206, 208, 214, 215, 217
Sun-Tzu, 231
Suppes, P., 132, 150
System integration, 244
Systems management, 194-195
poor performance factors, 194
processes, 195
Tang, V., 184, 197
Task-focused instruction, 158
Taylor, M., 3, 23
Teaching, learning, and technology roundtable (TLTR), 140
Teaching Theater, 212
Technical complexity, 186
components of, 183
Technical quality, 233
Technological change, and mobile computing, 93
Technology, and client/server projects, 180-181
Technology fees, 100
Technology refresh, 244-245
Teleclassrooms, 212-213
Teles, L., 120, 129
THOMAS, 10

Thor, C. G., 271
Thorin, S. E., 10, 23, 224, 229
Top-down innovators, 161
and technology, 151-153
Total quality management (TQM), 11, 266
Trainor, H. E., 52
Tuller, C., 84, 86
Turner, R. E., 251
Turoff, M., 120, 129
Twigg, C. A., 34, 35, 201, 202, 217
Tynan, D., 95, 108
U.S. Air Force, 231
U.S. Department of Defense, 231
U.S. Department of Education, 265
U.S. National Laboratories, 263
University and Industry Television for Education (UNITE), 126
Venkatraman, N., 43, 52
Virtual campus, 80
Virtual classroom, 208, 213
Virtual classroom environment, 203
Virtual universities, 69
Vygotsky, L. S., 119, 130
Wake Forest University, 97-98, 99, 100, 122, 128
partnership with IBM, 241-242
plan for the Class of 2000, 241-245
project life cycle, 242
strategic plan for technology, 109-117
Wilson, J. M., 93, 108, 211, 217
Wingspread Group on Higher Education, 2, 23
Wisconsin, University of, 263
Wisconsin-Madison, University of, 249
Wolfshorndl, A., 206, 217
Workplace simulations, 123-124
Wunderle, T. C., 53
Zemsky, R., 4, 23, 27, 35